The Depression and the Urban West Coast, 1929–1933

THE AMERICAN WEST IN THE TWENTIETH CENTURY
Martin Ridge and Walter Nugent, *editors*

The Depression and the Urban West Coast, 1929-1933

LOS ANGELES
SAN FRANCISCO
SEATTLE AND
PORTLAND

William H. Mullins

INDIANA UNIVERSITY PRESS
Bloomington and Indianapolis

Portions of this work appeared in *Pacific Northwest Quarterly*, 79 (1988): 109–18 and *Pacific Northwest Quarterly*, 72 (1981): 11–19 (rpt. in Thomas Edwards and Carlos Schwantes, eds., *Experiences in a Promised Land: Essays in Pacific Northwest History* [Seattle: University of Washington Press, 1986], pp. 323–37).

The paper used in this publication meets the minimum requirements of American National Standard for Information Sciences—Permanence of Paper for Printed Library Materials, ANSI Z39.48-1984.

⊗™

Manufactured in the United States of America

Library of Congress Cataloging-in-Publication Data

Mullins, William H., date.
    The Depression and the urban West Coast, 1929–1933 : Los Angeles, San Francisco, Seattle, and Portland / William H. Mullins.
        p.   cm. — (The American West in the twentieth century)
    Includes bibliographical references (p.   ) and index.
    ISBN 0-253-33935-9 (alk. paper)
    1. Depressions—1929—United States.
    2. Los Angeles (Calif.)—Economic conditions.
    3. San Francisco (Calif.)—Economic conditions.
    4. Seattle (Wash.)—Economic conditions.
    5. Portland (Or.)—Economic conditions.
    I. Title.   II. Series.
    HB3717 1929.M85   1991
    330.979—dc20   90-4752
1   2   3   4   5   95   94   93   92   91

*To the memory of
My Mother and Father*

CONTENTS

Foreword

The urban history of the twentieth-century West is fragmented because much research needs to be done before anything resembling a comprehensive story can be told. There is no doubt that American cities, East and West, had common problems dealing with growth, suburbs, sanitation, management, and a host of other issues. It is also true that their leaders seemed to have held shared values and to have approached community problems in much the same way. There were, however, certain regional issues of difference. But such generalizations can only be validated through comparative studies, and that is why this book is so valuable. This analytical and comparative study focuses on one specific problem: how the four largest West Coast cities provided relief for the unemployed and indigent during the Hoover years of the Great Depression. The leadership in the four major cities confronted a national and regional trauma of such magnitude that it compelled some of them to abandon a philosophy of social welfare that had characterized American thinking for generations. President Herbert Hoover, who embodied this philosophy, spelled out his enlightened version of humane individualism and tenaciously paid lip service to it even as his administration's policies began to deviate from it during his last years in office.

If President Hoover, whose contact with the human suffering and dislocation produced by the Great Depression was limited by the isolation of his office, came to realize its depth and tragedy, little wonder city and county officials who had to deal first hand with the depression's impact felt beleaguered. Almost overnight they faced increases in the locally unemployed, the migrant job seeker, and the demands of the welfare system, as well as problems of rising taxation to meet community needs and the gradual collapse of the community chest and other volunteer agencies. Step by step many were forced into accepting decisions and taking actions that they would never have dreamed possible a few years earlier.

Urban leadership was not alone in meeting the crisis; the average citizen in Seattle, Portland, San Francisco, and Los Angeles was asked to make commitments, both public and private, in response to a steadily declining economy. The values of enlightened capitalism and the merits of an essentially laissez-faire state were sorely tested. Year by year, from 1929 to 1933, citizens and community leaders came to realize that they faced problems of dealing with relief that grew in magnitude until they were beyond the resources of volunteer agencies, cities, counties, and even some states.

Change came slowly and unevenly in West Coast cities. People do not surrender their deeply held beliefs unless they confront overwhelming pressures that they cannot relieve, and even their response is often compromise rather than surrender. The thinking about how to deal with the newly unemployed urban worker during the depression did not shift overnight. In some instances, determined hardliners held out for the old values that called for letting the economy run its course until it righted itself regardless of human cost. Even advocates of change were not as radical in retrospect as they were perceived at the time. Moreover, the skills, methods, and models of bureaucratic leadership were even slower to respond to the urban crises. Persistence rather than radical innovation characterized the public and private response to dealing with relief and unemployment even after the onset of the New Deal.

William H. Mullins accomplished pioneering work in his painstaking study of how the West Coast cities dealt with the problems of relief and unemployment from 1929 to 1933. He has shifted the focus of the study of the Great Depression from the national and state scene, where individuals and grass roots problems are often overlooked, to the local setting, where the real struggle was waged against impoverishment and unemployment. He has presented the first comparative study of four major cities, and he has also brought their experiences into a national context by pointing out how similar problems were dealt with in the East. Mullins's narrative is a study of the modification of ideology in the face of severe conditions.

When the editors of *Fortune Magazine* observed in 1932 that "No One has Starved," they paid tribute to the leadership in those communities that had exhausted their resources fighting the Great Depression. The editors had also erred. By that time, as Mullins demonstrates, hunger was a reality in some West Coast cities. He also shows that what has been heralded by many historians of the national scene as major change meant little at the local level. There was much continuity of ideology and methodology in dealing with relief between the Hoover administration and Franklin D. Roosevelt's New Deal.

This book is one of a series dealing with the West in the twentieth century. The series is intended to provide the general public and the scholarly reader with a deeper understanding of an important aspect of the recent past of the American West.

Walter Nugent
Martin Ridge

Acknowledgments

A work that takes some time to come to fruition accumulates a large number of debts. Such is the case with this book. I want to express my special thanks to Otis Pease at the University of Washington, whose counsel I valued and encouragement I appreciated throughout the task. I am also grateful to Robert Burke for his assistance and efforts at crucial points. To Martin Ridge, who has read the entire manuscript more than once, I express my gratitude for his valuable suggestions, for his support, and for his direction. The book is better focused and more readable for his efforts. Dauril Alden, Charles Coate, Joe Hall, and Carol Zabilski have also read portions of the work. I have profited from their suggestions and corrections. A faculty development grant from Oklahoma Baptist University helped underwrite one more swing West to complete my research.

Members of the staffs at several libraries and archives generously offered their help and ideas along the way. I thank again those who lent assistance at UCLA Public Affairs Service, the Bancroft Library, the Oregon Collection at the University of Oregon Library, the Northwest Collection at the University of Washington Libraries, and the Portland Archives and Record Center. I am especially indebted to Bohdan Bucmaniuk, Records Specialist at the Los Angeles Board of Supervisors office, and Rich Burner and Karyl Winn at the University of Washington Manuscript Division for help in obtaining important records. Although everyone mentioned has contributed much to the final product, I take full responsibility for any shortcomings, whatever they may be.

Finally, my thanks go to my family who both endured and uplifted me throughout the research and writing of this book. I thank Michael and Julie, who would have rather done something other than wait outside a library. And, most of all, I thank my wife, Edith, for her typing, her loving support, and her encouragement when it seemed the project might never be completed.

The Depression and the Urban West Coast, 1929–1933

Introduction

The crash of the New York Stock Exchange in October 1929 set off a series of events without precedent in American history. As the "New Era" of prosperity withered and the Great Depression took its place, millions of Americans found themselves unemployed: some 3 million by the spring of 1930, 15 million by 1932.[1] The economic collapse had no parallel in U.S. history, and few Americans at the outset provided viable ideas that could have halted the economic slide.

President Herbert Hoover had a clear vision of how the political economy should function, which he stated explicitly in his inaugural speech:

> The larger purpose of our economic thought should be to establish more firmly stability and security of business and employment and thereby remove poverty still further from our borders. Our people have in recent years developed a new found capacity for cooperation among themselves to effect high purposes in public welfare. It is an advance toward the highest conception of self-government. Self-government does not and should not imply the use of political agencies alone. Progress is born of cooperation in the community—not from governmental restraints.[2]

Even as the depression deepened, the president, in a speech to Congress in December 1930, underlined his intention to stick with tried, true, and traditional remedies when he said: "Economic wounds must be healed by the action of the cells of the economic body—the producers and consumers themselves. Recovery can be expedited and its effects mitigated by cooperative action."[3] Hoover believed individuals should try to help themselves. If this failed, people with means should assist those in need. For Hoover the Red Cross was "one of the most beautiful flowers of the American spirit" because it exemplified philanthropic cooperation for the public welfare.[4] Government assistance was represented by the dole—a term used in disdain in the thirties.

Hoover, however, did not believe in passive government. His was not a "do nothing" administration.[5] Nonetheless, it operated within several philosophical constraints. The president believed that the national government should be only a catalyst or, at most, a coordinator for relief and recovery. The government could orchestrate the building of public confidence. As early as November 1929, business, labor, and farm leaders gathered at the White House to reassure the public that they would take the necessary steps to get the nation's economy rolling again. Promises, ultimately unkept, issued forth from the meeting: there were guarantees of no wage cuts, no strikes, and expansion of production. A balanced budget would set the tone by restoring confidence in the government's fiscal responsibility. The federal government would speed up public works construction, and encourage state and local government projects. The Federal Farm Board also purchased grain to stabilize prices. In May 1930 the president, trying to bolster confidence, declared that the worst of the slump was over.[6]

In its attempt to bring the nation out of the slump, the Hoover administration encouraged and guided, but tried not to interfere. In October 1930 the President's Emergency Committee for Employment (PECE) met for the first time. (The name was later changed to the less optimistic President's Organization on Unemployment Relief—POUR.) An advisory group, it collected and disseminated information and issued hopeful, encouraging statements. Although the president authorized $500 million of federally funded public works, the government took no direct hand in local relief operations. During the winter of 1930–31 Hoover reported that, according to directors of the community chest and the governors of the states, no one in America was starving.

The administration refused to intervene in local relief efforts, even while enlarging its own programs. To reduce unemployment, federal authorities planned more public works. As banks began to fail, the government formed the National Credit Corporation so that solvent banks might loan funds to banks in distress. The plan failed, as the stronger banks hesitated to imperil themselves by loaning to other, less stable institutions.[7] The Farm Board continued its struggle to stabilize prices, and in late 1931 the government distributed $125 million to land banks to prop up mortgages.

The year 1932 was the most aggressive of the Hoover presidency. Under intense congressional pressure, Hoover compromised his ideal of local self-help. Congress created the Reconstruction Finance Corporation (RFC) in January and expanded its functions in July. The RFC had $2 billion to subsidize public works and to loan to local governments for relief. Hard-pressed local officials welcomed the RFC, although its funds were inadequate, the administrators distributed them in a niggardly fashion (only $35 million had been dispensed by October 1932), and the whole operation was constrained by excessive fiscal propriety (loans, not grants, were channeled through financial institutions and public works projects had to be self-liquidating). The RFC furnished some relief, but it failed to stimulate the economy.

For over three and one-half years Hoover and the Great Depression tested the limits of self-help and the ideal of local responsibility free from federal interference. The depression placed Americans and their local communities under fierce pressures. By reacting to the depression with the tenacity of an idealogue rather than the pragmatism of a politician, Hoover forced the nation to demonstrate the bounds of its endurance. A historian of social welfare, Robert Bremner, effectively catches Hoover's position: "History abounds in examples of humanitarians who were ahead of their times. Hoover belonged to a different breed: the humanitarian behind the times."[8] Nevertheless, Hoover had gone further than any previous president in modifying the role of the federal government in the nation's political economy. Although Hoover's circumscribed solutions proved insufficient, he made it possible for his successor to go beyond the old ideals and form a new relationship between the people and their national government.[9]

Because so much attention is given to the change from Hoover to Franklin Roosevelt and the New Deal, historians tend to focus on national events. Yet, because of the nature of Hoover's programs, the story of the early depression years is better found in the experiences of cities and counties of America trying to work out solutions on their own. Unfortunately, there is not a wealth of information on the subject. For the most part, city biographies, which include the period as a part of their chapters on the depression, unpublished dissertations, the Lynds' pioneering *Middletown in Transition*, and Bernard Sternsher's *Hitting Home*, a collection of essays on local reactions to the Hoover years, are the major offerings. Charles Trout's work on Boston during the depression is an example of a more recent comprehensive presentation of a city's attempts to cope during the depression.[10] There are no comparative works that look at western cities.

By understanding local problems and responses—how individuals and institutions reacted and why they reacted as they did—it is possible to gain greater insight into the nature and substance of the United States during this period of change. This study of four major western cities provides an understanding of the early depression years and addresses a number of questions: What happened to American ideals—particularly ideals relating to individualism, self-reliance, and the work ethic—when they were challenged by the Great Depression? How well did urban institutions respond under intense pressure? How did the depression take shape in the West? Did a regional outlook affect the response on the West Coast? And to what degree do these years represent continuity or change in America, especially urban America?

Several themes emerge from a close examination of Los Angeles, San Francisco, Seattle, and Portland during the Hoover years. A central concept involves the political culture of the four cities—and, by inference, of the nation. At the outset of the depression a set of values and traditions governed Americans' beliefs about the role of government, their attitudes toward poverty, and their views on providing relief. It is ironic that Herbert Hoover, whom voters repudiated in 1932, best embodied these attitudes. In 1922 Hoover wrote a small volume entitled *American Individualism*. He not only presented his own philosophy in the book, but also described the prevailing outlook of the American people. The kind of individualism Hoover defined was not "rugged individualism"—a philosophy that held that a person succeeds or fails on his own. Instead he called for "an individualism that carries increasing responsibility and service to our fellows." Neighborliness, service, and cooperative self-help were the hallmarks of Hoover's brand of individualism. For Hoover each individual was responsible for coping with his own economic problems. But that did not mean persons or families unable to sustain themselves were left to survive as best they could—that would be the unfair and unkind strain of rugged individualism that Hoover condemned. Americans who were better off should assist those less fortunate than themselves, just as Hoover himself had done in the First World War and throughout much of his public career.[11] Private charity, especially as rendered by those who could best afford to support it, was to be the first bulwark against economic distress. If this should prove inadequate, local governments, and, if necessary, state governments could assist the private efforts. The intended result of this carefully prescribed hierarchy of response was, to the greatest degree possible, the preservation of individual self-reliance—the quality that Hoover and many other Americans viewed as fundamental to the American character, the backbone of society, and a quality that had made America great. If individuals cooperating with one another could handle the problems brought on by depression at the local level (and the president seemed confident they could), then extensive federal intervention ("interference") was unnecessary. If the national government could avoid handing out relief, the economic storm could be weathered without altering the relationship between the American economy and the federal government.

This somewhat paradoxical concept, best labeled "cooperative individualism," is used frequently in this study.[12] Although it smacks of middle-class righteousness, cooperative individualism was not a method of controlling "the masses." Local decision-makers, most of whom were middle-class or upper middle-class businessmen and politicians, believed they were doing what was right for their cities —and judging from the limited amount of protest and from scattered evidence from the less prominent, less articulate portion of the communities, it appears that there was substantial agreement that this was a worthy ideal.

Americans' adherence to cooperative individualism was demonstrated in a multitude of ways during the Hoover years. In the early going the community chests assumed almost full responsibility for relief. Local governments awoke slowly to the growing crisis, stirred about reluctantly before responding, and usually employed a private or quasi-private agency as the channel for assistance to the unemployed. When relief was provided, a work test was usually demanded. Businessmen acknowledged a responsibility to aid in the emergency and took part in relief programs in each of the four western cities. Self-help groups in Los Angeles and the Unemployed Citizens' League in Seattle, especially, are important examples of the ethos of self-reliance. Finally, the reluctance of the state governments of Washington and California, and to some extent Oregon, to provide much more than an expansion of highway construction to absorb the jobless testifies to the desire to keep the relief effort centered in the local community and avoid budget deficits. In short, the record of the Hoover years in the major West Coast cities is a test of cooperative individualism. And, at least in the beginning, the cooperative, generous side of this ethic balanced the exhortation to self-reliance.

But as the depression wore on the number of "have nots" increased and the assets of the "haves" diminished. Groups organized to lower their property taxes. Higher taxes were needed to furnish adequate relief, but many taxpayers had no desire to fund relief so directly at their own expense. Although relief bond issues passed in each of the four cities, government officials sought in earnest to trim budgets, assessments, and tax levies to satisfy their constituents. Declining community chest pledges failed to meet yearly goals. Selflessness, expressed through charity and a willingness to raise or maintain taxes to help others, gave way to fear and a drive for self-preservation. The spirit of cooperative individualism, exemplified in the actions and attitudes of the citizens in the early months of the depression, by the end of the Hoover administration had vanished—the will, and in many cases the ability, of the people to care for themselves or sacrifice for others had succumbed to unprecedented demands.

An analysis of the responses of Los Angeles, San Francisco, Seattle, and Portland to the Great Depression offers an opportunity to observe institutions and people being put to the test. Local governments created boards and commissions when existing welfare agencies failed. Usually these new entities represented innovative efforts. Private charities received public funds, prominent businessmen assumed the major decision-making positions, and in Seattle the unemployed themselves had a major part in the relief program. Private charities furnished the few social workers who had any experience with public assistance. The businessmen were natural choices to lead these organizations in an era devoted to the efficiency of the business place. The makeshift nature of the relief programs demonstrated that the communities had never before concerned themselves with the alleviation of poverty on a grand scale. The hybrid relief institutions suffered from a lack of professional leadership and some became victims of political manipulation. But, in the end, they failed principally because the resources to provide funding were inadequate in 1932; then their leaders looked to the state or federal government for help.[13]

Finally, to what degree, if any, was the western experience unique? From several studies of large and middle-sized communities, the problems these four cities faced and the structure of their responses were largely typical of what occurred around the nation. This work will compare, from time to time, the undertakings in the West with the efforts in other cities to demonstrate mainly the similarities, but also some differences, between the West and the rest of the country. First, contrary to many assertions of the day, the depression did not affect the West Coast later or to a lesser degree than the rest of the nation. The economies of Los Angeles and Portland were already in a decline similar to that recorded in Philadelphia and Boston before the crash. Los Angeles suffered economic problems as early as Detroit, Pittsburgh, Cleveland, or Chicago. Some statistics show the West may have even been worse off in the early 1930s.[14] And the opinion that a particular region had been spared the brunt of the depression was not unique to the West. Commentators in the Midwest, and even the Northeast, sought to buoy spirits in their locales with the same analysis.

The pattern and process of relief on the West Coast was also representative of efforts throughout the nation. Seemingly, all cities were slow to recognize the enormity of the problem. Each responded with private charity and a mayor's commission in 1930, undertook a major relief effort in late 1930 or 1931, and then fell short in 1932. A common characterization of the West was that it was a region more dedicated to individualism than other sections of the nation. As James Patterson observed, "much of the West retained a fervent belief in the virtues of self-help which clashed, sometimes sharply, with the ideals of public welfare endorsed by New Dealers."[15] Patterson referred to a later period, but his estimate was borne out at the state level in the Hoover years. The three western states adopted a policy that tilted more to rugged individualism than to cooperative individualism.

Several state governments, notably New York and Pennsylvania, intervened more quickly than the governments of California and Washington. Although Oregon, perhaps still impelled by progressivism, acted earlier, other states that responded rapidly demonstrated more staying power. In the end, Oregon was more concerned with efficiency than aid. There seems to have been a reluctance on the West Coast to provide state assistance.

At the city and county levels cooperative individualism was a value shared by much of the nation. New York City, Chicago, and especially Philadelphia sought to provide relief through private funds, and self-help groups formed in a number of states. In a national survey the Russell Sage Foundation discovered that city relief leaders consistently turned to more costly work relief programs to keep citizens off the dole and to preserve their self-respect. The spirit of cooperative individualism eroded nationally at about the same rate as in the West, and with the same effects. Budget trimming in the face of need was typical in most cities by 1932.

The western experience during the Hoover years of the depression replicated what was occurring nationwide. The U.S. economy had become a national economy. The depression rocked all sections of the country simultaneously and equally. The same cultural traditions and values guided most responses to the economic crisis well into 1932. Local administrators throughout the nation, partly out of allegiance to these traditions and partly out of necessity, made similar decisions. Disheartened, Americans in the West Coast cities, and throughout America, saw their values erode and their efforts fall short. Under great financial and psychological strain they had neither the ability nor the will to try to survive on their own. When put to the test, cooperative individualism was found wanting. By 1932 Herbert Hoover espoused an ideal no longer embraced by the American people. By 1933 not only the state of the economy, but also a shift in values made the West Coast and the rest of the country ready for the New Deal. Therefore, this study is more than the history of four West Coast cities. It also sheds further light on a neglected but important part of the nation's history during the Great Depression.

ONE

▄▄▄▄

Prelude

The four largest cities on the West Coast at the time of the Great Depression were Los Angeles, San Francisco, Seattle, and Portland. Each was the economic hub of its respective region, especially because each served as a rail center and, more important, as a shipping port for its hinterland. All four could be described as new cities—even though Los Angeles and San Francisco were some one hundred fifty years old—because they had only begun to establish themselves as major urban centers. In comparison to the great coastal cities of the Atlantic seaboard, Seattle and Portland lagged economically and socially. The relative economic immaturity of the West Coast, the lack of a solidly entrenched political system, and the absence of a political machine with the force of a Tammany Hall had an impact on the way the cities responded to the depression. Some of the institutions—one in Seattle in particular (the Unemployed Citizens' League)—that sprang up in reaction to the economic problems were without precedent. Among the four cities only San Francisco, during the 1906 earthquake and fire, had confronted a challenge of the magnitude of the depression. These cities were not well seasoned as they faced a crisis that would be the ultimate test of a community's ability to survive on its own.

Los Angeles, by far the largest of the four, had a population of over 1.2 million, according to the 1930 census. Los Angeles County approached 2.2 million. During the 1920s the city had boomed as its population increased 113 percent. The county grew 134 percent, and the state's population expanded 66 percent over the same period.[1] The growth of the Southland was unparalleled on the West Coast. The other three cities grew during the 1920s, but none by more than 25 percent. Los Angeles was the nation's fifth largest city by 1930. The residents were overwhelmingly native white in origin (79.3 percent), although there was a liberal sprinkling of citizens of Mexican origin, blacks, and Japanese.[2]

Los Angeles in the late twenties and early thirties had predominately a commercial and service economy. Although manufacturing had grown, almost tripling from 1921 to 1929, the city ranked only ninth in value added by manufacture.[3] The port, one of the busiest in the world from 1925 to 1931, shipped almost as much tonnage as all other Pacific cities combined.[4] The two pillars of the production economy were oil and agriculture. The oil boom began in the early 1920s, peaked, and went bust in late 1929. Even though depressed, petroleum was California's top industry in the 1930s, with most of the production concentrated in the Southland. Los Angeles County claimed the largest agricultural output of any county in the nation in 1937. After oil and agriculture the most important regional industries were movies and tourism.[5]

Los Angeles politics demonstrated the problems of a city that was in the process of discovering itself. Mayor John Porter came to office as the prosperity decade ended. The used car salesman's principal claim to the position was his honesty. This stood in marked contrast to the administrations that preceded and succeeded him into a newly built city hall, which has over its main entrance "Righteousness Exalteth a People." Much more than the other three cities, Los Angeles was afflicted with racketeering, bribery, and rampant violation of prohibition. Although charges were leveled at Porter, his real sins—at least in the eyes of the press —were inexperience, ineptitude, and an opposition to public power.

In 1930 the population of San Francisco[6] was just over 634,000, and the metropolitan area was approximately twice as large. It was composed predominantly of native white stock (69.6 percent) and foreign-born whites (24.2 percent).[7] Economically San Francisco depended on manufacturing to a greater degree than Los Angeles. Most occupations in the Bay City were associated with manufacturing (20.4 percent), trade (18.9 percent), and transportation and commerce (17.4 percent). Its port annually shipped $40 million worth of refined mineral oil and an equal value of fruit. As the port of the great San Joaquin Valley, San Francisco handled nearly 80 percent of the state's agricultural output.[8]

San Francisco had experienced volatile labor-management relationships. Until 1921 the Bay Area embraced the closed shop. From 1921 through the early 1930s management succeeded in enforcing the "American Plan," characterized by the open shop and company unions, even along the waterfront. Therefore, what could have been a source of confrontation and even violence during hard times had been eliminated before the depression. Not until the longshoremen's strike of 1934 would unionization become a heated issue in San Francisco.

Statistically, Seattle and Portland were similar in 1930. Seattle's population numbered 365,500 and Portland's just under 302,000. Native-born whites were in the majority in both cities.[9] More than the two California cities Seattle and Portland depended on agriculture and, most important, the lumber industry, for a healthy economy. Even in good years, loggers and agricultural workers invaded the cities each winter until the weather and job opportunities improved. Seattleites and Portlanders took high unemployment levels for granted when the days turned cold, gray, and damp. Seattle's wage earners worked primarily in manufacturing, agriculture, and transportation; the two major manufacturing enterprises were bread-making and grain milling. In Portland the lumber and food industries also provided the majority of manufacturing jobs. The Columbia River connected Portland to the interior Northwest. It was the nation's sixth busiest port in 1931— shipping lumber, wheat, wool, and apples.[10]

Each of the four cities experienced prosperity during the 1920s and was confidently expecting more. In fact, these expectations, spawned during a decade of economic advancement, generated a psychology of prosperity. Public statements, newspaper reports, and financial predictions all led to the same optimistic conclusion, that the 1930s would be as good or better than the previous decade. Despite the stock market crash, at the end of 1929 leaders of the urban West Coast, confident in the stability of its economy, were drawing up plans, and making overly optimistic (for any time) predictions of what was to come.

The reigning belief was that the West was too vibrant and had too many projects under way to be affected seriously. Throughout the Hoover years the leading pro-business newspapers, particularly in their January issues, invited leading businessmen of the community to express confidence that their city was moving forward. What these men thought privately is hard to determine, but their public stance year after year demonstrated that they promoted the psychology of prosperity. Makers of public and private policy carried this optimism through the first part of the depression, at least into 1931.

In 1929, at least on the surface, there was no good reason to challenge such an outlook. Most of the statistics and reports indicated the era of prosperity had a long time to run. Building and plant expansion inspired enthusiasm for the future. In Los Angeles, Procter and Gamble, Ford Motor Company, and Pittsburgh Plate Glass intended to build factories. Ford, along with Pacific Coast Cement, Racor –Pacific Frog and Switch, and Bethlehem Steel were supposed to be planning new plants or expansions in Seattle. Plans for a new federal building were being drawn up, Seattle City Light was constructing a hydroelectric dam, and the Denny Regrade—the leveling of a large hill in the middle of downtown—was nearing completion. In January 1929 the number of building permits in Seattle lagged behind only those in New York, Chicago, and Los Angeles, and the permits for 1930 were on the way to record-breaking levels by May. Portland was looking forward to automobile tire, silk hosiery, and canning plants.[11] In San Francisco, with the Hetch Hetchy water project under construction, the city sold bonds far into the depression. At the same time, the state and city cleared the way financially for constructing both the Golden Gate and the Oakland Bay bridges.

The most important business statistics from all four cities indicated that 1929 had been a good year, if not a sensational one. Bank deposits in 1929 increased 13 percent in San Francisco. In Los Angeles and Seattle deposits were up 3 percent over 1928, though only 0.5 percent in Portland.[12] In the late 1920s employment —usually a lagging indicator—was another highlight. The number of wage earners in Los Angeles increased by 12 percent from 1927 to 1930 and improved about 6 percent in San Francisco and Seattle from 1928 to 1929. Employment apparently reached a peak in Los Angeles and San Francisco in the late summer or fall. Other signs of a healthy economy included a 27 percent advance in profits and a new record for bank clearings in Portland, a slight increase in San Francisco's retail sales, and, in Los Angeles, a 22 percent gain in wholesale trade.[13]

But signs of a softening national economy appeared. Philadelphia was experiencing greater than average unemployment—the rate was as high as 14 percent even before the stock market crash. In Boston manufacturing declined in 1929, and the city's welfare obligation was exceeded by only those of New York and Detroit at the time of the crash.[14] The Pacific Coast economy was also slowing. The Twelfth District Federal Reserve, surveying the whole West Coast, noted business activity more active than in 1928, but in its November 1929 report indicated that employment, production, and building had turned down since the crash.[15]

The long term trend in issuance of building permits was downward. As early as 1925 in Portland and 1926 in Los Angeles construction had leveled off or decreased. In 1929 building in Portland was reported at less than half of what it had been four years earlier, and one source claimed 50 percent of all employees in the Los Angeles building trades were unemployed by 1930. Seattle, too, despite excitement over some short-term figures, experienced downward fluctuation from 1927, and San Francisco builders were on a five-day week by the end of 1929.[16] Building, one of the more accurate economic indicators, pointed to a slowing economy in each city. A depression was hardly predictable in 1929, but warning signs were evident.

There were other indicators of an economic slump as well. In Los Angeles the boom in real estate and oil prepared the way for the bust. By the mid-1920s property sales had begun to flag. And as oil prices slipped, fraudulent dealings, which the hectic pace of expansion had obscured, came to light in the petroleum industry. Inexperienced businessmen and politicians had created and led an artificially inflated, unbalanced economy. Los Angeles had grown up too rapidly and was now entering an unprecedented crisis. The Security Bank Business Index for Southern California, which measured nine items, including building permits, industrial employment, and bank debits, had been over 120 in mid-1929. It slid precipitously in the fall to a year-end low of 109. The slide continued, almost without stint, until spring 1933. The city's volatile economy and lack of experienced leadership forecast a difficult time ahead as Los Angeles sought to react even adequately to unanticipated problems.[17]

San Francisco was better established and probably better prepared to handle the depression than Los Angeles, if for no other reason than it had experienced more manageable growth. Its less spectacular boom times were abating by fall 1929. By December employment and payroll indexes in San Francisco were down from their four-year highs of June. California public employment bureaus throughout the state were having a far harder time placing the jobless in November. A San Francisco Chamber of Commerce business index told a slightly different story from Security Bank's figures for Southern California. Business conditions in the Bay Area fell off sharply in late 1929 and early 1930 but recovered mid-year. San Francisco's decline did not begin in earnest until late 1930.[18]

Slack times were also evident in the Puget Sound region. Of greatest concern was the lumber industry. The production of lumber had peaked in 1926. In that year Oregon and Washington milled 12 million board feet. Production had slid to 11.6 million by 1928, and a decline in the industry, which employed over half of the manufacturing workers in the two states, had a serious impact on the leading cities in the region. Agriculture affected Seattle and Portland too. In 1930, 20 percent of all gainfully employed Oregonians were in agriculture. Farm product sales, particularly rye and hops, declined in 1929. Apple prices in Washington during the first two years of the depression declined to an average price of minus thirty cents per box. Little wonder unemployment in December 1929 was worse than it had been in the last month of the two previous years. The Seattle Public Employment Office director correctly discerned that the decline was something more than a seasonal drop off.[19] Portland's economic slowdown may have come earlier—the employment office director there suggested the city's period of growth had concluded as early as 1925.[20]

The boom decade had come to an end by the fall of 1929, although few seemed to realize it—or at least few were willing to admit it. On the contrary, most economic leaders in the cities ignored the pronouncements of employment bureau chiefs, if they knew of them, and assured their fellow citizens—and themselves —that the economy was stable and healthy, even in the face of the stock market crash. Hindsight illuminates the signposts, but there was indeed evidence of economic problems in the late 1920s.

For some West Coast investors the stock market crashed in 1928. In early summer of that year the Pacific Coast Stock Exchange suffered the so-called Giannini Break. The prices of the holdings of A. P. Giannini, the founder of Bank of America, slid precipitously in June. The price of Bank of Italy stock plunged 160 points, Bank of America sank 120, and Bancitaly Corporation lost 86 points.[21] West Coast shareholders had had only a taste of what was to come.

The reckoning in New York, when it came, elicited a wide variety of responses and reactions from West Coast residents. Some were deeply affected economically and psychologically. At least one broker in Los Angeles committed suicide, although his suicide note indicated the breakup of a romance as at least an extenuating circumstance. A Portland physician, hard hit by a bank closure that seemed tied to the stock crash, lamented, "We have $2.25 in cash with everything tied up in the bank." Hiram Johnson, Jr., advised his father in Washington, D.C., that he had suffered severely as stock prices plummeted. In Seattle an investment firm went into receivership and a real estate broker filed for bankruptcy immediately after the crash. Financial leaders privately were understandably skittish at the end of 1929. A. J. Mount, president of the Bank of Italy, warned of tightening soon after the crash but hoped normal attrition among the bank's employees would alleviate the necessity of layoffs. H. R. Erkes, a Bank of Italy vice-president in San Francisco, perceived retail trade slowing in November 1929 and feared some "pretty serious effect on general business."[22]

Some observations exuded optimism or reassurance. A day after the crash A. P. Giannini wired a colleague, "Everything tiptop. Don't worry."[23] Much of the optimistic language, though, reflected a recognition of the seriousness of the panic in New York and belied an element of concern locally. Inevitably brokers shared with their clients the opportunity to pick up undervalued stocks and agreed with many national analysts that the episode had only been a necessary contraction after speculative excesses. Other West Coast commentators took pains to point out that business was good. The financial district might be reeling a bit, they claimed, but retailers were looking for a good Christmas shopping season in 1929. But the holiday crowds were not so large, and luxury items such as cars, radios, and refrigerators were not selling well.[24]

As 1929 faded into 1930 the optimists continued to speak brave words but acknowledged problems that were becoming more evident by the week. The president of Security First National bank proclaimed 1929 a good year in the *Los Angeles Examiner*'s special new year financial section but noted that overproduction troubled the petroleum industry and real estate and building were off a bit. The Washington State Chamber of Commerce maintained, "there has been no depression in the state of Washington since the first of [1930]," but then suggested the tightening it had just denied was because of the usual seasonal slowdown. Portland daily newspapers proclaimed the economy sound in November, then proposed a speed-up in public works to absorb the unemployed just a month later.[25]

Judging from these comments by 1930 there was increasing concern that the economy might not be quite right. But if business leaders were reasonably genuine in their public statements, the stock market crash had not shaken their confidence that prosperity would continue.

An economic study done in 1949 reveals dramatically that the uneasiness, which apparently only tugged at the fringes of the consciousnesses of West Coast business leaders and commentators in 1930, was the result of signs that a severe economic slump was beginning.[26] The authors of the book *Business Cycles in Selected Industrial Areas*, which studied Los Angeles, San Francisco, Chicago, Cleveland, Detroit, and Pittsburgh, concentrated on bank debits, retail department store sales, and manufacturing. They found a 71 percent decrease in bank debits in Los Angeles from 1929–33 and a 56 percent decline in sales over the same period. This put the city near the average rate of decline for the six cities. San Francisco showed the least decline with a 49 percent loss in bank debits and a 30 percent decline in department store sales from 1929 to 1933.[27]

Another examination of the period suggests each of the Pacific Coast states suffered even more than the national average in the Hoover years. While per capita income in the nation declined 28 percent from 1929 to 1933, income levels in California went down 29 percent, 31 percent in Oregon, and 33 percent in the state of Washington over the same period.[28] Finally, another report based on an examination of business cycles in California and the nation insisted: "so far as manufacturing activity in the aggregate is concerned there is virtually no difference between the impact of the Great Depression upon the California economy and upon the national economy. Moreover, the difference between the two regions in the subsequent recovery is negligible."[29]

These later studies contradict contemporary opinion that "Things are not nearly as bad in the West as in the East." Many visitors to the West throughout 1930 remarked at the cheerfulness and optimism they found, and they attributed this to a sounder economy. Local residents, too, after traveling in the gloomy East, were happy to get back home where the economy seemed more vibrant. As leaders in the West expressed their optimism and confidence for the new decade, they reinforced the belief that the West had been little touched and would come through unscathed because it was either different than the East Coast or sufficiently isolated.[30]

Commentators from other, supposedly more affected, parts of the nation echoed similar thoughts. Though they could not claim geographical insulation, observers in Milwaukee, Muncie, Rochester, and throughout Texas maintained that the national economic slide in 1930 was occurring somewhere else. The belief that the depression, in its first months at any rate, was someone else's worry must have been widespread.

In reality, however, Los Angeles and San Francisco—and one would reasonably suppose Seattle and Portland—not only were affected to the same degree as eastern cities but were also affected at about the same time. In a carefully illustrated section on business cycles the authors of the 1949 study, Phillip Neff and Annette Weifenbach, show that the Los Angeles economy turned for the worse at precisely the same time as the rest of the nation, September 1929. The San Francisco economy swung downward only one month later.[31] Despite local perceptions, the depression descended on the West Coast in the fall of 1929.

TWO

The End of Prosperity

1930

In early 1930 the general business climate on the West Coast still seemed salubrious. If some worrisome economic signs were being ignored, there was sufficient evidence to sustain the optimists of 1929. As the year wore on, however, it became clearer that prosperity had come to an end. Los Angeles, for example, saw $29 million worth of factory expansion, and new corporation filings improved over 15 percent—but this did not match the increase of 1929.[1] In the first quarter, or even the first half, of the year reports on business that were not necessarily glowing still revealed some positive momentum. The monthly Federal Reserve District report was among the first to signal a significant slowing of the economy. As early as January 1930, it announced declines in almost every major category it monitored. The trend intensified in February. For San Francisco both Dun's and Bradstreet's reports (they had not yet merged) began to be less positive as the second quarter closed. The two financial services sprinkled words such as *slow*, *quiet*, and *fair* in their private business summaries. The California State Chamber of Commerce, however, issued positive reports on building, retail sales, and employment.[2] At the end of the year San Franciscans, after they had read in the Federal Reserve Report that 1930 had been a year of business depression for the region, could draw hope from the *Dun's Review* forecast of a resurgence in Bay Area business.[3] The same pattern held true in the Pacific Northwest. The Washington State Chamber of Commerce, after the first quarter of 1930, confidently predicted increases in building and improved employment, but the Seattle business index declined from 126 to 114 from January 1929 to January 1930.[4] Meanwhile, Portland's retail and wholesale business had slowed over 50 percent by year's end.[5]

The common man felt what the business indexes recorded. From October 1929 to October 1930 factory employment decreased in Los Angeles by 23.8 percent and in San Francisco by 11.3 percent. The cost of living retreated over the same period (18.3 percent in San Francisco), but total payrolls declined as well—28.2 percent in Los Angeles and 13.7 percent in San Francisco.[6]

Retail trade figures demonstrate that the fears, or the reality, of enduring wage cuts and unemployment made a greater impact than falling prices. In Seattle and San Francisco retail sales advanced early in the year—a record Los Angeles sustained into the fall. By the year's end, however, Seattle reported a drop of 6 percent in sales and the San Francisco retail index declined from 114 to 107.[7]

Department store managers reported the Christmas trade lackluster, with the crowds opting for utilitarian gifts over luxury items.

Bank deposits are particularly crucial indicators of a community's financial health. Rising deposits demonstrate that individuals feel sufficiently well paid to save a portion of their incomes. Conversely, declining deposits indicate that people are drawing on their resources. A drop in deposits, coupled with a slump in retail sales, means people are not drawing down their savings for purchases. Instead, layoffs, or at least wage cuts, are eating into savings. Declining deposits are both a cause and an effect of a depression spiral. When savings are withdrawn, banks have less reserves to loan. As the money supply dries up the cyclical nature of a depression commences. Deposits, then, directly represent cash flow in an economy and indirectly provide some idea of wage and even employment levels.

San Francisco, the financial center of the West Coast—the Federal Reserve district headquarters were in the Bay City—suffered least in terms of money circulation in 1930. Deposits increased $150 million, about 8 percent. A. P. Giannini provided another sign of banking confidence. In September the Bank of Italy and the Bank of America merged to become what would ultimately be the largest bank in the country, the Bank of America. Giannini, at least, was moving ahead on his estimation that everything was "tip-top." Seattle banks, too, showed about a 1 percent increase in deposits, gaining approximately $5 million. Although this probably shows that the two cities were weathering the stock panic reasonably well, at least one source suggested that the cash-on-hand figure had more to do with loan demand (i.e., it was low) than it did with a healthy economy.[8] The statistics in Los Angeles and Portland told a clearer but less hopeful story. In Los Angeles deposits were down almost $60 million, about 4 percent. This represented a significant reversal from the increase of $218 million—about 19 percent —Los Angeles banks experienced from 1928 to 1929. Portland financial institutions lost $3 million in deposits in 1930. Although the Portland banks had been a comfortable $4 million ahead of 1929 through September, Portland's economy tightened severely in the final quarter of the year.[9] But there was evidence of financial problems in Los Angeles and Portland that was more stark than moderate declines in deposit figures. In Portland the Bank of Hibernia closed for an extended period of reorganization soon after the crash. In Los Angeles, the Bank of Hollywood, suffering a severe liquidity problem, closed, and accusations of fraud— about $8 million of losses—accompanied the Guaranty Building and Loan into receivership.

In an era in which governments did little to gather accurate employment statistics, building permits are a window on the employment scene. Building permits measure proposed construction—commercial, public, or residential—in a city and, consequently, provide an idea of the rate of employment in the building trades. Because this area of employment is so crucial to the economy, it is a sound measure of the overall strength or weakness of employment. Building levels also represent the general economic temper. Families build homes when they are confident of the future, and businessmen expand facilities when they expect growth and can afford to build. A decline in building rates is a sure sign of lack of confidence in the economy.

Votes of no confidence were cast in 1930 in Los Angeles, San Francisco, and Portland. Permits were down $19 million in Los Angeles from 1929 and $27.5 million since 1928. After its building boom in the mid-1920s Southern California became overbuilt as the onset of the depression sapped economic energies. Public works took up the slack, but controversies over public power delayed spending on water projects and later contributed to the defeat of power bonds earmarked for construction. In Los Angeles the building trades went into depression.[10]

As the decade opened, expectations for construction in San Francisco continued strong. The *San Francisco Examiner* added up almost $400 million in projects expected over the next three years for the Bay Area.[11] There were hospitals, army and air bases, auto and oil plants, sewers, streets, houses, and, most important of all, bridges to be built. In November 1930, Bay Area voters approved $35 million worth of Golden Gate Bridge bonds, enough to finance the project. In the same month the California Toll Bridge Authority sanctioned the $72 million Bay Bridge. These two projects would provide sustenance for a hard-hit construction industry. Because bond funds remained available for the two toll bridges, building continued on them through the 1930s. The bridges served the region as a public works project in the style of those that later New Deal agencies financed. These projects were critical, for, despite hopes, San Francisco suffered an acute decline in building in early 1930. Permits plummeted by one-third from $33 million to $22 million in the first full year of the depression.[12]

The story was much the same in Portland. Building permits in 1929 had totaled $15.5 million, but the 1930 figure was down some 22 percent to $12 million. Like bank deposits, building was ahead of the previous year's pace until September, when a last-quarter slump set in.[13] Seattle remained easily the bright spot on the coast. The late year expectations of 1929 for a private and public building wave were realized. Although the number of permits declined by more than 1,000, building increased $1.7 million to $30.8 million.[14]

These two major indicators, banking and building, paint a picture of an economy that was ailing, but hardly moribund, in 1930. Los Angeles, affected the earliest and the most thoroughly, saw its hopes for a second boom decade prove false. Portland also suffered more in 1930. The city was already in the economic doldrums by the late twenties because of the conditions of the lumber market. As a financial center San Francisco should have been hit hard by the crash, but bank after bank in northern California reported 1930 as a good year. Perhaps a degree of the fabled banker's conservatism, not so evident elsewhere, had been a reality in San Francisco.

Finally, considering the condition of its lumber market rival in Oregon, Seattle's banking and building condition proved a surprise. The depression may actually have hit the Puget Sound later than most places. If so, its fate was similar to that of Milwaukee, a city of comparable size. The Wisconsin city basked in prosperity in 1928 and 1929, but after encountering the problems of the depression somewhat later than much of the nation, Milwaukee had a more difficult time of it than most other cities.[15] Seattle, too, ultimately became a sorely pressed city. Perhaps the timing of the onset of the depression made a difference. Two cities, less affected in the first part of 1930, were later hit especially hard. At any rate, by 1930 the West Coast was a part of the Great Depression—but it is clear that the depression did not ravage the cities until late in the year.

A city's hinterland provides part of its economic context. Although a city of one-half million or more appears to dominate its outlying areas, the region surrounding a large metropolis has a great impact on its regional hub. If the market goes flat for what is grown or produced outside the city limits, the city will suffer. A useful way to gauge the economic impact of the outlying area on a city is to analyze the city's commerce figures. For the four great port cities of the West, waterborne commerce seems to have held its own or decreased slightly in 1930. Carloadings, however, were down on the West Coast. The greater problems evident in domestic commerce might be explained by the fact that the national economic slump preceded that of the rest of the world.

If Washington State orchardists really had to pay people thirty cents a box to take their apples, small wonder excess fruit showed up on New York street corners in the early years of the depression. In Washington surplus trees were pulled up and used for firewood.[16] Problems of overproduction extended to wheat and dairy products in the Northwest. The condition of the lumber industry, however, was worse than ever in 1930. By the first half of the year, mills were running at 63 percent of their capacity.[17] A multitude of sources—newspapers, employment bureaus, and private individuals—complained and worried about the fate of the lumber industry. Prices were low, demand was low, production was low, and they were all sinking lower. In the middle of 1930, an especially bright hope for Northwesterners, a tariff on wood products, suffered defeat in Congress. By January 1931 one Seattle newspaper lamented that production had reached pre–World War I levels. Portland milling in 1930 was 20 percent below the level of a depressed 1929.[18]

Los Angeles and San Francisco faced an oil glut of major proportions. In February petroleum industry leaders met in Los Angeles to discuss an oil conservation program. Unlike the conservation programs of a half century later, it would operate at the level of the producer rather than depend on consumers. The oil companies planned to conserve by artificially controlling the supply and, thus, the price. Whether born out of these cartel tactics or simply a reaction to low demand, California oil production was down 22 percent—40 million barrels—during the year.[19]

Another major industry of Southern California, tourism, took an interesting twist even in the early years of the depression. Auto travel into California rose in the summer tourist season—perhaps as much as 22 percent.[20] As the year came to a close, Californians became concerned about the quality and the motives of the visitors to the Golden State. The *Los Angeles Examiner* assured its readers that 91.7 percent of the cars coming into California were carrying financially well-off travelers planning to stay only for the winter. Indeed, the period 1930 to 1934 represented a low point of immigration to California.[21] Those who could afford to do so moved west, but in the 1930s many people who might have sought their opportunity along America's western shores simply could not afford it. The images from John Steinbeck's *Grapes of Wrath* derive from later in the decade. Nineteen-thirty witnessed a lull in geographical mobility.

Those who went to California looking for work rather than relaxation were not welcomed with open arms. Southern Californians were worried about migration not only from the East but also from south of the border. C. P. Visel, head of the Citizens Committee for Coordination of Unemployment Relief in Los Angeles, wrote to Colonel Arthur Woods of the President's Emergency Committee on Employment sharing his concern about the influx of 20,000 to 25,000 illegal aliens. Visel suggested holding federal hearings to alarm the aliens and send them packing somewhere else.[22] Although Southern Californians seeking cheap labor did not agree with the policy, the federal government began deporting illegal aliens in the 1930s. To others, however, the issue of unemployed outsiders invading the city became a major one as more and more Angelenos found themselves looking for work.

The West Coast economy tightened steadily in 1930. There was a noticeable slowdown in trade, manufacturing, and business. Money was not circulating as it had before. Although the entire year was hardly a loss, these negative forces intensified in the fall of 1930, reaching even the most out-of-the-way trades. In Portland the *Oregonian* reported that rather than police raids putting a dent in the Chinese lottery business, it was the "general financial depression" that limited the gambling operation.[23]

Nevertheless, the fortitude and optimism that characterized the response of many to the Great Crash continued through most of 1930. The main source of this surety was undoubtedly the confidence of the business community engendered by a decade of perceived prosperity. Business and political leaders of the four communities acknowledged some financial problems but did not admit, especially at the first of the year, that anything approaching a general financial depression was occurring or was possible. The financial forecast feature that the newspapers published at the beginning of each year gave businessmen the chance to wax their most optimistic. Chamber of commerce boosterism, so typical of the twenties, shot through many of the statements. Presidents of railroads, building and loan associations, utilities, banks, film studios, and, of course, the chambers of commerce all gave assurances of a plentiful decade to come. Citing the past, they confidently extrapolated the future. They predicted even greater growth, assuring their readers and themselves of the fundamental soundness of business. They prepared to build on that foundation. For example, the *San Francisco Examiner* asserted that the opening of the Stock Exchange Building in January symbolized "Faith in the future of the Pacific Coast and . . . unwavering confidence in San Francisco as the financial, manufacturing, and shipping capital of this western empire." And the *Oregonian* welcomed the new decade by proclaiming "That Oregon prosperity will continue throughout 1930 and far into the indefinite future seems as assured as those things can be."[24]

Editorials throughout the year reiterated this early confidence. The *Los Angeles Times* repeatedly reminded its readers that the city was the economic "white spot" in the nation. A progress section appeared in the *Seattle Star* in May. This seventeen-page pictorial and verbal salute to economic enterprise in Seattle featured new construction and spotlighted a variety of businesses and plants that symbolized the city's economic well-being.

Another variety of 1930s optimism admitted to some economic unsettling but focused on the upturn that was sure to materialize. One main theme was that the stock exchange drop was only a short episode that squeezed out speculators and made the entire economy healthier. The "white spot" editorials in the *Times*, for example, cautioned that the unemployed must not be overlooked. George Greenwood, president of Seattle's Pacific National Bank, proclaimed business basically sound but warned businessmen to move with care in the first part of 1930. Charles Martin, soon to be an Oregon congressman, implied the existence of problems even as he pointed at the "knockers" of business and prosperity in Oregon. He counseled these less-than-optimistic commentators to go to the wailing wall until they recognized how good they had it. Similarly, the *San Francisco Examiner* admonished its readers not to pay attention to howlers of gloom, especially in the face of prosperity. And the editor of the *Seattle Daily Journal of Commerce* called on citizens to stiffen their spines and stop wailing.[25] The Hearst newspapers —the *Examiner* in Los Angeles, the *Call-Bulletin* and *Examiner* in San Francisco, and the *Post-Intelligencer* in Seattle—ran small features entitled "Good News for Good Times." The editor of this section sought out signs of economic stability or resurgence to reassure the readers that, even if some people were becoming a little apprehensive, the economy was sound. The *Examiner* sponsored "Good Times Week" in October to celebrate not continuing prosperity, but the return of prosperity.[26]

Optimism, even among the boldest, then, was anything but monolithic. Some acknowledged problems, mainly in the past tense. Others used their optimism to bolster both a flagging confidence and a flagging economy—the two growing realities that fed on one another. In the spring of 1930, though, a number of prominent people in each of the cities recognized that something serious was wrong with the economy, and many of them were not necessarily taking or dispensing a dose of optimism as the cure. Even as early as December 1929, Mayor John C. Porter of Los Angeles noticed that winter unemployment was heavy, although he assured others he was not alarmed. In Portland the chamber of commerce had formed an unemployment committee and distributed an unemployment questionnaire by January. Two Portland Chamber of Commerce officials shared their concerns in their correspondence. Chamber president Raymond Wilcox wrote: "The situation, while probably not worse than in other leading cities of the nation, is one that commands the serious attention of every thoughtful person in Portland and Oregon." A few days later L. C. Newlands, head of the chamber's unemployment committee observed, "There is an unusual number of people unemployed here now;" he went on to urge a speed-up of Portland construction projects. In San Francisco, Hiram Johnson, Jr., expressed his worries to his father in January, writing that the city's economy was "dull" and that he had never seen things so slow.[27]

Some newspaper editors also pointed out economic problems, even as the weather warmed and seasonal employment picked up. Papers aimed especially at a blue-collar audience railed at what they perceived as their competitors' empty optimism. The *Los Angeles Record* ran a two-week series in April, "Forty and Out of Work," the tale of a former bank teller now down and out, fruitlessly in search of a job. The *Oregonian* received a diary of a fifty-eight-year-old unemployed "wanderer." The man described his despair—no jobs, spending his last quarter on some hot cakes—and his joys—a lunch at a Lions' Club soup line. The diary ended ominously as the wanderer threatened to break into jail—or just turn on the gas. The *San Francisco News* editorialized on the seriousness of unemployment in the city; it soon became a daily theme. The editor of the *Portland News* averred in July that his paper had been printing the facts on unemployment because he sought to report the news fully. And the *Seattle Post-Intelligencer* warned against printing "ballyhoo" to ward off discouragement, an offense the *P-I* was surely guilty of. Even Seattle's business paper, the *Daily Journal of Commerce*, warned in May that the unemployment levels might not be temporary.[28]

For some, the pressures reached the breaking point by the fall of the year. A San Francisco auto dealer shot one of his partners and took his own life. In Los Angeles a jobless cook committed suicide and a mortgage company executive killed himself, apparently after misappropriating $9,500.

Earlier in the year, the almost apocryphal Death Valley Scotty—Walter Scott—showed up in Los Angeles declaring, "I've been cleaned out in the stock market. Yes sir, I've been taken for a cleaning. Six million berries."[29] Los Angeles, long a hot-bed of racketeering, suffered a crime wave great enough to merit national attention—perhaps induced by the declining economic conditions. A *Portland News* reporter posed as an unemployed worker—a feature approach that virtually every newspaper tried out during the depression—and discovered misery, joblessness, and sleeping accommodations beneath the Burnside Bridge.

Portland City Commissioner R. E. Riley received two desperate appeals. One came from a newly arrived physician who sought night work so that he could keep his office open in the day to pay for his equipment. The other letter writer asked for work and pointed out, incredulously, "A few years ago we paid income tax, but now, we don't have enough to eat."[30]

John Anson Ford, later a Los Angeles County supervisor, related stories with happier endings. When Ford was thrown out of work he cashed in his savings bonds and all but one life insurance policy to pay the mortgage. After a short stint as a principal of a night school, he found a job in advertising, his field. Ford's parents assisted a neighbor family of six by sharing their own small supply of food. Not long thereafter, the neighbor started a rental business that ultimately was capitalized at several hundred thousand dollars.[31]

As the realization grew that the period of prolonged prosperity was over, there was no lack of proffered remedies. Letters to the editors in papers all along the West Coast suggested everything from William Randolph Hearst's national campaign for a $5 billion "prosperity loan" to road camps for transients. In May a *Los Angeles Record* reporter began a series of back-to-the-land articles describing the lures of country living and yeoman farming. So many wrote letters of interest and endorsement in response to his articles that he became the full-time back-to-the-land editor. A letter writer to San Francisco Mayor James Rolph suggested the California equivalent of New York apple sellers. In the Golden State oranges, of course, would replace apples.[32] Especially in the California cities, but in Portland and Seattle as well, some who focused on the unemployed were more concerned with their own security. They suggested a round-up of vagrants, especially aliens, who were taking Americans' jobs. These demands increased with time, especially in Los Angeles.

Critics of the capitalist system added their voices to those making suggestions. Upholders of the single tax advocated, inevitably, a shift of the tax burden from business onto the real estate speculator. A Bay Area commentator thought too much efficiency was the culprit. And Norman Coleman, president of Portland's Reed College, denounced the dog-eat-dog competition of capitalism and hoped for a more planned economy.[33] In 1930, though, it appeared unlikely that many shared these sentiments for a drastic overhaul of the American economic system.

Most of the ideas for wrestling with the economy and unemployment were more traditional and predictable. They came mainly from chamber of commerce members. A strongly advanced remedy was buying, or "buyology" as a *San Francisco Examiner* editor put it. He challenged his readers to keep struggling with the steadiness of the persevering ant.[34] The *Los Angeles Times* ran a feature entitled "Now Is the Time to Buy," which pointed out opportunities for cheaper purchases brought by the deflated dollar. The *Times* exhorted consumers not only to step up their purchases, but also to buy locally manufactured items. San Francisco's celebration of "Buy at Home Week" in August provided no remarkable results in retail sales figures. The *California Eagle*, a newspaper aimed at the black community of Los Angeles, worked a variation on this theme. The *Eagle* frequently admonished its readers that in a time of economic problems no Negro should patronize any establishment that refused to employ Negroes.[35] In a depression, the editor implied, it was more necessary than ever to support one's real friends, a sentiment shared by every segment of the community.

In all four cities private construction and public works gained the greatest advocacy. As early as March and April of 1930 both chamber of commerce leaders and newspapers called for increased building to offset unemployment. Typical was the *Oregon Daily Journal*, which led off a March editorial, "When the unemployed reach numbers in the thousands . . ." and went on to call for accelerating construction projects in the area.[36] At the onset of winter the Portland Chamber of Commerce asked the city and county governments to provide supplemental expenditures and a diversion of funds for public works. To the north the *Seattle Daily Journal of Commerce* echoed the same plea. Wyllie Hemphill, Seattle chamber president, assured his listeners in July that things were not as bad as rumors indicated, but he noted defensively that four months earlier he had urged Seattle to get busy on work projects to help the unemployed.[37] Leaders in all the cities asked federal, state, and local governments to support public works projects vigorously. The state of Oregon, most responsive to such a call, accelerated its highway work. San Franciscans probably had the most to capitalize on, as the Hetch Hetchy project was being finished and the bridge projects were starting up. The San Francisco Chamber of Commerce recognized its opportunity and printed in bold type on the front page of its October newsletter, "Break Breadlines! Build the Bridge!"[38] Los Angeles, too, looked to construction projects. The *Examiner* saw a hope of absorbing the unemployed through approval of water bonds and claimed 2,061 more would be employed if voters approved public power bonds.[39]

The push for building projects to take up the slack in unemployment included more than major public or private undertakings. Those paint-up, fix-up chores that had gone untended for so long, editorialists suggested, now could be done by hiring men who badly needed the work. This ultimately became a major response to unemployment.

Advice for stemming the mounting tide of joblessness did not entirely flow from the top downward in 1930. Many citizens in the four cities urged their suggestions on the business leaders. Primarily this advice had to do with who worked, how long they worked, and for how much. The laboring community itself seemed to be divided on these issues, and when issues of pay and working hours became enmeshed, the advice got hazy. Labor union leaders and wage earners in general, of course, declaimed against cuts in pay. Five major employers in Seattle declared as late as August their companies would make no wage reductions.[40] Labor and management representatives seemed in accord about the five-day work week. The shortened week was supposedly a method by which work could be spread around, and, perhaps, wages would remain relatively stable. The probusiness *Los Angeles Times* was a proponent of the idea, and many labor leaders endorsed it. But one must wonder if they had really agreed on the same thing. The *Times* clearly advocated five days' wages for five days' work—in effect a one-sixth wage cut. The labor leaders meant the same thing by their five-day week plan, but only under the stipulation that management hire additional workers to fill the gap. A cut in the work week alone was unacceptable. The five-day week did become a popular remedy but did not result in increased employment.

Another issue concerned two-income families and the practice of moonlighting. Should both husband and wife work when other families had no breadwinners? In 1930 the answer seemed to be no, and in 1931 and 1932 many West Coast observers became emphatic about it. One job per family was enough when so many families had none.

The least painful solution was to bring dollars from the outside. Chambers of commerce being what they are, business leaders in the West acted on this hope with a great deal of vigor. In November 1930 the Seattle business community responded to a "call to arms" at a town meeting and organized a Committee of 59. In San Francisco, true to their Gold Rush heritage, it was the Committee of 49, and in Portland the On to Oregon committee was formed. The mandate of each committee was to sell the city and the region to the rest of the world and to promote new industry, tourism, and population growth—taking care, of course, not to attract unemployed workers. As the economy deteriorated, booster-ism became more organized.

The public reaction of community leaders and opinion-makers was merely evolving in 1930. Early in the year, before the evidence of a fall-off in the economy was widespread, the statements of most people in the public spotlight were hopeful and optimistic. By spring only a few seemed to recognize that any significant slowdown was occurring. Then, as acknowledgment of some problems grew, most policy-makers responded with the rhetoric and ideas of the 1920s. Men of promi-nence tended to emphasize the psychology of economic slumps. Dispelling doom-sayers, encouraging waverers, cautioning against a negative attitude that would send the economy reeling was the order of the day. The nation in 1930 continued to hold businessmen and business practices in high esteem. Underconsumption, not poorly managed production, was the first culprit that most commentators pub-licly identified. The consumer needed to get out and buy; the manager need not stop outproducing demand.

While observers advanced the solution of simply continuing the good times of the 1920s, they also pressed vigorously for a remedy that ultimately played the major part in extracting the nation from depression—the speed-up of all con-struction and an expansion of public works. With perhaps the exception of San Francisco and its bridge projects, the dimension of the solution was limited in 1930. There was little desire for the federal government to initiate and subsidize public projects just to get people back to work. When Herbert Hoover urged an increase in public works at all levels, including the national level, in November 1929, he was actually in advance of many local opinion-makers in the West. Few, if any, public statements revealed concern that problems were so serious that local, or perhaps state, authorities could not handle them. The mindset developed over eight or more American generations was not so easily changed. The ideas commu-nity leaders advocated for combating economic problems and unemployment were constrained by a historic attitude and underwritten by personal and national suc-cesses in the 1920s. In 1930 the people and their president were in substantial agreement about conditions, remedies, and the role of the federal government. There was no reason to change.

What about the condition of the people themselves—those caught in the eco-nomic rip tide, those who would draw the attention of their concerned fellow citizens for the next years? How many people struggled under the burden of wage cuts or were without a job? What were their thoughts? The federal government did not immediately embark on anything resembling a careful and sophisticated process of information gathering, and when it did—the census of unemployment, which accompanied the decennial census of April 1930—many emphatically dis-agreed with the results.

This lack of nose counting necessarily leads to impressionistic descriptions of the unemployment levels. The impressions, however, correspond with reports from the rest of the nation. Philadelphia in 1930 suffered a 44 percent increase in unemployment over its already inflated level of 1929. Boston's welfare costs shot up 32 percent, in Detroit 100,000 had registered for help by the end of 1930, and soup lines had formed in Tulsa.[41]

The situation in the West was as grim as anywhere. About March or April, when employment levels should have picked up, there was no seasonal rise. Concern about unemployment remained quiescent during the summer, then emerged in the fall, about November. This reaction paralleled the downward swing in building statistics, and the first shudder of anxiety among the more optimistic observers. The downturn in the seasonal economic cycle (the slowing of construction as West Coast weather turned showery) converged with joblessness to create a distinct impression of unemployment in the last third of the year.

Whether the unemployment rate had been unusually high all year is difficult to ascertain. There is evidence that low employment existed as early as spring 1930. This was well before leaders of the four communities recognized it. The *Los Angeles Citizen* quoted an organized labor report stating that the jobless rate peaked in the city in March 1930, after there had already been a severe drop-off in the fall of 1929. The head of Los Angeles County Charities estimated his agency's case load had quadrupled by March. The U.S. Employment Service reported that in May a large surplus of laborers remained in San Francisco, even though unemployment rates had declined since early spring. As early as February, Seattle newspapers ran both editorials and articles on unemployment, and two local unemployment offices estimated that between 15,000 and 35,000 were out of work. Whatever the figure, employment was in more than a seasonal decline well before the end of the year. The job crisis was worst in Oregon. Estimates of the unemployed ranged between 10,000 and 20,000 in Portland. The state labor commissioner estimated that the February jobless rate for the entire state reached as high as 25 percent.[42]

The official federal figures showed a much less drastic situation. President Hoover authorized a count of the unemployed in urban areas as a part of the spring census. In April, conditions improved as the weather warmed and the rain abated and more outdoor jobs became available. But this seasonal moderating (and in the first comprehensive census of unemployment there was hardly such a thing as a seasonal adjustment) cannot explain the divergence between local reports and the federal figures. The census-takers found 20,000 unemployed in Los Angeles, a jobless rate of 3.6 percent of the population, or 7.7 percent of gainful workers. In San Francisco 21,000 were unemployed for a rate of 3.4 percent of the population, or 6.4 percent of the normal work force. In Seattle 12,000 were looking for work, or 3.4 percent of the population and 7 percent of the work force. And in Portland the census recorded the worst situation of the four with over 13,000 unemployed—4.4 percent of the population.[43] Although these percentages should represent the most reliable data, they are hard to accept in the light of different statistics and comments from throughout the nation. Officials in Rochester, New York, for example, estimated in November that unemployment was twice as high as the federal census-takers had set it in April. James Patterson maintains the average unemployment rate from 1910 to 1929 was between 8 and 10 percent. If this was so, the census may have missed by half. The census-takers also failed to include those "temporarily laid off" as unemployed. In April 1930 many of the newly unemployed would have optimistically placed themselves in this category.[44] For whatever reasons, the 1930 census of unemployment seriously underestimated the number of jobless workers everywhere in the country. It is easier to believe this than it is to believe that so many became unemployed so rapidly in the fall of 1930.

Breadlines formed in Los Angeles in June, and police confronted transients and vagrants in San Francisco by the end of the year. The California State Chamber of Commerce economic report ratified local concerns—the December rate of employment in the state was 20 percent below the five-year average. Seattle and Portland were experiencing the same kinds of problems in autumn. The Seattle Public Employment Office noted that laid-off workers came from all walks of life. In a telling aside in his report, the agency head asked that the office be moved away from the Volunteers of America breadline because he did not want his respectable but unemployed clients to be tinged with the down-and-out image associated with the charity effort. In both Portland and Seattle the number of positions the employment office could find for their applicants dropped drastically in December. Placements ran about half the October level and were the lowest of the year. The Portland jobless figure fluctuated. In November A. W. Jones of the Public Employment Office estimated it at 16,000 to 18,000—a May estimate had ranged as high as 20,000—and the *Oregonian* estimated unemployment had risen 4 percent from August to September.[45]

Besides the business statistics, the comments from community leaders, and the somewhat uncertain employment figures, there was one other indication of economic problems resulting in unemployment—the reactions of the jobless themselves. Through the early depression years the unemployed were calm. The absence of violent protest through 1933 characterized both the West Coast and the nation as a whole. Robert and Helen Lynd judged that in Muncie, Indiana, class consciousness was rudimentary at best.[46] This observation describes the situation in the larger West Coast cities. Some of the nation's jobless did join Communist Unemployed Councils. A council formed in each of the western cities and became a center for avowedly Communist agitation.

Just how "Communist" the unemployed councils were, or how much Communists influenced the unemployed is a matter of conjecture. Estimates of the number of Communists in San Francisco demonstrate this. In the spring of 1930, representatives of the Pacific American Steamship Association worried that 2,000 Communists were boring into the city's unemployed. A San Francisco police captain thought he detected 5,000, while immigration officials thought 300 to 355 Communists must be in the city. The *Examiner* estimated only 175 card-carrying Communists to be in San Francisco.

In Los Angeles the International Unemployed Conference organized in early 1930 to seek ways of combating the depression. According to an American Civil Liberties Union publication, the conference had become Communist dominated by April of that year. Even without Communist leadership the International Unemployed Conference stridently criticized capitalist leadership. In a letter to the Los

Angeles County Board of Supervisors the conference wrote: "Call this slowing down of industry a business depression if you will, but that does not lessen its severity." The letter also protested the fraudulent propaganda of the Los Angeles Chamber of Commerce that lured "poor suckers" to the Hollywood underworld of motion pictures, tide flats, and alkali cactus.[47]

This kind of radical verbal heat in 1930 kindled reactionary fires up and down the West Coast, especially in Los Angeles. The Los Angeles police and *Los Angeles Times*, acutely anti-Communist, insisted the city was a hot-bed of activism. The *Times*, especially, gave front-page space to any kind of unemployment activity, presenting the events as a threat to the safety of Angelenos. Reports of "Reds" rioting graced the pages of the *Times*, and an editorial pointed out that most of those arrested in a February riot bore Russian names.

In March 1930 the unemployed, led by Communist organizations, staged marches all over the United States. The manner in which the leaders of the four cities responded to the marches is instructive. In San Francisco and Portland the parades of unemployed occurred peacefully. The mayors of the two cities spoke with the marchers when they arrived at their respective city halls, and in San Francisco, where 1,200 marched, the chief of police participated in the parade. Portland Mayor George Baker met the marchers' demands of immediate direct relief, free rents, a seven-hour day, and five-day week with sympathy and promises of an employment clearinghouse. In Seattle the police—chamber of commerce "cossacks" to the prolabor newspaper—broke up a march of one hundred or so demonstrators. And in Los Angeles a show of force met perceived threats to the American Way. Some one thousand police stood ready to repel the marchers with blackjacks and clubs. The night before the parades, police had staged raids and arrested some of the militant leaders. Mayor Porter refused to confer with marchers.

Throughout the United States the unemployed demonstrated a number of times, but they did so more to draw attention to their plights than to overturn society. Only Cleveland experienced a jobless riot, but Los Angeles witnessed as much ongoing unrest, which at times broke into violence, as any city.

To a degree, Los Angeles officials brought this on themselves. Of the four cities, Los Angeles was controlled by leaders most hostile to any kind of demonstration. In the 1920s the city had organized the Intelligence Bureau of the Metropolitan Police Division—commonly known as the Red Squad. This special law enforcement group was active throughout the Hoover years, and it became a part of Los Angeles's response to the depression. Southern Californians seemed to approve. Some accepted it as a necessary evil, but many Angelenos considered the Red Squad a bulwark against radicalism. The head of the squad during the era, William Hynes, outlined the premise of the enforcement group: "The policy of this department . . . has been concerned mainly with the rights and privileges, and interests of the vast majority of the law abiding citizens of Los Angeles and not with protecting the asserted rights of known enemies of our government or with their fantastic and hair-splitting free speech rights."[48] If anyone questioned this attitude as less than correct in upholding the law, Police Commissioner Mark

Pierce set them straight: "The more police beat them up and wreck their headquarters the better," Pierce stated. "Communists have no Constitutional rights and I won't listen to anyone who defends them."[49]

Community leaders and police in the other three cities also experienced problems in dealing with the militant unemployed, and they were concerned about Communists and radicals in their midst. Portland police cracked down on vagrants, broke up a jobless union, and hired a spy to infiltrate the Communist hierarchy. Sixteen indictments resulted from the latter action. Police in Seattle met a succession of marches by force and physically broke up a protest meeting of the unemployed. As each city became acutely aware of the economic and employment situations, it appears only San Francisco leaders felt secure enough to deal relatively peacefully with those most strident in pointing out the problems.

To cope with their growing problems it was crucial that each city possess not only the financial strength to carry on but also a willingness to provide for the unemployed. Each city worked with its own set of advantages and constraints as it sought to meet the needs of its citizens.

A major policy of the Los Angeles city government throughout the depression was retrenchment. And retrenchment was the order of the day as the 1930–31 budget process got under way. The city council hoped to pare as much as $1 million from the previous year's budget. Assessments had been lower than expected, and, according to Mayor John Porter, the city faced "subnormal conditions."[50] Ultimately the council agreed on a budget that was $660,000 less than 1929–30. Remarkably, after suffering a $1.6 million shortfall in 1929–30, Los Angeles showed a surplus of almost $6 million at the end of the 1930–31 fiscal year. It was the last surplus of the Hoover years.[51] As the council considered cuts it turned to public works and the wages of city employees. The council voted to cut thirty-eight projects, estimated to save $2 million. Council members did, however, appropriate $227,000 to be sure the Los Angeles Coliseum would be ready for the fall 1930 football season. The council passed an ordinance to cut most employees' work week to five days, allowing a skeleton staff to serve on Saturday mornings in eight key offices. These decisions foreshadowed some important trends. In Los Angeles, as in the other three cities, there was a great deal of tension between advocates of property tax cuts and those seeking increased expenditures or, at least, minimal cut-backs to keep as many as possible employed—at public works projects or on their jobs with the city. In Los Angeles, more than any of the other three cities, those who were most concerned about escalating tax levies controlled the decisions.

In San Francisco, Seattle, and Portland the 1931 city budgets were higher. Fighting the same problem of lowered assessments as Los Angeles, the city and county of San Francisco increased both its budget and its property tax rate. Seattle and Portland, expecting higher assessments, raised their budgets. Portland lowered its tax levy but, when assessments fell, experienced an unbalanced budget.

Because cities do have a base of property on which they can levy taxes, their potential to raise money is extensive. There are, however, both obvious and subtle limits to this. Obviously, political realities do not permit an open-ended increase of taxes as a community is pressed down by its needs, such as the relief for the unemployed. At some point, homeowners and other property owners object. This happened in each city as the depression progressed. In the struggles over taxes the ideals of Hoover's cooperative individualism encountered the greatest challenge. Sacrificing for others less well off meant accepting higher tax rates in a time of insecurity and lost income. Taxes and city budgets were a supreme test of Hoover's faith in American values and of Americans' perception of themselves.

In addition there were legal limits to the opportunities to sacrifice for others through the tax structure. Each city had a debt limit tied to its assessed valuation. California law mandated a 15 percent limit. That is, a city was allowed to carry a load of bonded indebtedness of up to 15 percent of the value of all taxable real estate and personal property. In Los Angeles there was a 12 percent lid for acquisition and construction of public utilities and a 3 percent limit on general purpose obligations. San Francisco's limit was 12 percent, not including water bonds. Portland's limit for the city and dock was 7 percent.[52]

City authorities were in a vise. As the needs of the unemployed mounted, relief took a larger and larger chunk of budget appropriations. Decreasing property valuations meant tax levies would have to increase simply to maintain budget levels, a dismal prospect for property owners. And, because of the generally poor condition of the nation's financial community, there was no market for municipal bonds even though the cities were well below their legal indebtedness limit. Marketing bonds became progressively more difficult. Maintaining budgets and tax levels proved virtually impossible. As economic conditions worsened, cities struggled harder and harder to find the funds to respond to those conditions.

THREE

Tried and Found Wanting

By the end of 1930 economic problems and unemployment could not be ignored. Urban leaders, and citizens themselves, finally grasped, still imperfectly perhaps, the magnitude of the problem at hand. The reaction, for it was not assertive action by any means, was spontaneous and commensurate with the level of realization. No help was expected from the federal government. President Hoover had met with business and labor leaders and extracted assurances that they would cooperate to assure a sound economy. The President's Emergency Committee for Employment, set up in October, advised mayors on how to cope with their unemployment problems but did no more than that. In December Congress did pass a $116 million public works package to expand employment, but this had little impact on the rapidly deteriorating situation.

The efforts put forth to deal with these problems provide insights into the value structure of Americans, especially those on the West Coast. Because neither well-developed programs nor contingency plans to meet economic catastrophe existed in some welfare directors' files, citizens fell back on familiar schemes that had proven effective in lesser crises of shorter duration. There were also a few professionals who could help establish emergency relief. In short, 1930 was a year first of discovery, then of trial. The citizens still perceived a reasonably manageable problem and placed their faith in tried solutions. In most cases these were found wanting.

In a nationwide study of emergency relief made in 1930 and 1931, Joanna Colcord of the Russell Sage Foundation found evidence of particular values that governed the relatively traditional responses to the depression in the Hoover years.[1] Cities chose not to provide the unemployed with direct relief. Administrators believed that the jobless would not spend the money wisely and that direct relief would only intensify their aversion to work. Work relief was the only acceptable solution for the able bodied. Colcord pointed out that work relief, as opposed to a dole, had two distinct advantages that Americans endorsed: it benefited the community and it did not demoralize the relief recipient. Both the worker's morale and the work ethic were thereby served, and the taint of the dole was avoided. Of the twenty-eight work relief programs Colcord surveyed, most were virtually indistinguishable from existing public works programs.

Moreover, she noted many city programs, in their efforts to adhere to the established values, focused on the nature of the relief program and failed to pay attention to the needs of the recipients. This was not unusual, given the general nature of public welfare at the time. The social work community, of course, had long abandoned the notion that poverty revealed a character flaw or some other deficiency in the recipient's make-up. By the 1920s most professionals accepted the progressives' belief that the economic environment was a principal cause of poverty. Social workers had also adopted a progressive devotion to efficiency. This, combined with a twenties proclivity for applying good business principles to anything, led to the rationalization of charity and, consequently, concern for the program rather than the impoverished. On the eve of the depression, Colcord observed, the professionals believed—not unlike the businessman-engineer-president —that poverty literally could be managed. As poverty became unmanageable and "normal" people began seeking assistance, the view of social workers and the president soon diverged.

From the little evidence they left, the poor seemed to share in the general ethos. The jobless seemed poor candidates for radicalism. Those who have studied poverty and the poor in America theorize that an initial lack of suffering, then the debilitation of lost jobs, the necessity of relief, and, finally, the loss of hope caused or deepened apathy among those in need. "For the new poor, especially," James Patterson suggests, "the shock of hard times was overwhelming. Unemployment made them ashamed, defensive, reclusive." Patterson quotes a victim of poverty: "Always going to be more poor folks than them that ain't poor, and I guess always will be. It ain't that's the government's fault. It's just right truth that's all."[2]

The attitudes and values Herbert Hoover commended to the nation were in fact the people's own. The responsibility belonged to local governments or private entities but not to the federal or even the state government. The jobless would work for their relief checks so their moral fiber could remain strong. The strength of these beliefs was ratified in Los Angeles, San Francisco, Seattle, and Portland in 1930.

The California Pauper Act in force in 1929 stated:

> Every county and every city and county shall relieve and support all paupers, incompetent, poor, indigent persons, and those incapacitated by age, disease, or accident, lawfully resident therein, when such persons are not supported and relieved by their relatives or friends, or by their own means or by state hospitals; or other state or private institutions.[3]

Although the reference to relatives and friends is a telling one in terms of prevailing values, the thrust of this statute meant that California counties had legal responsibility for the welfare of their citizens ("city and county" is a reference to San Francisco's unique form of government). In Los Angeles, then, the legal burden was on the county, although the city was hardly exempt from moral responsibility. The County Department of Charities administered public welfare under the direct jurisdiction of the Los Angeles County Board of Supervisors. In addition to the general hospital, sanitarium, cemetery, and other similar institutions, the superintendent of charities oversaw the Bureau of County Welfare, which handled all noninstitutional relief cases such as the unemployed.

Prior to 1930 the task of the welfare services was caring for the physically and mentally infirm, not dispensing relief to those whom a business panic had thrown out of work. In the 1921 economic downturn, the state of California increased its public works budget by $10 million while local municipalities helped with direct relief.

The qualifications for receiving relief funds from Los Angeles County were strict and inappropriate for people who had lost steady jobs for the first time in their lives. For example, relief was denied to anyone owning property valued at $2,500 or more. Those who owned less had to agree to a county lien on their possessions if that property was worth $250 or more. The county established a family budget and refused aid to those who exceeded it. Moreover, the claimant had to prove he had no relatives to depend on and had to be a resident of the county at least one year and California for three.[4] Although the relief process became more professional by 1930, not the structure, the professional understanding, or the rules for eligibility fit the victims or the scope of the depression.

Because it was not under legal mandate the city was understandably even less prepared to handle major relief problems. The Municipal Social Services Department mainly approved private charitable organizations and regulated their solicitations. The Social Services Department also ran the Christmas Clearing Bureau, established the Municipal Service Bureau for Homeless Men in 1928, and the Associated Women's Committee for Women's Unemployment Relief in 1931. The Bureau for Homeless Men, the major direct, city-financed contribution to unemployed assistance, was a clearing house that referred clients to private agencies. In 1929 it handled over 6,800 applications. The case load for the last half of 1929 increased 267 percent over the last half of 1928. It is difficult to be sure whether the increase was because of better organization and better articulation with other agencies or whether it marked the beginnings of the economic slowdown.[5]

Although the county had the ultimate responsibility for sustaining the jobless, private institutions assumed the primary burden during most of 1930. The Los Angeles Chamber of Commerce did more than simply exhort consumption and propose building projects. As early as March the chamber had formed a committee to look into the jobless problem. By September, chamber president John Austin, who later became the POUR director for Los Angeles, announced the chamber would coordinate welfare and public employment agencies to expand assistance to the unemployed. By the end of the year the efforts at coordination had become regionwide as D. W. Pontius, president of Pacific Electric Railway, headed a Southern California study group to ascertain the extent of the problem and seek available means of relief.

Many long-standing private organizations joined the relief efforts. A response unique in scale for any of the four cities was the Parent Teacher Association (PTA) milk and lunch program. As school opened in 1930 local PTAs realized that some Los Angeles families were in desperate circumstances. Using its own funds and later subsidized by tens of thousands of county dollars, the PTA began to identify children and, in some cases, adults in need. In October 1930 the organization distributed 3,032 half-pints of milk and 1,276 lunches every day at Los Angeles County schools. For over 250 children this was the only meal consumed the entire day.[6]

Several religious organizations in Los Angeles enlarged their operations to respond to the situation. The Catholic Welfare Bureau—the largest private charitable agency in the city—served primarily Roman Catholics in need but did not turn away others. The bureau's main outreach was through Family Service. Similar to the Municipal Service Bureau, Family Service directed people in need to the local agencies that could be of the greatest help. In 1930 21,600 received such assistance. The Catholic Welfare Bureau was not only a clearinghouse. It also provided housing for the homeless and set up an employment bureau, and St. Vincent de Paul—the international Roman Catholic charitable organization—assisted 2,020 families during the year. The Jewish Social Service Bureau, a part of the Jewish Federation of Los Angeles, provided the same services for the Jewish community. This bureau aided those who were not receiving county relief and provided a supplement to those whom the County Welfare Board was helping. There is no record of any Protestant organization that assisted the unemployed in 1930. This may be because Protestants were a majority in the city and relied on community agencies. Individual church histories from each city seem to include little reference to depression-related relief for their congregations or for their neighbors. The most frequent concern expressed in these brief recountings was whether the church could pay its mortgage.

Private secular organizations served the needs of those unable to find work. The Midnight Mission was a central spot in Los Angeles for transients. Originally founded to assist drifters wandering in and out of town, the mission was packed by the end of 1930. An emergency dormitory with 300 beds accommodated the overflow beginning in November. During the Thanksgiving season the mission fed 2,000 jobless in one day. Mary Covell, mission director, reported that 130,890 received beds and 315,982 meals were served to single men in 1930.[7] Covell also had a hand in establishing the Los Angeles Food Conservation Warehouse during the early years of the depression. The warehouse served as a companion for the Midnight Mission, providing food for families. Covell, with the help of others, turned an old Southern Pacific Railroad building into a distribution center. Warehouse officials handed out thousands of dollars of donated goods every week to recipients who obtained tickets for a week's supply of food from other agencies. The food was donated or provided at low cost. Several tons of sugar, which federal agents seized from bootleggers, went to needy families by way of the warehouse.

A number of agencies that could not by themselves serve the variety of needs of those who came to them combined for greater efficiency. This multifaceted group, which included the Red Cross, the Volunteers of America, the American Legion, and five other agencies, functioned under the financial aegis of the community chest, although not all of them were chest charities. Finally, to aid farm workers, the Farm Labor Bureau opened its doors in August. The bureau directed farm workers to jobs throughout the state and, thus, removed them from idleness on the streets of Los Angeles.

The hoped-for neighborliness of cooperative individualism exhibited itself in numerous job drives, fund raisers, and individual contributions to assist the unemployed. These less structured, grass roots efforts were not annual but were responses to the prevailing conditions. The *Los Angeles Record* was especially active early on, assisting those who had lost jobs. In June the newspaper provided free advertisements for both job seekers and those who could furnish positions. By the Fourth of July the paper reported itself "swamped" with eager takers.[8] In the fall the *Record* urged citizens to call the Division of State Employment with any job opportunity, no matter how small. Two thousand placements materialized out of the campaign. In Los Angeles there were labor fund raisers, actors' benefit performances, a radio auction, a forget-me-not campaign for war veterans, and, after the merits of selling flowers or shopping bags were debated, the jobless purveyed apples on the street corners.

The *Los Angeles Examiner*, and others as well, warned that charity money be put to good use. "It is right to take care of our own first," the *Examiner*'s editor proclaimed, as he worried over spending public and private charity funds on professional panhandlers and aliens. For many Angelenos, not just the editor, serving only citizens of Los Angeles was sound stewardship.

Another method of giving assistance was to spread the work. Those who were relatively secure in their jobs made major sacrifices to assist fellow employees keep their positions in the face of layoffs. At a metal-working plant workers voted unanimously to accept a five-day work week to enable the hiring of ten additional employees. The city workers' job fund was the most publicized instance of workers sacrificing a portion of their salaries for others. The job-fund campaign originated in the Los Angeles Fire Department, then spread to the engineering, police, and health departments, and finally expanded to the whole city. In December city employees on their own initiative set up booths where individuals could register to donate 1 percent of their salaries. The first phase of this project lasted from December to August 1931 and raised $114,469, which provided 28,140 days of work for those who otherwise would have been laid off.[9]

Those who had fallen victim to unemployment also began to join together in 1930 for some bootstrap tugging. A *Record* reporter interviewed Paul Davis, an unemployed Angeleno, who described a barter system. The *California Eagle* endorsed a national job-finding convention scheme for Afro-Americans. And in April the International Unemployment Conference came together to help the jobless get food and work. Almost immediately Communists elected their candidates to every office, and the organization turned to direct action against the authorities rather than pursuing a course of self-help.

In all four cities, wherever the private response was structured rather than spontaneous, the community chest usually provided leadership. Before the onset of the depression, the community chest oversaw and solicited funds for a wide variety of organizations, most of which had a special target group or cause. As the needs of the general public increased, the chest became an integral part of both the public and private response to declining conditions. In many cases throughout the nation, city authorities worked closely with the community chest, often funneling public funds through the organization because its administration and its component agencies were the most capable and most experienced in rendering service efficiently and well. This mingling of private and public funds was common on the West Coast.

The community chest in Los Angeles was a three-part organization. The finance committee raised funds, the council of social agencies decided what funds each constituent agency received and oversaw the agencies' work, and the public relations department apprised the public of the chest's needs and accomplishments. Many of the major private charities in Los Angeles came under the umbrella of the community chest's funding and oversight. The Catholic Welfare Bureau, St. Vincent de Paul, the Jewish Social Service Bureau, the city's Municipal Service Bureau for Homeless Men, and the Midnight Mission were chest agencies.

The Los Angeles Community Chest depended heavily on the well-off. In 1929, 2 percent of the contributors gave 65 percent of the gifts.[10] The chest spent just over $3 million and ended the year with a surplus of some $2,000. This was the first time in five years it had functioned in the black and the last time the chest would come close to such a feat for some time.

The 1931 fund drive began in October 1930. The *Los Angeles Times* pointed out in a supportive editorial, "At no time since the war has thoughtful and constructive giving been so essential." Spurred by recognition of this necessity, chest officials set the goal for contributions at $3.2 million—about 7 percent higher than ever before. In an ongoing irony of the depression, just as there was surely a greater need, there was less ability on the part of the community as a whole to fill the need. The struggle for funds went on for almost two months. Campaign workers placed a good deal of pressure on those better-off citizens who had always provided a large proportion of the budget. In at least three different businesses employers informed their employees that they must contribute one day's wages or be fired. Each business reported 100 percent participation.[11]

Despite such pressure and harassment the drive fell short. The chest collected less than $2.7 million—a 15 percent shortfall. The chest would fall well short of the needs in 1931, but there was little that its officials could do. One answer was to pare the operating budget. From 1930 to 1933 employees endured a 25 percent pay cut, and the general manager received a salary of $6,000 a year, the lowest of any director in a large city. But even these savings were insignificant compared to the need. Much more than private charity was needed.

In December 1929 agency officials, institution heads, and leaders of business and labor met at city hall to determine the best course of action to absorb the unemployed. They agreed that a simple increase in public works projects would be the correct action. A meeting this early in the course of the depression, and the results of the meeting, fit the traditional pattern of awareness and concern. Something had gone awry, but officials did not sense that problems were so serious that they needed to take more meaningful and concerted action.

In October 1930, Mayor Porter confidently reported that the city had neither begun nor contemplated any general campaign to aid the jobless.[12] In fact, both the city and county were expanding their public works programs, and soon a greater effort would be made to assist the unemployed. The mayor, in his announcement on the nonexistence of a general campaign for the jobless, did mention aqueduct work on the major Owens Valley project underwritten by a $38 million bond, which voters approved in May, and noted that the city had put 60,000 jobless men to work on fire breaks in March.

A. C. Price, county assistant superintendent of charities, wrote to the county board of supervisors in July, "I believe [the board of supervisors] are evidently thoroughly familiar with the present situation in Los Angeles County" as he successfully requested an additional $50,000 to finish out the fiscal year.[13] The board also sped up public works projects, which included a large appropriation for work on the Los Angeles Coliseum, the site of the 1932 Olympics.

As the season for major outdoor construction was ending, Angelenos began to admit that they were facing problems. In late October the chamber of commerce became more active on the unemployment issue as John Austin called for a city –county conference to establish a cooperative program for responding to the problem. Throughout November several public and private leaders formulated a plan to alleviate unemployment and created an organization to carry it out. The chamber–city–county coalition proposed a three-part solution: speed up public works, make no city or county layoffs, and buy locally. The county underlined its commitment to provide relief to only the deserving poor by promising a work test for transients. Anyone seeking relief in the form of room and board would have to perform work to receive aid. The prison work farm was the alternative for any vagrants who sought to evade the work test. As plans progressed politics intruded. Political rivalries produced two relief committees. County Commissioner Frank Shaw, the chairman of the board of supervisors Welfare Committee, controlled one body. Shaw was a political rival of Mayor Porter, so it was no surprise that a city committee, which Porter controlled, also came into being.

The city began confronting the problem of raising and dispensing funds. After the city attorney ruled a mandatory 1 percent city worker contribution scheme illegal, municipal authorities designated money for relief. By January 1931, Porter reported that Los Angeles had channeled $100,000 through the community chest, set aside $40,000 for more fire break construction, and the Department of Water and Power had appropriated $200,000 for 500 extra jobs for the coming year.[14] Fire stations served as registration headquarters for those who sought the relief work. The city created three priority categories: residents with dependents, residents without dependents, and, finally, single men and nonresidents. So many of the first category signed up that only they received work. In two days 2,000 had registered. By the end of the first month 14,000 requested relief.

It was the county, of course, that had the legal responsibility to provide relief. County officials met to consider the best plans and discussed simply encouraging citizens to buy now and buy locally. But ultimately they established substantially the same program as the city—a central registry through the public schools. The board of supervisors appointed Harvey C. Fremming, a deputy state labor commissioner and president of the Long Beach Central Labor Council, as director of the Employment Stabilization Bureau—an agency created to help the unemployed find jobs.

In the fiscal year 1930–31 the county and city each spent $5 million. Besides public works the county found shelter for the homeless and sought jobs for almost 26,000 relief cases, only 15 percent of which they placed.[15] The county offered direct relief where necessary—if the recipient was infirm or physically handicapped—but both county and city preferred to provide work relief for those seeking aid, even though it was more expensive. The concern for the work ethic Joanna Colcord found in her study outweighed cost-cutting or efficiency.

The county, swamped by applications, sought to pull in the welcome mat. Police met arriving trains to escort transients to city and county labor camps. The supervisors demanded that all county-contracted work be done by resident employees and embarked on a program of deporting illegal aliens, one that picked up momentum in the succeeding years.

The state of California was not particularly vigorous in contributing financial assistance. Governor C. C. Young set up the State Unemployment Commission, which studied the unemployment problem with the primary purpose of planning for future emergencies. Although almost half the men on the governor's board were residents of Southern California, little came to Los Angeles. And the new governor, former San Francisco Mayor James Rolph, showed little inclination to go beyond study committees. In his January 1931 inaugural address, Rolph came out against any tax increases; later he admonished the counties to shoulder much of the relief burden.[16] The governor and state legislature did little for any city or county until 1932. The federal government lent assistance by increasing California's highway appropriation 181 percent for the first quarter of 1930 and later adding another $3 million in an emergency bill.

Elements of the Los Angeles response were repeated in the other three western cities, although there were interesting variations. The first reaction to unemployment in San Francisco was to provide charity, and private agencies bore by far the bulk of the relief load. The community chest's Associated Charities and other private groups spent just over $143,000 during the first quarter of 1929, though only a fraction went for unemployment relief. The city and county government, even before the depression, seemed more willing than Los Angeles to subsidize these private efforts. In the winter, when unemployment was at its seasonal height, the city usually contributed $20,000 to the Associated Charities to aid displaced men and families. In 1929, $60,000 of public funds went to a wide array of charitable causes. Public and private roles, however, reversed dramatically in 1930, and by the first quarter of 1931 public expenditure on charity, which the board of supervisors now set aside primarily for those out of work, increased tenfold to $599,000. This far outstripped the $216,000 that private agencies spent on unemployment relief and customary needs during the first quarter.[17]

Fund drives fared somewhat better in San Francisco than in Los Angeles.

The community chest met its $2.3 million goal but had to extend its March drive several days to go over the top. The Jewish Fund found itself 7 percent short at the end of its solicitation campaign. Concern and action emerged at the grass roots as the economy worsened in the autumn and winter of 1930. The pastor of Grace Trinity United Church asked his congregation to fill in cards to indicate available odd jobs. He also exhorted them to help by going into the highways and byways to buy. Veterans staged a military ball to aid the jobless, and labor unions provided their halls as clearing houses for the unemployed.

Another staple among the private remedies, the paint-up, fix-up campaign, was tried in San Francisco. The *News* ran a "Mr. Fix-it" column and gave front-page coverage to its subsequent "Give a Job" campaign. Every daily newspaper and a variety of radio stations pitched in. According to the *News*, well over 1,000 found some opportunities—but, as the newspaper itself admitted in June, this made only a dent in the need.[18] The private efforts in San Francisco—aid dispensed by long-standing agencies or new responses that the declining economy stimulated—were inadequate.

Although public officials in San Francisco seemed more comfortable in their relief roles than did their counterparts to the south, they assumed this responsibility almost as slowly. The proscription against public intrusion into what was perceived as a private matter forestalled a major governmental response until early November. In the meantime the city sold bonds, which the voters had already approved, to finance and speed up public works. During the year, the city spent several million dollars improving streets, building schools, working on the harbor, and planting trees.

These efforts proved insufficient. By the fall of 1930 the mayor and board of supervisors saw that something beyond an acceleration of planned works was needed. The groundwork for the city's relief plan had already been laid during the summer. A group of San Francisco's most prominent people—including Andrew J. Gallagher, a member of the board of supervisors; Frank McDonald, a labor leader; Selah Chamberlain, a welfare worker; Fremont Older, the venerable newspaper editor; and Mortimer Fleishhacker, a banker—formed the Citizens' Committee to Stimulate Employment. This group sought to fulfill the promise of their title by promoting various job-making schemes. The paint-up, fix-up plan grew out of their planning. By November the committee realized it could not succeed alone. The city took over the committee and through it began moving seriously against the problem of unemployment. The board of supervisors immediately appropriated $50,000 to establish a program of work relief. Both Los Angeles and San Francisco followed President Hoover's pattern of action—in fact the pattern used nationwide—for handling the economic displacement. When the private sector—in San Francisco, the community chest and the Committee to Stimulate Employment—proved unable to handle the problem, local government stepped in with something more than a general program of public works.

The unemployed lined up at the Exposition Hall in the Civic Center to register to work on street repair projects, sewer maintenance, or harbor improvement. Although these jobs benefited the city, they were undertaken primarily to create work for the jobless. The supervisors limited work relief to the married unemployed. Each successful applicant worked three days at $5 per day. By the middle of its first month, the program employed 1,400 men out of the 4,132 who had registered, and the city appropriated another $150,000 for this relief program in December.[19]

As the expenditures for relief rose, the mayor and supervisors looked anxiously at their budget while continuing to appropriate for public works. The board set aside money for a junior high, street improvements, sewer work, and port construction. In late October the *San Francisco Chronicle* reported that the city would spend up to $1.5 million on works projects over the near term. But the mayor could foresee a $1 million deficit for the next fiscal year, and the city treasurer prohibited any further allotments.[20] At that point San Francisco became the first of the four cities to go to its voters for help. The board of supervisors called for a bond election for $2.5 million, to be used solely for relief. Officials were overly optimistic when they estimated that half would be used during the 1930-31 winter and the other half would be spent during the following winter, if necessary.[21] City leaders came out in force to support the bonds, and newspapers offered advice on how to ensure the best political environment for the bond election: keep everything else off the ballot. The chamber of commerce gave its approval. San Francisco voters in February ratified the bond proposal by a margin of seven to one.

San Francisco also received help from the state and federal government, though it was not extravagant. California reserved $1.3 million for public works projects in the Bay Area, and the increased federal highway appropriation helped the region as well.

The government of San Francisco consistently seemed more alert than the city or county of Los Angeles to the needs of its citizens. Even though the Bay Area was probably not affected as early nor hit as hard as the Southland, the responses of the public officials demonstrated a greater willingness to face the problems of the depression. Whereas cooperative individualism was a tenet almost forced on jobless Angelenos, and the cooperative, helping aspect of that creed was not all that widespread, some of the values restricting a vigorous public response were beginning to be modified in San Francisco.

The story of the emergence of relief in Seattle is similar to that of the two California cities. Once again, the first response was substantially an intensification of already existing private efforts followed by a growing awareness in the fall of 1930 that more was necessary. But perhaps because the economy was not slipping so quickly or because traditional values remained unshaken, Seattle public authorities did not expand their role as quickly.

The community fund, as it was called in Seattle, traditionally handled special charity cases, such as the disabled and orphaned. King County's Public Welfare Board took responsibility for unemployed families and singles. Much of the time, and apparently more so in 1930, the county board channeled funds through private welfare agencies to those in need. Even in relatively good times, the charity operation was a cooperative venture linking the public and private sectors. The city of Seattle assisted the unemployed through its Public Employment Office, which endeavored to find jobs. These were usually part-time placements. The agency was especially active in the winter, when transient laborers moved to the city.

The slogan for the 1930 Seattle Community Fund was "The need is greater."[22] But the story was the same in Seattle as elsewhere. For the same reason that the need was greater, the contributions were smaller. The fund drive fell short by about one-half million dollars.[23]

In Seattle few private organizations that operated outside the purview of the community fund could or would pick up the economic slack. Organized labor raised funds for food and operated a soup kitchen by the end of the year. Beyond that the three daily newspapers seemed to be the primary impetus behind any private efforts to alleviate unemployment and hunger. The *Star* was the catalyst for a fall paint-up, fix-up campaign in Seattle, which, of course, fell well short of the need. The paper also conducted a successful food drive in December. The *Times* and the *Post-Intelligencer*, which held year-end charity fund drives, proudly proclaimed that their goals were exceeded. The Seattle Police Sunshine Club Christmas operation was also a success. From all accounts, however, the extent of private charity was more restricted in Seattle than in the two California cities.

The same held true for the public response in 1930. Seattle sped up public works projects, but, unlike Los Angeles and San Francisco, the city had not formed a relief commission by year's end. Throughout much of that year the Seattle City Council studied a whole array of public works projects. A March vote authorized $1 million in bonds for the construction of the Aurora Bridge on the main north-south highway in the city. Street paving and works in the parks absorbed more men. By the end of the winter, the city had spent $125,000 in excess of its public works budget, but this was an increase of only $115,000 over the city's customary relief appropriation for the slack season.[24]

Even late in the year Seattle officials lacked a sense of the nature and scope of the economic problems in their city, and they were satisfied to adhere to tried and true methods to respond to them. In November 1930, Mayor Frank Edwards acknowledged to the city council that street and sewer improvements should be undertaken in the "near future" to "relieve existing conditions" and spoke of $2 million of public works to alleviate some of the joblessness. Edwards, referring not to an additional $2 million but to a somewhat enhanced 1931 public works budget, more acknowledged the unemployment situation than responded to it.[25]

Like his fellow mayors, Edwards in November appointed a panel to find jobs. This group obtained lists of the jobless from the Public Employment Office and other private charity organizations such as Goodwill or the Salvation Army. Public commissions and private industry could draw from these to fill any openings they might have. The year-end statistics of the city's Public Employment Bureau imply that this approach was not fruitful. In 1929 the bureau placed 26,560 men and women in paying positions. In 1930 the bureau report showed some 15,000 job seekers placed.[26] Even though this latter figure may not include job placements through the mayor's commission, it indicates the paucity of positions available.

Seattle's civic leaders, aware of the joblessness, did not seem as willing as their California counterparts to meet the unemployment problem head on. The expansion of public works constituted a response, but no program specifically designed to help the jobless, and certainly no proposal for a bond issue for the unemployed, came forth from the city's leadership.

Seattle received little help from the state government. Governor Roland Hartley firmly believed that the state had no part in providing relief. The only assistance, then, was an appropriation that Congress voted for public works in the Greater Seattle Area. The construction of a federal building, a hospital, and an immigration station and improvements in the naval yard at Bremerton were included in this $7 million expenditure.

The Oregon pauper law, similar to the California statute governing the provision of charity, stated: "When any poor person shall not have any relatives or such relatives shall not be of sufficient ability, or shall fail or refuse to maintain such pauper, the said pauper shall receive such relief as the case may require out of the county treasury."[27] In Portland a number of agencies, public and private, were in place in 1930 to fulfill this mandate. The major instrument of outdoor charity in Portland was the Public Welfare Bureau. The bureau originated in 1888 as an arm of the First Congregational Church of Portland. In 1921 it became Multnomah County's disbursing agent for outdoor relief, receiving funds from both the county budget and the community chest. Portland, too, blurred the lines between private and public agencies. The Public Welfare Bureau, for example, possessed the kind of professional staff most able to administer funds. As in the other cities, Portland officials relied on professional social workers and others with at least a modicum of experience through the depression.

Besides the Public Welfare Bureau several organizations that had always assisted down-and-outers continued and expanded their work. The YMCA, the Salvation Army, and the Volunteers of America, of course, all had their counterparts in the other cities. In Portland each of these provided meals in exchange for labor, for a nominal fee, or for no charge over a short period. In addition, Grandma's Kitchen furnished free soup with no questions asked, and the Commons gave free lodging and a meal to anyone who chopped some wood.

Individuals, service organizations, churches, and newspapers in Portland responded as they discovered growing poverty in their city. The *Portland News* ran free want ads as early as May and offered $.75 to any unemployed person who sold a three-month subscription to the paper. The *Oregonian* provided "Give-a-Job" coupons for its readers to indicate full- or part-time work they could provide. The Rotary and Kiwanis clubs and the Police Department's Sunshine Division collected food, fuel, and clothing and sought jobs for the unemployed. The Sunshine Division and the *Oregonian* joined forces to erect the "World's Largest Christmas Tree," meant to draw forth gifts and donations for the needy.

The private relief effort in Portland seemed strong, but the status of the Portland Community Chest belied this. The average $2 per capita donation was $.75 under the national average, and, according to the *Oregon Daily Journal*'s estimate, the lowest per capita level in the West.[28] The original community chest goal for the fall 1930 drive was $700,000, which the organization's officials presented as the minimum possible in a period of severe need. By the time the campaign for funds had ended, the people of Portland had done as they had for the past eleven years, failed to meet the goal. The shortfall was almost $200,000. Even though community chest officials then cut the minimum goal to $603,000 the city of Portland was still $60,000 short as 1930 came to an end.

A variation of this dismal picture appeared in a report made by a committee the governor appointed to study relief in Oregon. It indicated that throughout the state the lack of funds and the widespread belief that the economic slump was temporary caused difficult problems, even undernourishment of children.[29] Despite the number of charitable groups and programs, Portlanders would or could not meet the needs. In Oregon, help from the local and state government was essential from the beginning, and officials at these levels responded with some liberality.

Such a reaction, especially coming from the state, contrasted sharply with experience in the other cities. The administrations in all three coastal states were Republican through the election of 1932. In California and Washington, where conservatives Rolph and Hartley governed, there was no assistance for local unemployment in the beginning and precious little as the depression wore on. Oregon acted more quickly, perhaps because its population was small and relatively concentrated. Another possibility is that Oregon, once on the cutting edge of progressivism, was less tied to conservative traditions. For whatever reasons, in February 1930, Governor Norblad called an Oregon economic conference to discuss the state's problems. The conference resolved "That this meeting hereby records its impression of the present economic situation as being one of encouragement, but needing local and general pressure on the actual starting of projects already financed to the end that labor may be better distributed in employment throughout the season. . . ."[30] The idea of speeding public works was hardly original, nor was the state labor commissioner's opinion about relief: "While destitutes must be relieved, a dole is always damaging to the individual though temporarily helpful."[31]

Despite conventional methods and conventional sentiment, Oregon was unique on the West Coast. The governor characterized state action as important, and the state acted to meet the problems. As early as April 1930, Oregon considered how highway funds might be used to help the unemployed. In September the labor commissioner sought ways to work with the U.S. Department of Labor to establish a clearinghouse for the jobless. And by December the governor had formed the State Emergency Employment Commission, which was far more active than its California counterpart. At the same time the state highway commission inaugurated a plan to put 1,750 men to work on the state road system for six months. By mid-1931 the highway commission had spent $657,000 on relief road work and planned to spend almost $3 million more of state and federal highway funds during the rest of the year.[32]

That the state recognized the problem and was attending to it energetically did not mean local authorities were doing nothing. The priority of responsibility in Oregon, as elsewhere, caused local authorities to bear the primary share of the load. The Public Welfare Board spent $11,500 of county funds in January 1930. This expenditure dropped to $6,000 in July, then shot up to $13,000 in December. This almost doubled the previous year's outlay. The county spent over $100,000 on relief in 1930, ultimately running a $15,000 deficit in the relief budget.[33] In addition, Multnomah County put over one thousand men to work on roads during the final three months of the year.

Portland, too, met the problems of unemployment with energy, provided by Mayor George Baker. Baker, Portland's mayor since 1917, seemed to enjoy the office as much as Portlanders enjoyed him. This former theater owner, an empresario and gregarious showman, served as Portland's definition of dapper. As an administrator, he was less flashy, tending to react to problems rather than take the initiative. Politically he was a probusiness conservative. Contrary to his tendency to let style outrun substantial achievement, George Baker led his city in the early thirties vigorously and with some success.

In March the mayor acknowledged that joblessness was acute and held an unemployment conference to hasten public and private projects. As in the other cities the unemployment pressures eased somewhat during the summer, and the mayor grew silent on the subject of depression. Then, at the end of October he proclaimed, "I disagree with any idea seeking to discount the problems here or elsewhere. I feel the time has come to force the situation as it stands. . . . the condition is general and we must call a spade a spade and prepare to meet the problem."[34]

The mayor directed that every cent lopped off city budgets and those of all other local government entities go into a fund for the unemployed. He demanded that every city department find public works to provide jobs. And, as he sought old buildings to demolish for urban renewal, he declared with characteristic hyperbole, "I'll wreck the town if it will give employment."[35]

Mayor Baker did not act alone in confronting his city's problems. In January, on the cue of the U.S. Chamber of Commerce, the Portland chamber formed a committee on unemployment, conducted a survey, and announced recommendations for speeding construction work and creating jobs. In October this group became more active. The unemployment committee formed several subcommittees to coordinate public works, survey the unemployed, and encourage Portlanders to speed up maintenance work and rotate workers to provide wider employment. Under the direction of Ben Selling, a respected philanthropist and business leader, the committee publicized these and other ideas. Among its less traditional schemes was a kind of capitalist's approach to unemployment—a workingman's bank that would loan $25 a month to married Portlanders at 6 percent. The loans would become repayable after six months at $2.50 a week.[36]

The convergence of private and public efforts formed the structure of Portland's response to the depression. Out of a mid-November meeting at city hall the Civic Emergency Committee (CEC) emerged. This new committee, composed of community leaders, joined with the city and county officials to oversee work relief. T. Harry Banfield, president of the Iron Fireman stove company, served as chairman, and G. B. Herrington, chairman of the Portland Chamber of Commerce

Unemployment Committee, was the vice-chairman. One hundred six different organizations were represented on the committee, although businessmen held the balance of power.[37]

The CEC immediately sought funds for emergency relief and prepared to administer the program. Again the public and private efforts merged easily, and no concern was expressed about where lines between the two might exist. At least one commentator later accurately observed that the CEC kept much of the decision-making power in its own hands. This alienated some politicians who believed the relief efforts should be guided by public officials.[38] The CEC pressed both private and public leaders to find jobs, speed construction, and rotate employees, and it lobbied for increased budgets for public works and unemployment relief. In addition, the committee began to register the jobless at polling places throughout the city to create lists of eligible workers for those who could supply additional jobs.

Before the end of the year the CEC, with the help of the local governments, was placing the unemployed in public works jobs. Multnomah County sought a $100,000 budget item to battle unemployment, and the city asked for $500,000. Out of this the Multnomah County Tax Supervising and Conservation Commission, a board of oversight that ruled on local governmental budgets and kept a ceiling on taxes, authorized a total of $300,000—the full $100,000 for the county and $200,000 for the city.

To spread the money as widely and as equitably as possible, the CEC selected only heads of families who received $.50 an hour, or $4 a day. The relief work was rotated so each worker would receive $24 a month. Given the limited funds available—or at least appropriated—this seems to have been a reasonably equitable arrangement, especially if the president of the Portland Community Chest correctly estimated that $18 a month would support a family. If it took, however, $48.20 per month, which a governor's panel suggested, Portland families surviving on work relief must have been sorely tested.[39] There was one other problem. The *Portland News* complained that overhead costs and the necessity of providing as many relief jobs as possible would imperil the jobs of regular city workers, and, indeed, the day after this concern was aired thirty-five regularly employed park workers were laid off. Ironically, work relief had caused unemployment.

Portland's relief response, though not as generous as San Francisco's, was as well organized as that of any of the other cities. Moreover, by the end of the year, while Los Angeles was beginning to match the jobless with positions, San Francisco was concentrating on pushing its bond vote, and the city of Seattle had yet to begin to draw up any thorough list of the jobless, Portland had put a large number of its unemployed to work using a plan that would become familiar in the other three cities.

The state of Oregon, too, had become much more involved than California or Washington. Two things might explain this. State politicians were more influenced by progressivism than the leaders of the other states who embodied the general political ethos of the 1920s. This tradition left Oregon officials more in touch with the needs and desires of the common man. Important, too, is that

Portland, with an economy so tied to lumber, had been in the economic doldrums as long or longer than the other cities. If it was a case of greater sensitivity, it must be added that officials had a longer time to become sensitive.

Oregon did become involved with relief more quickly, but by 1932 state officials had backtracked a good deal in the name of efficiency. Conversely, several states to the east did far more to assist their cities than did Oregon, California, and especially Washington. As early as 1931, Philadelphia was spending $2.4 million of a $10 million grant that the state of Pennsylvania distributed. Wisconsin, like Oregon a progressive stronghold, helped out Milwaukee with $1.6 million in 1932. Ohio increased its relief budget 60 percent by 1932 from an already generous $15.5 million in 1928. Illinois sent the bulk of $18.7 million to Chicago's Cook County. New York, with its Temporary Emergency Relief Administration, provided millions to local communities. By the end of 1931, twenty-four states had followed New York's example and created their own state relief organizations.[40] This activity at the state level contrasted sharply with the relative lassitude of the Pacific states.

Beyond the relatively small increase in public works and the formation of the President's Emergency Committee for Employment (PECE), the federal government offered little help. According to PECE chairman Arthur Woods, his committee was created to "let various places know what others are doing as a guide for their own efforts."[41] That would not be of great help to the four West Coast cities because they were doing essentially the same things in 1930, and their responses matched the basic contours of the local relief efforts nationwide.

At first, in the spring, it had appeared that the traditional providers of help —the Salvation Army, the Red Cross, the Catholic Welfare Bureau, and, above all, the community chest—could handle the needs of the jobless. But unemployment grew noticeably in the fall and outstripped the resources of the private charities. Two problems confronted these organizations and confounded their response. First, few of the agencies had ever considered assisting the able-bodied unemployed as a significant part of their mission. Second, none had ever dealt with so many jobless people, and they were not prepared financially to do so now.

The problems of the depression breached the traditional bulwark of private charity in rather short order on the West Coast and in most cities, but in some places private undertakings were far more hardy. Most notably, Philadelphia raised approximately $15 million in donations for relief in 1930 and 1931. Philadelphia's private effort at aiding the unemployed was remarkable, well conceived, and well administered, although it did run out of funds in June 1932, leaving 57,000 families stranded.[42] According to New York's mayor, James Walker, the city charter prohibited spending money on relief, so private charity carried the load in that city into 1931. The Emergency Employment Committee, a group of private businessmen, collected over $8 million during the winter of 1930. "Voluntary" contributions of almost $2.5 million from city employees and teachers kept things going into the new year.[43] Boston also relied on private relief to an unusual extent. Thwarted by an uncooperative legislature, a large debt load, and a tight debt lid, Mayor James Curley and the city council finally opted for private fund drives in 1931 and 1932. The appeals netted a total of $5.6 million—made up in part of city employee contributions—but this fell well short of the need. Chicago was able to raise $5 million in 1931, but that too was inadequate. Throughout the country private charity played a major role, but the lesson was the same: it was not enough. Most city leaders, including those in the four western cities, recognized this—or, more accurately, were forced to this conclusion—by fall 1930.

In 1930, West Coast administrators began to act, but not all that forcefully, and they continued to look to the private sector for assistance. Principle (a reluctance on the part of local governments to usurp the role of private charity) and pragmatism (the need for experienced professional and business leadership for the emerging programs) joined to produce a combined public–private response in each city. Public funds were funneled through the community chest. The mayors and local business leaders formulated policy together. And the unemployed themselves would help run one of the programs.

As rising unemployment overpowered traditional approaches, there were no new responses to the challenge. The variations in 1930 were variations only of degree—more public works in San Francisco, fewer in Seattle, better and earlier planning in Portland. But unemployment remained, and prevailing attitudes about work, charity, and individualism had a sterner test to come.

Because the response to the depression was so resolutely confined to the local communities, the effects of politics at the national level and at the state level in California and Washington were tangential. Elections provide insight into the minds and changing values of the electorate, but the victorious candidates in 1930 —and, in some cases, 1932—did little to change the course of the depression or the nature and scope of the reactions to it. The West Coast was solidly Republican in the 1920s. Democrats failed to win any seats in the California State Senate in three elections in the decade. From 1900 to 1930 Oregon Democrats made up less than one-third of the registered voters. Democrats in Washington usually occupied less than 10 percent of the seats in the state legislature.[44]

In California, and especially in Oregon, something of a two-party system existed because the Republicans were riven into conservative and progressive factions. Hiram Johnson of California and Charles McNary were the two most prominent western progressives. Johnson, as active as anyone from the West in advocating an expanded federal role during this period, joined with George Norris and Robert Wagner against the roadblock of Hoover vetoes. Johnson castigated the Reconstruction Finance Corporation (RFC), Hoover's greatest concession to the principle of intervention, as little more than a trickle-down solution.[45] The California senator obviously had little use for Hoover and in 1932 supported Roosevelt for the Presidency.

Charles McNary, a boyhood acquaintance of Hoover's, got along only marginally better with the president. Hoover opposed federal farm-price supports, the centerpiece of McNary's legislative agenda in the twenties. McNary seemed to bridge the progressive–conservative rift and stayed loyal to his party in the 1932 election as he sought, and got, the top Republican leadership position in the Senate.

In the 1930 general election he won every county in Oregon. As a progressive he supported the Wagner–Garner Bill to expand relief (Hoover vetoed it), lined up support for the RFC, and was a strong supporter, along with most of the Oregon and Washington delegations, of public hydroelectric power. As an Oregonian, he constantly pushed tariff protection for the lumber industry.[46]

Wesley Jones, a Republican, and C. C. Dill, a Democrat, were the senators from Washington. They, along with Samuel Shortridge of California and Frederick Steiwer of Oregon—both Republicans—took much less visible positions than their progressive colleagues. Dill and Steiwer did push dam building on the Columbia River. Dill took much credit for persuading Franklin Roosevelt to build a high dam at Grand Coulee in Washington.

In 1930, at the national level, Democrats took control of the House of Representatives when Republicans lost fifty-two seats. The Republicans barely clung to a majority in the Senate. The elections did not go so badly for the Republicans on the West Coast. In Los Angeles, Republican representative Joe Crail won his seat handily. In San Francisco the Republican won the nomination of both parties by cross-filing. Ralph Horr defeated incumbent John Miller in the Republican primary in Seattle, then won the general election. In the four cities only Democrat Charles Martin in Portland defeated a Republican incumbent. Martin, a retired army general, was the former commandant of the Canal Zone. A registered Republican and, as was later proved, a conservative, Martin won the Democratic nomination as a write-in candidate because no Democrat had filed. His platform emphasized public power, development of resources, and a national referendum on prohibition. His opponent, Frank Kroll, promised to work with the administration to end unemployment, called for public power on the Columbia River, but in general stood for free enterprise.[47] Martin won by 14,000 votes. The elections of 1930 were not a clean sweep for the Republicans, but westerners were not prepared to reject their national leadership.

State leadership, except in Oregon, had relatively little impact on the search for relief. Washington's Governor Hartley—elected in 1928—remained solidly in favor of rugged individualism. California's James Rolph, a popular Republican, won the governor's chair in 1930. Rolph, who had been San Francisco's mayor for nineteen years, defeated the progressive incumbent C. C. Young in the 1930 Republican primary. The race featured some complex maneuvering. During his term, Young expanded aid for the handicapped and pushed an old age pension law through the legislature. Although he increased state expenditures, he left a surplus. Rolph, more conservative than Young, was a "wet." Young and a third Republican candidate, Buron Fitts, the Los Angeles District Attorney, were both "dry's." As his two opponents split the dry vote, Rolph won the primary. The colorful "Sunny Jim" then swamped his Democrat opponent with 72 percent of the vote in the fall election. In his term as governor, shortened by death, Rolph expressed sympathy for those out of work but did little beyond augmenting public works. Mainly because of a drop in revenue, the state surplus of $30 million became a deficit of $9.5 million by 1933.[48]

Angelo Rossi, a San Francisco supervisor, succeeded Rolph as mayor. Although not as flamboyant as his predecessor, Rossi was a popular mayor. The former florist had been president of the Downtown Association yet garnered widespread support among labor. As finance chairman of the board of supervisors, he was economy-minded—a quality that became important as he led his city during the depression.

In Oregon the Republicans, after a roundabout primary process marked by tragedy, retained control of the state governor's chair. George Joseph, an advocate of public power, won the Oregon Republican primary. Before the general election Joseph died of a massive heart attack while viewing National Guard maneuvers. The Republican Central Committee selected the more conservative Phil Metschan to replace the deceased nominee. This caused a great deal of consternation in the liberal wing of the party and, after some haggling, ended with Julius Meier running on Joseph's platform as a write-in candidate. Meier, a member of a prominent Portland merchant family, supported public power and seemed generally cut out of the progressive Republican pattern. Both the state Grange and the state Federation of Labor supported him. In a heavily Republican state Meier defeated his Democrat opponent by a two-to-one margin and prevailed over Metschan by three to one. The election of Meier, then, served to keep the state on a course strongly influenced by a progressive outlook, and Meier continued to do more for relief than his Republican counterparts in California and Washington.

FOUR

Hitting Home

1931

The year 1930 was one of growing awareness on the West Coast of the severity of the economic crisis. The unease about the economy that exhibited itself in the spring gave way to concern by the fall. In 1931 this concern verged on anxiety. Many who had never imagined themselves being affected by a downturn in the economy were thrown out of work. Leaders who had depended substantially on expanding and intensifying traditional methods in response to economic problems now had to go beyond their long-held ideas about the individual's responsibility for himself and the relation of local government to charity. In 1931 the preservation of values could no longer be the preeminent concern. The more elemental quest for security, even survival, became the issue in the second year of the depression. The depression was hitting home.[1]

An overview of business conditions in the four major West Coast cities presents a disheartening story and demonstrates how the depression touched the consciousness and the lives of the populace. The Southern California economy fell off drastically. The Eberle Economic Service reported that Southland business was 30 percent below normal at the opening of 1931 and 50 percent off the pace by the end of the year.[2] The decline in value of manufactured products from 1929 told the same story all along the coast. From 1929 to 1931 Seattle manufacturing decreased 40.5 percent. Portland lost almost as much, 40.4 percent, over the same two years. Manufacturing slipped 38 percent in Los Angeles and 34 percent in San Francisco.[3]

These statistics merely begin to demonstrate the impact of the depression on people's lives. In Los Angeles a one-time millionaire declared bankruptcy, Richfield Oil went into receivership, and the failures of two major financial institutions not only revealed fraud but also implicated three California Supreme Court justices in questionable dealings regarding a receivership procedure. Business failures climbed 27.5 percent in Los Angeles from 1929 to 1931. Even more jarring, the asset value of the failures had increased 194.4 percent—larger, seemingly more stable operations were having a hard time.[4]

In Portland, Ralph Lloyd, a California investor who had grand plans for developing a portion of the city and boosting the local economy, began to get cold feet. By May, Portland had experienced 363 foreclosures, and the city considered delaying street and sewer projects in areas where taxes were 10 percent or more in arrears to avoid placing further pressures on teetering businesses.[5] A year-end letter from Representative Charles Martin to his son Sam may have reflected the national gloom, but it also caught the feelings in the Northwest. Martin, counseling his son not to purchase any more stocks, wrote: "The prediction is freely made here [Washington, D.C.] that by February they are not going to have any market at all." He also directed his son to use any extra cash to pay the mortgage on their office building and further suggested that they not pay property tax on some of their real estate holdings. Apparently, short-term tax delinquency was not all that risky by this time.[6]

If one took cues only from the newspapers in San Francisco and Seattle, the gloom would not have seemed so thick. The Bay Area dailies, minimizing or avoiding Federal Reserve reports to the contrary, happily pointed to chamber of commerce declarations that business trends were up—at least they were up for certain business endeavors over certain portions of the year. An interesting example of the San Francisco Chamber of Commerce's effort to cast the best light on business is a page from its 1933 *Economic Survey*. The chamber admitted freely that several local indicators were down but hastened to point out that, while the number of business places in San Francisco dropped 11 percent from 1929 to 1931, the nationwide decline was 18 percent. Likewise, if San Francisco wages were off 31 percent, wages nationwide were down 38. And the nation's 27 percent drop in wage earners exceeded the Bay Area's 25 percent layoff rate. Optimism was merely a matter of perspective.[7] Seattle newspapers publicized a new $3 million Ford plant and the opening of the largest J. C. Penney store in the chain. Fourteen new industries had located in Seattle by mid-summer, the papers boasted. Actually by the end of 1931 the city had lost 134 of the 1,219 manufacturing concerns functioning in 1929.[8]

The Federal Reserve's *Monthly Review of Business Conditions* in the twelfth district contradicted the optimists. Although there had been some degree of economic stability in the early months, the *Review* reported, business activity declined for the year, with both wholesale and retail sales showing especially sharp drops. Prices had fallen as well, although not so drastically as 1930. Finally, throughout the West, industrial production was at half of its 1929 high by the end of 1931.[9] Despite the penchant of chambers of commerce and local newspapers to emphasize the bright side, there were abundant reasons for a growing feeling of anxiety.

The two bellwethers of the economy, bank deposits and construction, clearly corroborated the existence of the economic malaise to which the general business and manufacturing figures pointed. Deposits in Los Angeles were off $184 million, or 16.5 percent, and banks recorded noticeably fewer check transactions at the beginning of spring. Deposits in San Francisco and Seattle were down 9 percent and 12 percent, respectively.[10] The decline in deposits revealed a critical cash flow problem throughout the economy—less loan money was available and people had less to spend.

Bank and savings and loan closures rocked all four cities. Two important financial institutions that shut their doors in Los Angeles declared they would be able to pay back to their depositors only seventy-five and eighty-five cents on the dollar. In San Francisco much concern attended a power struggle over the control of the TransAmerica holding company. As Bank of America deposits dropped throughout 1931 and TransAmerica omitted its dividend, matters appeared serious. President Elisha Walker embarked on a series of measures aimed at clearing bad loans from the ledgers, consolidating the operation, and liquidating some holdings. At that point A. P. Giannini decided to regain control over TransAmerica, which he had relinquished, and did so in a proxy fight in early 1932. The Bank of America and the Giannini empire had gone through turmoil. Although none of the events threatened the corporation, the end of 1931 and the reestablishment of Giannini's power surely must have been a relief to many corporate officers and shareholders.[11]

Important factors in bank closures were gross mismanagement and plain dishonesty. Reports of poor decisions, fraud, and embezzlement surfaced in three of the four cities in the first two years of the depression. But poor stewardship or criminality were not the only causes of bank failures. The waves of problems that the stock crash sent rippling out over the nation's economy were too much for many reasonably well-run banks to withstand. In Seattle at least two banks closed their doors voluntarily in 1931 and returned their customers' money; the state banking commissioner shut the doors of two other banks. Institutions cursed with embezzlement stood even less chance. Two such afflicted Seattle savings and loans went into receivership when they could not make up their losses.[12]

Los Angeles and Portland witnessed similar closings. The case of mismanagement of the Hibernia Savings and Loan in Portland, the city's fourth largest in size of deposits in 1928, presents an insight into bank failures of the period and into what seems to have been the most frightening bank panic among the larger West Coast cities during the depression. The Hibernia was one of at least six financial institutions to close in the Portland area in 1931. As the state bank superintendent closed Hibernia's doors in late December 1931, the *Oregonian* described its plight: "[The] capital structure of the bank has become impaired due to the slump in the bond and security quotations."[13] In more straightforward language the Hibernia management had invested a goodly portion of the bank's assets in stocks and bonds, and now those assets were a fraction of what they had been. This was not unusual in the early 1930s as supposedly conservative bankers perhaps perceived a "sure thing" in the New York Stock Exchange and had invested in it too heavily. In the case of Hibernia poor judgment was the problem. In other cases cover-ups, panic within management, and personal investing at depositors' expense complicated matters.

After the Hibernia closed its doors, anxious depositors of banks all around Portland made what the *Journal* described as an "assault." By 10 A.M. of the morning the bank superintendent announced the Hibernia closure there were 3,000 worried customers in the lobby of the United States National Bank set to withdraw their savings. Apparently a phone campaign—a whispering campaign initiated by "Reds" according to United States National president John C. Ainsworth—had suggested to as many as 10,000 depositors around Oregon that the Hibernia closure was only the tip of the iceberg. A frantic run on the United States National and First National banks, the two major financial institutions in the city, lasted several days. The American Legion and Oregon Manufacturers Association assured the public of their confidence in the local banking system, and, probably more important, the banks enforced their right to require a withdrawal notice, which could delay withdrawals for a number of days. Only then did the panic subside. Whether it was an insidious campaign against the financial institutions or, as one study suggests, merely the playing out of people's fears as signs of a weakening economy became more evident, the possibility of such a widespread panic lends credence to the idea that the average citizen, in Portland at least, was well aware that the economic problems threatened his own security.[14]

The circulation of money slowed on the West Coast in 1931 because one of its main impellers, construction, slumped severely in all but San Francisco. Bay Area building permits, up through September, fell by just over $1 million for the year—about 6 percent. Seattle, where building increased in 1930 as both private and public builders carried out major projects already in the works, had to withstand a crushing 69.5 percent decline in building permits in 1931. Portland endured a second hard year with a 51 percent loss from 1930, and building permits were down 44.4 percent in Los Angeles.[15]

Retail trade reflected the same ills. With the exception of Oakland, San Francisco area retail sales declined the least of any West Coast city in 1931. But, again, this was the only perspective that could see any hope in month after month of declining trade. The year-end figures confirmed a 9.5 percent decline for San Francisco. In Seattle retail sales were down 17.7 percent from 1930, and in Los Angeles department store sales dropped 12.2 percent.[16] Both sales volume and deflation were taking their toll. In San Francisco, for example, a price war in the milk industry depressed the price to nineteen cents per gallon, a nickle below the break-even point. In Seattle food prices dropped by 15 percent or more, and, although Christmas business was as brisk as ever at the Bon Marche, Seattle's leading department store, less money was taken in because of the lower prices. Cost of living statistics in California reinforce these specific examples. In December 1929 the index for San Francisco was 160.8 (1914=100), and, for Los Angeles 168.7. By the end of the next year the index numbers were 151.5 and 158.1, repectively. By the end of 1931 the index had dropped to 138.1 in the Bay Area and 145.1 in Southern California.[17]

The rigors of deflation became especially evident at the pay window for those who were still employed. There were fewer deposits because paychecks were shrinking. Despite the promises businessmen had made to the president just after the crash, 1931 became a year of major battles over wage scales. From spring through the fall, builders and construction workers in San Francisco wrangled over a wage cut. The contractors' association agreed in April to maintain the pay rate. But by August the builders had voted unanimously for wage cuts. Only after ten days of controversy could the two sides agree. The settlement instituted a wage board to arbitrate and maintain pay levels to the end of the year. A month later, management and laborers agreed to a five-day week and a six-hour day, paid at the same scale—in effect a cut in hours to bring about a lower wage.

Other companies took up reductions during the year throughout the West. The Southern Pacific Railroad in December announced a 10 percent cut for all nonunion employees; two weeks later it deepened the slash to 15 percent. The American–Hawaiian Steamship Company was able to reduce wages, it claimed, because so many unemployed offered their services aboard ship for lodging and meals only. In Portland, street railway workers incurred a 10 percent reduction in wages, but the major problem in that city came over public school teachers' pay. The school board claimed unpaid property tax had caused a $1 million shortfall in the school budget and called for pay cuts beginning in October. Yet such cuts were illegal in mid-contract. The board then suggested pay warrants—that is, debt obligations issued by the district. The teachers could cash them with whoever was willing to become a creditor of the school district. Others suggested that teachers from families with two incomes take a year off. This solution was aimed clearly at female elementary school teachers. The issue was still at an impasse as the year ended.

In the Northwest wage scales for timber workers were, of course, of great concern. In May 1931 industry heads voted to maintain existing levels. Despite this avowal, Washington payroll figures seem to indicate something else. In 1930 the average logging wage was at seventy cents an hour, in 1931 it dropped to fifty-six cents an hour, and by 1932 it had sunk even lower, to forty-four cents an hour.[18]

Amid these wrangles, compromises, promises, and unreached agreements, workers' earnings fell all along the West Coast. Table 1 indicates the decline in pay in three of the four cities over a six-year period encompassing the Hoover years of the depression. Average wages slid 10 percent or more from 1929 to 1931 in each city. The drop of 25 to 40 percent in wages per capita indicates the compound effect of pay reductions and layoffs and highlights the pernicious

TABLE 1
Wage Levels, 1927–1933

	Average Wage (annual)		
	Los Angeles	*San Francisco*	*Seattle*
1927	$1520	$1460	$1440
1929	1480	1500	1450
1931	1285	1370	1310
1933	995	1080	1070

	Wages (per capita)		
	Los Angeles	*San Francisco*	*Seattle*
1927	$90.10	$102.00	$84.50
1929	93.00	108.00	92.50
1931	53.60	72.50	58.50
1933	42.50	48.50	41.00

From "Table showing relationships between industrial factors in Seattle, San Francisco, Los Angeles, and Oakland 1921, 1923, 1925, 1927, 1929, 1931, and 1933." (Typescript) John Anson Ford Collection, Henry E. Huntington Library.

effect of the deflationary spiral. Less and less money circulated in the depression-wracked economy, causing less demand and, consequently, lower wages and less employment, which in turn propelled the spiral on another downward swing. Analogies of a spiral or lines on a graph tend to obsure the reality of labor relations in 1931. As the depression became personally threatening, laborers pressed to protect their paychecks, while managers sought to sustain profits or limit losses by cutting overhead, especially labor costs. Major tensions were developing.

Finally, the news from the hinterlands of the cities offered little hope. Despite the rise in California fruit and field crop tonnage, the produce was worth less because of the depressed prices. The Pacific Northwest lumber industry collapsed. If anything, the oil industry in Southern California was in worse shape than agriculture or lumber. Production was down 18 percent from 1930, and oil stocks had dropped 75 percent in value since 1929.[19] By 1931 the depression had hit home all along the West Coast.

In the face of all this, a relatively large number of leaders in the private sector still expressed little or no concern. By 1931, westerners appeared a little more enduring in their optimism than the rest of the nation. Although the citizens of Muncie, Indiana, even as late as 1933, continued to view the depression as a temporary phenomenon, baleful statements were not difficult to find around the country. The New York City Commissioners of Public Welfare averred in late 1931 not only that things were bad today but also that they would get worse tomorrow. And Kansas newspaper editor William Allen White lashed out at 1930, writing. "You went to hell and aren't worth remembering. There ought to be a hole in the calendar where you stuck up your dirty face. You . . . did everything that a bad year could do."[20] In contrast, some western optimists, if their public statements accurately represent their beliefs, seemed almost oblivious to conditions. In its April edition *The Nation* quoted Los Angeles Mayor John Porter: "The situation is not at all alarming. We do not find it necessary to feed our unemployed men here. In San Francisco I saw free soup kitchens. There are none here." The presidents of Southern California Edison and the Security First National Bank agreed that the depression had had no great effect on California, maintaining that 1928 had been a worse year. John T. Flynn, a business writer, was just as optimistic about Portland, saying it was in "very good condition," in fact "just about the best I've seen anywhere."[21]

Other positive thinkers along the West Coast acknowledged the problems even as they tried to rally their communities and reverse the psychological momentum. The Retail Merchants Committee of the Portland Chamber of Commerce, for example, suggested the word prosperity be substituted for depression wherever possible in business advertising.[22] The optimists tended to use two rationales. One was a variation on the belief widely held immediately after the crash that depression would not come West. By 1931 this notion had little merit, but some still maintained that the depression was affecting the region to a lesser degree. The encouragement offered by W. Kenneth Hayes, the financial writer of the *Los Angeles Examiner*, was typical: "It would be idle to deny that 1930 was a poor year . . . But it would be just as mistaken to deny that Los Angeles fared better than did most sections of the country." Other commentators suggested diversification, expansion, and lack of overdependence on an industrialized economy helped the West escape the brunt of the economic problems.[23] The other comparative tack was the idea of the upward swing. Businessman after businessman recited the same litany in the New Year's special financial sections: the economy had taken a tumble, but it would pick itself up and prosperity would return in 1931.

Others fretted about the state of the economy. Incoming San Francisco mayor Angelo Rossi spoke of the "present depression" and expressed his determination to do something about it. *Seattle Star* editorials throughout 1931 decried false optimism, declaring that times were hard. Louis Meyer of MGM studios noticed Americans were becoming "picture conscious," that is, choosy about what they went to see. And in the midst of Los Angeles's 150-year birthday celebration some complained that the money could be better spent to relieve depression-caused problems.[24] Many San Francisco business leaders in January 1931 admitted to real problems and resolved to do better in 1931.

Although cautious optimism seems to be the most typical public stance of leaders, a growing number of people, including several community opinion-makers, had become disillusioned about economic prospects. The author of the *Annual Report* of the Catholic Welfare Bureau put his finger on a major source of the pessimism. "With 'white collar' workers and business and professional men," he wrote, "types of human beings who never dreamed of being in want, thrust by the economic depression into the swelling ranks of needy how did the [Catholic Welfare Bureau] board meet multifarious problems?"[25] Others expressed the same idea, but not so grandiloquently. Hiram Johnson, Jr., despaired about an economy that did not bottom out. Isadore Zellerbach, of the paper manufacturing and timber family, sent out doleful Christmas greetings, "1931 has been quite a trying year for us all." Portland's *Oregon Daily Journal* and the Eberle Economic Service in Los Angeles judged that their cities had never before faced such a crisis. It was a year of "major depression" and "drastic decline."[26]

The continuing downturn of the economy hit everyone. In Portland, Mayor Baker claimed 95 percent of his appointments were with people seeking relief, and a Los Angeles executive agonized over able-bodied, well-educated men of the finest sort who came into his office and simply cried because they could not find a job. The Los Angeles County Library reported an upswing in borrowings, especially among titles that gave advice on how to set up businesses with little capitalization. The librarian noted that books on placer mining and prospecting were heavily used. More ominously the *Los Angeles Examiner* reported a widening crime wave in 1931.[27]

Having acknowledged the depression and its growing severity, correspondence, newspaper columns, and annual reports were filled with all manner of solutions and strategies to deal with hard times. The most frequently mentioned suggestions involved significant changes in the tax structure, in working hours, or in the relationship between the local government and state or federal authorities. But advocates of the quick fix or easy fix had not abandoned the field. Tourist money was still hoped to be a remedy in Los Angeles. "Buy Oregon" was a theme, and advertising strategems such as a "Don't Let Down Club" and a "Prosperity Queen" contest, with a Studebaker sedan as the grand prize, sought to nudge Seattleites into a better frame of mind.

The hope that 1920s-type ballyhoo could improve the economy gradually dimmed. Even the *Seattle Daily Journal of Commerce* editorialized against it, on the theory that too much commentary, optimistic or pessimistic, was being written about the depression.[28] The editor meant to lessen the consciousness of depression, but he was correct in another way. Writing about problems was not enough: the time had come to develop workable plans to attack them.

The most popular remedy remained increased public works. In 1931 this solution took a few different twists, found more widespread acceptance, and was discussed in terms of much larger projects. Newspaper publisher William Randolph Hearst provided one of the different twists by calling for a $5 billion prosperity loan. That is, $5 billion of federally underwritten bonds should be dedicated to public works projects. The Hearst papers in each of the western cities, of course, editorialized in favor of their publisher's plan and in the process brought in support from a large number of local politicians—including the San Francisco Board of Supervisors and the Seattle City Council—business leaders, and even competing newspapers. Opinion leaders in each city endorsed their local projects as likely beneficiaries of a prosperity loan: aqueducts in Southern California, bridges across the San Francisco Bay, highways in Washington, and a major downtown riverfront development in Portland.

As the need and the desire for large public works projects grew, taxation became a major battleground. The depression-spawned needs of the out-of-work collided with the fears of the still-employed. Jobholders worried that wage cuts combined with the increased demands of the tax man would place their possessions, especially their houses, in jeopardy. As different individuals and groups tried to resolve this problem, the complexity of the dilemma was illustrated in many ways. Mayor Rossi, a Los Angeles city councilman, the *San Francisco Chronicle*, and the *Seattle Star* suggested corporate or excise taxes to help alleviate the pressures of unemployment. But a *Seattle Times* reader advocated lower corporate taxes to stimulate profit, increase production, and make jobs. And the *Los Angeles Record* published a front-page piece entitled "Sweat on Taxpayer" aimed at revealing the burdens and inequities of the tax system.[29] This represented only the surface of the tension that was growing in 1931 and 1932.

Proposals for rearranging the work week and the wage scale, which first cropped up in 1930, found wider circulation in 1931. The shorter working day or work week, in fact, was the most debated solution of the year. Proponents hoped to stem layoffs and avoid wage cuts—unobtainable goals in the economic crisis of 1931. Nevertheless, the shortened work week found wide support. The Los Angeles Labor Council and Chamber of Commerce endorsed it. A Portland Committee of 100 planned out a work schedule, and a number of West Coast newspapers suggested the idea. To labor and business leaders alike this was a good way to secure employment and avoid a reduction in wages. As in 1930, it is not clear if both groups meant the same thing as they set forth their plans. It may be that labor accepted a smaller pay envelope to assure more jobs and the same wage scale. Ultimately the plan failed. In each city wages continued to decline as layoffs mounted.

A solution to which few besides Hearst had given much consideration before 1931 was state or even federal assistance. By the second year of the depression community leaders recognized that their resources were insufficient to cope with the growing unemployment. This willingness to break out of the pattern of local responsibility was strong in Oregon. Throughout the summer debate took place over whether there should be a special session of the Oregon legislature. Organized labor and the director of the Public Employment Bureau called for it most strongly. State legislators from Southern California voted 14 to 8 to hold a special session of the state legislature to discuss taxes, the state budget, and a diversion of state funds to counties for relief.[30] San Francisco's Mayor Rossi spearheaded an attempt to "develop a unified system of relief" by bringing major California cities together to fight unemployment. Rossi's eye was especially on the problem of passing the needy from city to city. The Seattle City Council joined with the Senate's progressive coalition and others vainly imploring President Hoover to call a special session of Congress to deal with unemployment. Editorials in the San Francisco and Seattle labor newspapers called not only for federal relief but also for a dole and for a system of unemployment insurance from the federal government.[31] The reality of a growing problem began eroding the restraints of tradition.

Finally, proposals emerged for a substantial reorganization of the social economy—not along class lines but along the lines of professional pursuit. Newspapers in each state reported, encouragingly, on the "back to the land" movement, and the Oregon state labor commissioner supported a $10 million bond to resettle Oregonians on logged-off land.[32] If a number of people in the West began seeking their agricultural roots in a time of economic collapse, the Annual Grange Reports indicated they should not have bothered; things were no better on the farm.[33]

The statistics and comments reveal a great deal about the economy, but it was jobs that the economy was destroying and the jobless who occupied the minds of those who sought solutions. The central problem, unemployment, was serious. The 1931 figures, though not much more reliable than the 1930 compilations, revealed this clearly. In three of the four cities the unemployment rate was at or above 20 percent. Only San Francisco had, perhaps, kept below this mark. Fifteen percent were unemployed in January 1931, but, according to a newspaper report, 18 percent of those working in March 1930 had lost their jobs by April 1931. In Los Angeles 105,220, or 20 percent of the work force, were jobless. A tenth or more of these had been looking for work for three months or more. By January the Seattle unemployment rate was at 23 percent of the gainfully employable. This meant somewhere between 30,000 and 36,000 individuals were without a job in the Puget Sound country. In October the Unemployed Citizens' League, a self-help group in Seattle, estimated that unemployment in the city's neighborhoods ranged from 34 percent to 83 percent in West Seattle. These were almost surely exaggerated figures. Just as surely the 23 percent was too low an estimate by year's end.[34]

Figures for Portland are not so readily obtainable. One source indicated employment in November 1931 was 17 percent lower than it had been toward the end of 1930, and several authorities pointed to at least 30,000 idle, a 20 percent unemployment rate.[35] Far more poignant was the Oregon Emergency Employment Commission's report, *Unemployment in Oregon*, which maintained that the need was so evident statistics were superfluous. This report, anything but bureaucratic, went on: "Notwithstanding the coming of spring in Oregon the situation is heartrending if not actually unprecedented. From all directions comes the urge to extend the emergency work. Everyone concerned would be more than happy to comply with such an appeal if possible."[36]

Reports from the relief agencies and employment offices added further evidence. In Los Angeles, San Francisco, and Seattle the loads had increased 250 percent from one year to the next. In Portland the same increase occurred from February 1931 to April.[37] Not only were the numbers of jobless increasing, but, more seriously, the unemployed were no longer willing or, more likely, able to take care of themselves.

These statistics are compelling testimony to the problems, but they convey neither the complexity of the story nor its feeling. Despondent people committed suicide. Unscrupulous employment agencies took advantage of desperate job seekers. Embarrassed by their inability to secure work, fathers could not bear to return home, and the number of desertion and failure-to-provide cases shot up. In a representative letter to a Portland city councilman, Harry Aldrich poured out his tale of unemployment, illness, and what he deemed bad management. He ended his letter pleading for as little as six days of work a month and declaring that if he could not make ends meet, "I shall have to walk off and leave my family as I will not accept charity direct."[38]

City editors recognized stories featuring the personal plight of the unemployed would attract readers. By 1932 at least one newspaper in every city had sent out a reporter to pose as a person thrown out of work and to describe what it was like to be "out there." In late 1931 and early 1932 the *San Francisco Examiner* sent Elenore Meherin to report on what it felt to be a jobless, broke working girl. In her first attempts to find a job she was thwarted by a lack of personal recommendations. Seven separate agencies informed her that if she had no local employment references she would be unable to obtain immediate employment of any kind. The only available jobs turned out to be the most menial housework or waitress positions, and a long waiting list stood between her and the cafe position. Her attention turned to food and lodging. Here she experienced somewhat better luck. In her days pounding the pavement several organizations helped Meherin get by. The Guardian Club picked up her meal tab because she was an unemployed woman. The YWCA put her up for the night in its boarding house but without much hospitality. The Salvation Army, the Volunteers of America, and, ultimately, the city's unemployment program gave her assistance. Even the city jail was good for one night's lodging. As the reporter in mufti met with genuinely unemployed women, the despair of being without a job, and without hope of finding one, began to hit home to her and her readers. There were really no alternatives to continually searching for employment. Many shuddered at having to accept welfare and considered especially the city's attempt at relief the last resort because it so completely labeled them as living off charity. Physically the life of an unemployed woman in San Francisco was not excruciatingly difficult. The psychological experience, however, was what left the scars.[39]

Most of the unemployed in each of the four cities acted as Elenore Meherin reported: calmly persevering, trying to pull themselves up, and accepting help from others when absolutely necessary. But in each of the cities there were those who had no intention of quietly sitting by and enduring. Although the number of Communists was probably far fewer than most citizens believed—a speaker in Seattle claimed there were 5,000 Communist party members in that city— by 1931 the opportunities for radical agitation were surely greater than ever before.[40]

In February especially, but throughout the year, unemployed in the four cities marched to make their demands known. As in 1930 their reception varied with the city. San Francisco and Portland marchers received peaceful police escorts and the mayors met larger parades at City Hall. In Portland the city council actually adjourned to hear Fred Walker, an avowed Communist, read a long list of demands. It included unemployment insurance, no evictions, and relief, to be administered by a combination of factory councils, trade union men, and unemployed councils. Before Walker was through he asserted that people were starving and the community chest was turning them away. "You're a liar," Mayor George Baker responded. The council then reconvened and denied each demand unanimously. This confrontation and exchange marked the moment of highest tension in Portland.[41]

The Seattle City Council also permitted the jobless to attend and be heard at a session in January, but a March demonstration ended in arrests. In San Francisco the marchers succeeded in shouting down Mayor Rossi and police arrested several unemployed individuals in a soup kitchen riot, but, on the whole, the city was quiet most of the year.

Once more tempers flared in Los Angeles, and the police and some city leaders perceived a threat to the peace from the Communist-inspired unemployed. In February, when there were parades in each of the other cities, there were none in Los Angeles—not because the unemployed had somehow become disorganized at the first of the year, but because of the attitudes and actions of the city council and the police. When the council denied marchers a parade permit in February, Chief of Police Roy Steckel made his viewpoint abundantly clear. "If your parade is going ahead against the wish of the city council then some of your people will be killed. If it takes bloodshed to protect constituted authority then there will be bloodshed."[42] The march was called off, and representatives of the marchers met with the city council. There was no bloodshed in February, but such was not the case during the rest of the year. The jobless took to the streets in Los Angeles more often than in the other cities. Each time, as often as once or twice every month if the strongly anti-Communist *Los Angeles Times* is to be believed, the police met the marchers and violence was the outcome.

Whether their frustration and anger manifested itself in rhetoric or bloodshed, a number among the jobless were upset and organized enough to demonstrate about it. Yet what Elenore Meherin found while posing as a jobless young woman conveyed the attitude of the majority of the unemployed far better than the tension-laden confrontations that gained more column space.

The number of unemployed grew as the year wore on. The problems of jobless-ness outran anyone's solutions. Wages fell and the work weeks shortened. Relief needs were greater, but city and county budgets were smaller. Tensions increased because the problems were unacceptable and seemingly unsolvable. The tensions, however, did not crystallize along class lines. They were more complex. Although management and labor may have wrangled over wage cuts or layoffs and the police and elements among the jobless might have eyed one another warily, confrontations were few and relatively mild, taking on even a subtle quality. Many perceived the conflict as a battle against more intangible forces—a fight waged against the economic crisis, against fate. It was fought for the future, and, most of all, for security. The drive to preserve one's own security, however defined, in the face of forces engendering monumental insecurity was the theme of 1931. And in 1931 few lashed out, confronted, or pointed a fault-finding finger at others. Instead the response was more a gathering in, a protecting of one's self and family, in any way possible, from the events pervading every part of the nation. The prevailing belief was that responsibility continued to rest with the individual whether em-ployed or out of work, and as long as that was accepted it was unlikely that major confrontation or class conflict would develop. The quest for security in its many forms could display a selfish side in an environment of insufficient resources. But at least as often a sense of responsibility to and for others—cooperation—tended to moderate single-minded attention to one's needs. The quest for security and the ideals of cooperative individualism were contradictory, and they began to strain against one another in 1931, but neither could be characterized yet as the truly dominant response of Americans to the problems of the depression.

This pull of a traditional concern for others against an elemental concern for one's self and one's own showed up in many places, but one of the easiest places to detect was in city finance. The relief effort in each city severely and unexpectedly drained city finances. How would the shortfalls be made up? Despite the urge to pass the buck to the county, state, or even national government, the solution during the Hoover years would have to be deficits or taxes. And it was on this latter reality that the milk of human kindness began to sour. A sense of responsibil-ity to others did not extend to risking the house through higher property assess-ments.

As the political leaders of each city made up their annual budgets, they realized that relief was not only occupying a larger and larger chunk of their projected expenditures but also was putting their cities into debt. Simultaneously, in the face of declining personal income, many citizens were demanding lower taxes. The bonding capacity of each city (the amount of debt a local government could incur by selling bonds based on property values and its ability to collect taxes on property) declined over the first three years of the depression. Not only did assessments drop in the deflationary conditions, but each city also increased its indebtedness as it sold public works bonds and work relief bonds. Moreover, as the national economy continued to deteriorate, there were even fewer buyers for municipal bonds than in 1930. In short, as the pressures for more relief mounted, it was more difficult for the four local governments to raise money through either bond sales or tax increases.

That is not to say that the budgets of the cities were all that burdensome. The Bank of America *Business Review* noted that San Francisco's tax rate was the third lowest in the nation. Los Angeles ran on the smallest expenditure of the nine largest cities in the nation. The Portland budget was one-fifth the size of Los Angeles's, and Seattle actually cut back on public works from 1931 to 1932.[43] Nonetheless, pressures for slashes in the municipal outlays mounted in 1931 and became even stronger in 1932.

In 1931 these pressures were especially strong in Seattle and San Francisco. The impetus for budget paring in Seattle did not come strictly from concerned citizens. In their annual messages, both Governor Roland Hartley and Mayor Frank Edwards made appeals for cutbacks in state and city spending to forestall tax increases. In fact, the two officials suggested that tax cuts would be a desirable result of efficient government.[44] The national financial markets also put Seattle on notice as Moody's investor service lowered Seattle's bond rating from "Aaa" to "Aa." Several newspapers and the Municipal League endorsed the prospect of lower taxes, and community clubs and the Property Owners Association lobbied hard for a reduction in assessments. The target of their meetings and rallies throughout the summer was a $3 million reduction in the 1932 city budget.

A large number of taxpaying middle-class voters in Seattle, because of either layoffs or salary cuts, were hard pressed for money. By early 1932 only 55.5 percent of Seattle's registered voters were paying property tax—a 14 percent decrease from 1928. Especially hard hit was the blue-collar worker. From 1928 to 1932, 42 percent fewer unskilled laborers were paying their property tax, there was a 20 percent decline among the skilled, and among the semiskilled an 11 percent drop-off. Tax paying among the lower level white-collar group, such as salesmen, clerks, and secretaries, declined 17 percent. The rate of payment among higher level white-collar workers decreased less than 5 percent. Principally, lower and middle segments of the population, who felt the economic pinch in 1931 and early 1932, demanded lower taxes. In Seattle these hard-pressed citizens and the community clubs won. The 1931 city budget was less than that of 1930, and the budget adopted in October 1931 for the following year included a $2 million reduction, representing a 3 mill drop in the tax levy.[45]

San Francisco confronted the same debates but with a somewhat different outcome. Real estate agents, especially, sought a lower tax levy, and some warned of a wave of bankruptcies among property owners.[46] The city faced a projected deficit of $1.2 million, as the board of supervisors began budget hearings. Because the city charter did not permit any further deficit spending, either severe retrenchment or a bond sale seemed inevitable. San Francisco had 65 percent of its bonding capacity remaining, so a precipitous cut in spending was not absolutely necessary.[47]

There was support in San Francisco for an expanded budget, or at least a larger appropriation for relief. A number of newspapers and Adolf Uhl, a defeated candidate for mayor, asked the board to approve the proposed $350,000 in relief. The supervisors authorized the entire amount even as they succeeded in paring the whole budget package by $155,000 and keeping the millage rate the same. Part of the savings derived from placing most city employees on a five-day work week.

The city of Los Angeles, too, reduced its budget for fiscal year 1931–32. The cut was $350,000, $1 million less than the 1929–30 budget.[48] Although property values were not declining precipitously, the city had to raise the tax levy about one-half mill. The council also sat on a reserve fund of over $5 million—a revolving fund that picked up any slack in between tax collections.[49] The only concern for the city was its bonding capacity. The unused margin of bonded indebtedness stood at 29 percent in 1931, but only $6.7 million dollars (13 percent) was available for bonds that could assist relief activity.[50]

The county of Los Angeles had to pick up the slack left by the city. While the city appropriated all of $50,000 to the community chest and $23,500 more to social services, Los Angeles County increased its appropriations 120 percent over the previous year by adding almost $1 million to its 1931–32 relief budget.[51]

In Portland public pressure for budget cuts surfaced as well, even as the municipal and county budgets increased. Moreover, the amount set aside for charities in Multnomah County increased each of the first three years of the depression. Adding to the difficulty, the unused portion of Portland's bonding capacity had fallen below $1 million, and by the end of the year the city had nearly lost its ability to market bonds.[52]

In the second full year of the depression the nation discovered the depth of the problems it confronted and realized the economic cycle was not turning upward. On the West Coast, leaders set about searching for a cure, or at least relief. In this they hampered themselves to a degree. Their abilities and attitudes proved an impediment to this quest. Both the tradition of capitalistic free enterprise and the ethos of individualism restrained officials from moving too swiftly or operating on too large a scale. Much was left to the self-reliance and the goodwill of those better off. And there was the matter of fiscal responsibility. Property owners and the cities as a whole refused to sacrifice themselves to accomplish a job that many believed was better left in private hands. Cutting taxes and balancing budgets were just as important locally as at the national level. And so, even if the events of 1931 drew a response from the four cities that was more innovative, more thoroughgoing, and, perhaps, less begrudging than that of the previous year, it was a response still circumscribed by intangible traditions and tangible financial realities.

FIVE

In Search of Relief

While the national government debated planning and coordinated relief efforts, cities and counties in 1931 sought to meet their problems in a far more concerted manner than they had in 1930. During that first year of depression, solutions had an air of spontaneity and administrators expected an intense but short-lived downturn. The responses of 1931 were more carefully planned than in 1930 and had the advantage of more consistent funding than in 1932.

In Los Angeles the community chest, still the spearhead of the private effort and a channel for some public funds, continued to encounter financial difficulties. In the spring officials made an emergency appeal for an additional $265,000 to provide assistance for the jobless through the rest of the year. Chest publicity emphasized that many flocking to relief centers had never before accepted charity. Only $61,000 was collected in the spring campaign. In the summer Los Angeles County officials came to the rescue, all but promising they would not cut back on the $400,000 per month they were spending on relief assistance. Assured of this and accepting a $100,000 loan to finish out the year, community chest officials breathed easier, at least until the fall fund-raising campaign. The target for 1931–32 was $3,321,000, just $100,000 over the previous year's unmet goal. Fully $1.35 million of the total was for family welfare and relief, including a special emergency fund of $600,000 that officials specifically earmarked for jobless relief. The fund campaign dragged past its planned conclusion in November into December. Then, on 2 December ecstatic fund-raisers announced the campaign had gone over the top, by $3,475.[1] The money would not be enough, but reaching the drive's goal was a remarkable feat. In the depths of depression many of the contributors were undoubtedly in the midst of their own economic crises. The Los Angeles Community Chest had exceeded its goal in a year in which 25 percent of the chest campaigns around the nation had fallen short by 10 percent or more.[2]

The scope and variety of the spontaneous private reactions to the depression in Los Angeles were equally remarkable. These responses weigh in the balance on the side of cooperative individualism and amply demonstrate that the quest for security was not by 1931 the only, or perhaps even the primary, reaction of Angelenos. The Parent Teacher Association (PTA) continued its school milk program in 1931, and, with the help of the county, the city, and other private charities, expanded the program to lunches. Even through summer school sixty-three school cafeterias were open six days a week to dispense meals. In outlying districts not convenient to schools PTA members opened their homes to feed children. Despite the effort, ill and half-starved children showed up when the regular school year opened. Some of them, those who had not attended summer school or who, because of the pride of their parents, did not choose to eat at the schools, had to be hospitalized.[3] In October the county board of supervisors appropriated $12,000 to carry the program through December.

Many others assisted in various ways to alleviate some of the physical suffering of the jobless. A sandwich shop owner gave ten tickets a day to organizations that then distributed the tickets to the unemployed for a free meal. Other examples of small-scale but helpful charity efforts included a food canning center, a food and clothing distribution warehouse, and free transportation to farms and orchards so unemployed could pick crops for others without incomes. An air circus, a Moose Lodge vaudeville show, and a Christmas benefit featuring a full slate of Hollywood celebrities helped raise relief money. The holiday season brought special fund drives, free dinners, and Christmas baskets for the needy (including a basket from the Women's Breakfast Club with rouge, lipstick, silk stockings, perfume, and powder for unemployed women).

The Midnight Mission continued to be the primary overnight residence for transients. Its record, however, was spoiled when an investigation of its sanitation practices revealed that Mission management had been scavenging scraps from restaurant tables for twenty months. The County Welfare Department and community chest immediately appropriated $3,000 so the Mission could carry on a more healthful service.[4]

Different segments of the population helped care for their own. In the black community the Industrial Council adopted the slogan "I am my brothers' keeper" and set up a distribution depot for the needy.[5] An Eastside Employment Committee also formed to assure blacks would get their fair share of city relief work and to keep tabs on community needs and problems. Forty-three women's clubs combined to form the Associated Women's Committee. The group supported single unemployed women and sought meaningful relief work for them in city offices.

Church-related groups were also active. A small Free Methodist Church provided a church service and a meal to as many as two hundred a day. The indefatigable Aimee Semple McPherson fed over 40,000 and clothed another 50,000 during the year. The Angelus Temple band added to the uplift by performing during the meals.[6] The whole of the Catholic Welfare Bureau report was an impassioned document. The report indicated the expenditure of $182,000 on 17,000 families and 2,600 more single people and added an emotional outcry against the depression, against those who would criticize the bureau, and for those in need.[7]

The unemployed endeavored to help themselves in creative ways. The *Los Angeles Record* featured the photo of a young man wearing a sandwich board. The legend on the board read: "Harvard student would like to make a good permanent business connection with a reliable concern. Majored in journalism but can do clerical, secretarial accounting and secretarial work. References furnished if necessary. Can also drive any make of automobile."[8] The *Record* supplied his address but apparently not a staff position.

Apple selling came to the streets of Los Angeles in 1931 when the Associated City Employees Relief Organization supplied apples raised on city property in the Owens Valley. Unemployed women, children of needy families, and incapacitated men did the selling. In just over two months of vending they raised over $55,000, most of which went to women who were heads of families.

The jobless in Los Angeles continued to organize. In January a Socialist, William Busick, announced a list of demands and vowed to gather in 20,000 jobless followers. Less threatening to a city with an almost hyperactive Red Squad was George McLain's Unemployed Voters Association. This one thousand–member group sought luxury taxes on fights, the theater, and night clubs. McLain's organization illustrated another way a person could help himself. McLain received $1 from each member as they joined and $100 from anyone who cared to serve on the board of directors of the organization. Although not many such swindles were reported, the needy were not insulated from the wiles of the confidence man.

Everyone involved understood that private assistance was critical to sustaining the community, but by 1931 substantial public funds were necessary as well. Despite the county's legal mandate to provide public welfare, the city of Los Angeles assumed a part in the relief effort, albeit more reluctantly than the other three cities. The city and county employment commissions, established at the end of 1930, augmented and adjusted their plans several times to meet the pressures of unemployment that mounted almost beyond belief. During the 1931–32 fiscal year, the city spent $5.7 million on relief while the county furnished $15 million.[9] For the most part the city's share went into public works, but several hundred thousand dollars bought food, paid utility bills, and furnished assistance to transients.

The city responded casually at first, then, assisted by a relief-bond issue, moved to its peak effort in mid-1931. Early in the year the city's relief organization, the Citizens' Committee on the Coordination of Unemployment Relief, began to define itself and its mission and also started to encounter problems. Working from the committee's plans, the city evidently hoped to get by as cheaply as possible. City officials appropriated funds for firebreak work and the Department of Water and Power furnished jobs on substantial construction already under way. The Citizens' Committee, headed by C. P. Visel, focused on what the private sector could do. The committee would coordinate job agencies, push a fix-up campaign, encourage Angelenos to buy local products to further local employment, and recommend rotation of work.[10] Almost from the moment the goals were announced, the needs exceeded them. The *Los Angeles Record* found in February what it claimed to be a closely guarded secret report and quoted Visel: "NO direct results have been noted through the job clearing house," even though 14,000 had registered. The *Record* reported Visel paid committee incidentals out of his own pocket.[11]

Reacting to the fact that 14,000 were already registered, and probably responding to Visel's report as well, the city council took stop-gap measures in early February. Funds for ditch-digging relief work came out of the remainder of a $38 million bond issue passed in 1930 for the Owens Valley water project. An additional $100,000 was transferred to the general fund from the Department of Water and Power budget, which contained a sizeable surplus. Even as councilmen looked for more available bond money or public works funds, it was clear much more was needed.

Almost immediately a plan for a $5 million bond issue for work relief, which had been submerged in a committee, rose to the surface. The council asked the people to endorse it at a special election scheduled for early March—less than a month away. Three million dollars would go to street construction, and city parks and playgrounds would receive $1 million each. The council anticipated that the bond would fund 16,000 jobs. Civic organizations, business groups, newspapers, and professional bodies all gave it a hearty endorsement. Will Rogers went on the air to support its passage. A billboard donated by Foster and Kleiser tugged at voters' heartstrings with the picture of a little girl asking voters to "Give My Daddy a Job—Vote for the Bonds for the Unemployed, March 5, 1931."[12]

Those worried about the impact on taxes opposed the measure. Several realtors gave their public approval, but the Realty Board of Los Angeles was against it. The effect of the bonds, the *Los Angeles Times*, a supporter, speculated, would be a 2 mill increase. The Municipal League was opposed, since it believed the county was better prepared to provide the relief work and feared the bond issue would end up being a great pork barrel for city councilmen.[13]

On 5 March about 25 percent of the registered voters turned out to give the $5 million bond issue their approval. The people gave each of the three issues more than 81,000 "yeses" and less than 36,000 "no" votes; the bond easily secured the necessary two-third's majority.[14] Perception of the need outweighed more personal concerns about increased taxes, but this would be the last general purpose bond passed in the city of Los Angeles during the Hoover years.

Almost immediately the Municipal League's concerns seemed to be coming true. Mayor Porter asked the Public Works Department to decide on and supervise the $5 million worth of work. The city councilmen strongly disagreed, maintaining that they should keep the power of planning, which they had always possessed, and not lose their authority to direct some of the funds to their districts.

The wage scale on the newly created relief work was also hotly debated. As in other cities, the issue was more political than a concern over a minimum living wage. Would these men, especially skilled workers, be paid a prevailing rate? Organized labor, of course, strongly maintained that they should. More thrifty, or more conservative, councilmen lobbied for a lower-than-standard wage. The prolabor faction on the council won the day, determining that $4 per day was fair. This matched the county's work-relief wage level and the prevailing wage but fell below the Civil Service standard. Compared to the figure most frequently quoted around the nation—$2.40 for each day's labor—this was a generous wage. Cities in the Upper Midwest and the East, such as Cleveland, Chicago, Buffalo, and New York City, however, paid from $4.80 to $5.14.[15]

The bond issue failed completely to address women's needs. The work was going to be heavy manual labor, which in 1931 was deemed inappropriate for women, at least in an urban setting. A number of women's organizations sent representatives to the city council soon after the bonds passed to remind the councilmen that as many as 15,000 women were out of work. The council responded with sympathy but maintained they would violate Civil Service codes by placing women into the relief jobs.[16] They had violated the codes, of course, in establishing the wage scale for street and park work. The council at first promised to find as much clerical work as possible for women in administrating the men's work, but finally they appropriated $120,000 for women's relief. The mayor, labeling it a dole, at first refused to sign the appropriation. He relented on the condition that the outlay go for food or shelter and not be given outright. This money along with a $22,500 appropriation in 1932 helped fewer than 3,500 unemployed women.[17] Yet this meager response demonstrated a consciousness and concern that matched or exceeded that of the other cities.

By borrowing from other funds until the city could market the bonds, the men's relief work got under way within a week of voter approval. Relief officials selected workers from lists of the unemployed that had been compiled at fire stations throughout the city in 1930. Tough eligibility requirements assured Angelenos that only their own and only the most deserving would get relief work. The rules required a recipient to have been a resident of the city for at least one year. Married men would get five days of work and the unmarried would receive three days as their names came up in the rotation. By early April, 3,000 men were toiling on streetworks, parks, and playgrounds. Through spring and fall the unemployed worked in two-week rotations, one week on and one week off. In September, as work relief funds began to run low and unemployment failed to abate, the city went to a three-week shift to spread the work, and the incomes, a little thinner.

To a reasonable person in March 1931 the bond vote had been a solution, in fact a generous solution, to the economic displacement. But the crisis continued to worsen. In Los Angeles $5 million provided only a respite that did not even last out the year.

On 30 September, as relief funds neared exhaustion, Mayor Porter called a conference on unemployment. A wide range of possibilities were discussed. The conferees suggested more bonds, more taxes, a loan scheme for potential home-owners who might be willing to build a house, and the continuation of current programs. Nothing positive resulted from the meeting. In November the mayor announced that the work relief fund was exhausted, and the city hoped the community chest, which was in the midst of its fund-raising campaign, would receive sufficient contributions to make up the difference.

Individual city employees had been generous in taking up the slack. Through much of 1931 they continued to contribute voluntarily 1 percent of their salary for relief assistance. Their goal was $30,000 a month, although they managed only $20,000. The program was inactive during the fall, but when the bond money ran out the contributions recommenced. In six months another $100,000 had come in, virtually all of which went to laid-off city employees.[18] The depression by the end of 1931 exceeded the allotted resources of the city of Los Angeles as well as its willingness to provide any more.

Because of its legal mandate to provide charity, Los Angeles County could not simply choose to abdicate the relief responsibility. The county, however, could winnow the list of applicants seeking public welfare. The priority for relief placed the physically and mentally incapacitated first, then came families with small children, families with no male breadwinner, and finally families with no children under sixteen. Under normal conditions assistance, usually without work in return, would have been given to the top two or three categories. In the early 1930s, however, there were plenty of able-bodied but jobless family and single men who applied to the county for assistance. The prevailing ethic demanded they perform some amount of work for relief payments. The board of supervisors ruled in January 1931 that all who could had to work for what they received from the county.[19] Consequently, the County Welfare Bureau continued to dispense direct relief only to those unable to work and also oversaw a good deal of work relief. The county's initial work project was cleaning the usually dry Los Angeles River bed. Apparently, this test saved a substantial amount of relief funds. The supervisors reported 60 percent declined relief or walked away.[20]

Relief expenditure, nonetheless, increased tremendously. The bill for outdoor relief in the county went up 178 percent from fiscal year 1928–29 to 1931–32. The family relief expenditure of the county welfare department rose 214 percent.[21] According to the supervisors' *Annual Report* for 1931–32, the Welfare Bureau tended to over 63,000 relief cases—a 55 percent increase over 1930–31—and provided more than 267,000 hours of relief work for those able to labor. The report estimated almost 10 percent of the population of Los Angeles County had sought assistance during the year.[22]

In addition to providing help to the standard charity cases and furnishing much more work relief than ever before, the county continued the Employment Stabilization Bureau. This agency, the only significant addition to the county's already existing public welfare apparatus, located work or obtained aid for over 30,000 county residents during the first half of 1931. Despite this impressive record, the bureau head, Harvey Fremming, resigned because he believed Supervisor Frank Shaw, who had been the driving force in founding the agency, was using it to stabilize his own political employment.[23] Indeed, Shaw's prominence throughout the early 1930s as an advocate and guide in the relief effort helped him win the Los Angeles mayor's office in 1934.

The county had problems finding sufficient funds to provide for its responsibility. Superintendent of County Charities, W. H. Holland, who oversaw the entire county relief program, came to the board of supervisors in April asking for an extra appropriation of $1 million to get to June, the end of the fiscal year. He explained that the reserve fund, which usually held $5 to $6 million, was almost depleted. The board granted him only $506,000. This marked the origin of a more serious problem. From April or May through the fall of 1931, the county charity operation became a political punching bag, ostensibly because of the budgetary shortfall. It may, however, have fallen victim to political maneuvering on the board of supervisors—a genuine possibility considering the ambitions of the politically astute Shaw who chaired the welfare committee.

Holland's first response to being denied his full request was to turn down a $125,000 request from the city of Long Beach. The board then slashed the welfare budget for June by $100,000. On 5 June, Holland closed his office at noon, declaring the County Welfare Bureau was $22,000 in arrears and could go no further. The supervisors responded with an additional $250,000.

At that point, the county launched an investigation into the charity operation. The inquiry supposedly concentrated on the eligibility of welfare recipients. At issue, however, was whether the board of supervisors had underfunded the relief effort—violating the law—or whether Holland and his staff had done a shabby job of administering it. Shaw's Employment Stabilization Bureau became the focal point of the investigation when Holland discovered to his dismay that he was supposed to be overseeing the bureau, which, according to a Reconstruction Finance Corporation administrator, was one of the most inept, disorganized operations in the country. Suddenly, on 7 July, Holland declared that ten years in one position was long enough and resigned, effective in January.[24] Clearly, he yielded to pressures that included charges of mismanagement. Behind the scenes two supervisors apparently executed a political trade-off. Frank Shaw had pressed for the demotion of the head of the county general hospital, while Supervisor Hugh Thatcher sought Holland's scalp. Holland and Dr. Neal Wood, the superintendent of the hospital, stepped aside the same day.[25]

The controversy did not cease with Holland's resignation. In mid-August the supervisors received a two hundred-page report that pointed to carelessness in the administration of county relief and saw the possibility of saving $500,000 if the Welfare Bureau were reorganized. Specifically, the investigators from the Bureau of Budget and Efficiency cited the Welfare Bureau's leadership for imprudence, or excessive generosity, depending on one's viewpoint. The central administration—that is, Holland—possessed an attitude, the report asserted, that the money was the county's, so why not spend it. This, along with a penchant for allowing the undeserving to get back on the county rolls, fostered a welfare mentality among recipients in the county. In fact, investigators charged that some families were coming to the point of seeing welfare payments as their right. Although evidence does indicate poor administration, in 1931 these particular allegations spoke precisely to the community's concerns about relief activities. The report called for decentralization of the budget, standardization of operation, and a return to the original intent of the pauper act—simple relief only to those in need and entitled to aid. District directors of the Welfare Bureau estimated 15 percent or $643,000 could be saved.[26] Under this increased pressure, Holland accelerated his departure date to 24 August, and the board of supervisors turned over a portion of the report to the grand jury for its inspection.

It is not entirely clear what to make of all this. Surely, Holland fell victim to politics, but doubtless the Welfare Bureau could have been run better, and the Employment Stabilization Bureau was politicized and chaotic. The Budget and Efficiency investigators were from an internal watchdog agency. The disagreement between Holland and the board brought on the investigation, but those who filed the report presumably had no political ax to grind. They pointed to some degree of mismanagement since 1927. Perhaps Holland had never been a paragon of efficiency, and under the extreme demands of the depression he was incapable of overseeing his agency. But it is equally possible that a man who had been administering charity for ten years had a different philosophy about it in 1931 than most Angelenos. Of the four cities Los Angeles was the most prudent—or least generous

—with its relief funds. Holland and his values may have been under review in the wrong city at the wrong time. Whatever the case, his successor, W. R. Harriman, in his first public announcement, reported that welfare cases had increased by 600 over the previous ten days, and the supervisors gave him approximately $2 million more to work with for 1931–32.[27]

Not a great deal of assistance came from beyond the boundaries of Los Angeles County. Through 1931 the federal government provided encouragement and tried to stimulate regional cooperation but did nothing directly in Southern California. John Austin, a Los Angeles architect and the former head of the chamber of commerce, was the federal government's representative as the local director of the President's Organization for Unemployed Relief (POUR). Austin's mandate was to gather a group in Los Angeles County to study, advise, and coordinate unemployment efforts. The new body would not replace any of the already functioning commissions but would orchestrate the efforts of each group to bring about maximum efficiency. A guiding idea of the Los Angeles POUR was that "relief plans be based on a theory that unemployed are seeking self-preservation, without losing their self-respect by being reduced to charity doles." The committee also hoped to eliminate red tape and prorate employment in the area.[28] Beyond lending encouragement and coordination, POUR pressured the Los Angeles Department of Water and Power to transfer $3 million of construction funds to the city's general fund for relief. The city utility was not persuaded.

Harvey Fremming went to Washington, D.C., in early 1931 to determine what Southern California could expect in the way of federal works during the year. He brought back only hopes, not promises, of federal funds for about $4 million worth of construction. The federal government did provide one concrete economic boost during the year through the distribution of the veterans' bonus loan in March. Los Angeles was a distribution center for Southern California and Southern Nevada. As much as $25 million would be handed out to more than 100,000 men over a short period of time. The *Times* predicted an influx of money, transient men, and chiselers during the month.[29]

There were two more sources of cash flow for the Los Angeles economy in 1931. One was the Colorado River aqueduct project. Although it was not under construction within the boundaries of the county, the Colorado project was sure to absorb a number of residents as employees as long as it continued. In September the people of the county approved $220 million in bonds that assured support for the continuation of construction. The Reconstruction Finance Corporation provided a helpful boost to the project in 1932 by purchasing $40 million of its bonds.

California, the other source of funds, began $1.5 million in road projects in the fall. Although this put jobless to work in the area, county and chamber of commerce officials complained about the economic effect of a one cent-per-gallon increase in the gas tax to fund the work and fretted over the program getting underway too slowly.[30]

California, especially Southern California, was a prime destination for transients and aliens. During the Hoover years the influx was not of legendary size, but many Californians were prepared to ward off the swarms of potential emigrants from other states and Mexico if they should come. The Los Angeles Chamber of Commerce, in a reversal of its normal role, in 1931 moved toward what later became known as the "Bum Blockade." A committee of the chamber wanted National Guard troops stationed at the state's borders to keep undesirables out. Southern Californians printed cards, to be distributed throughout the nation, informing unwary hopefuls that there were no jobs in the region. And in November 1931 the board of supervisors resolved that

> all National Broadcasting [sic] companies be and are hereby requested to cooperate with the State of California in broadcasting throughout the country the facts concerning unemployment in this state in order that misguided unemployed may be reached quickly throughout the country and saved from unwise migration to California which can, because of stringent state charity laws and local policies against employing any but bona fide residents, end only in disillusionment and increased suffering and despair.[31]

The stringent state charity law the resolution mentioned was enacted in September 1931, and when applied it alleviated some pressures that had been on the counties. For the county to be responsible for charity, according to the amended law, the recipient now must have been a resident of the state for three years. In the 1931–32 fiscal year Los Angeles County sent well over 7,000 men to private agencies, citing the change in the law. Even charity medical assistance was denied to those no longer eligible under the law.[32] The increased residency requirement may have had a broader effect. Arizona officials reported in January 1932 that the number of east-bound jobless slightly exceeded those headed for California.

If a jobless person, especially a single man, should press on despite the discouraging words, he would have found a welcome as cold as advertised. A Los Angeles Times reporter, sent out to identify with the itinerants, returned with a gritty tale. A fellow could mooch for about a week by hitting four or five agencies for a bed and a couple of meals a day, the writer reported. If you were willing to do some work the Municipal Service Bureau would put you up for a week or more. During 1931 the service bureau received almost 40,000 applications for this sort of help; about 13,000 were repeaters. After that the only choice was the state work camps, which were designed to discourage any long-term dependency, or even residency.[33] Other observers noted that all-night movie theaters and boxcars furnished sleeping accommodations.

To make the life of a drifter even less palatable, the city barred begging, promising a $500 fine for any placards, cups, horns, or instruments used in soliciting charity on the street. In the first months of 1931, until the YMCA provided help, police picked up juvenile beggars and put them into lodging houses with older men. The Times, in particular, became enthusiastic about the work test for single unemployed men—four hours at hard labor for room and board. The county shipped some transients to the Arcadia Military Balloon School. The city council of the exclusive suburb of San Marino responded with an unintended pun: they were concerned about so many "floaters" being in the neighborhood.[34]

Aliens from Mexico also concerned the citizenry and surely attracted the attention of county officials. As the depression deepened, Southern Californians began to segregate Mexican aliens in the public schools; and law authorities made arrests indiscriminately.[35] The county board of supervisors settled on repatriation as a solution to the alien problem. As they sought to encourage Mexican citizens living in the Los Angeles area to return to their native land, harrassment and mass arrests of illegal aliens were initially the methods of encouragement. When they saw their countrymen, both legal and illegal residents, being rounded up, many Mexicans, the board believed, would voluntarily leave for Mexico. The assumption was accurate, but this method was not as effective as the supervisors hoped.

The county's next step was to underwrite repatriation. On the surface the whole process appears insensitive and discriminatory. Francisco Balderrama, relying especially on the testimony of Rafael de la Colina, the Mexican consul in Southern California, however, demonstrates well that repatriation benefited both the county and those who went back to Mexico. By 1932, in fact, the consul urged the board of supervisors to repatriate those who were not receiving relief. Unemployed and suffering from economic and social discrimination, many Mexican aliens were in fact eager to return home.[36] If the consul's promises were carried out, the returnees received land in Mexico of equal value to that which they owned in the United States. According to the county's report 85 percent of those repatriated found employment in Mexico.[37] Only California employers, who were losing a cheap source of labor, strongly protested the repatriation.

Even though it paid for transportation, the county believed it came out far ahead. In its 1931 *Annual Report* the Welfare Division congratulated itself on "vision and farsightedness." W. H. Holland said, as the operation began, that the county would be "ridding ourselves of a large number of Mexicans who have been or are in danger of becoming dependents on the county."[38]

The Mexican National Railroad agreed to a county-paid fare of $14.70 per adult and half that for children to take the repatriates to their former homes in Mexico. Trains left throughout 1931 as more and more aliens decided to return. The superintendent of charity returned to the board at least nine times during the year for additional funds as the Mexican response exceeded county expectations. The board approved every request. In all, 13,332 were repatriated between 1931 and 1934. Of these 10,343 left in 1931 and 1932.[39]

The primary responses of all four western cities were in 1931 again similar in their main contours, substantially because their ideas were all born of common sense, existing financial and bureaucratic structures, and prevailing values. There were, however, variations on those common themes. San Francisco functioned differently, for example, because the city and county government was combined. But there was more. Financial pressures did not engender the kinds of political difficulties Los Angeles experienced. San Francisco was more willing and able than the Los Angeles city or county government to appropriate funds for relief. San Francisco's generosity is difficult to explain. The unique government configuration may have made a difference. It may have been due to the comparative strength of the Bay Area's economy, or, perhaps, both the residents and leaders of San Francisco were a little more openhanded and a little less concerned about the debilitating effects of charity on the recipients. There is evidence for each possibility.

Whatever the reasons, while private agencies increased their relief expenditures in 1931, the city and county of San Francisco took the major responsibility. Private charities, which continued to deal with unemployment relief as only one aspect of their load, did not drastically change their spending levels from 1929 to 1931 ($535,000 in 1929 and $711,000 in 1931). The city–county government, however, greatly expanded its role. In 1929 it designated $20,000 specifically for unemployment relief. This increased almost sixfold in 1930 to $118,000, and in the next year the municipal government poured over $2.4 million into relief for the jobless. The combined private and public expenditure for 1931 increased a whopping 583 percent over 1929.[40]

In 1931 the community chest, still the mainstay of San Francisco's private relief effort, cared for more recipients but experienced increased difficulty in soliciting contributions. Its executive committee, recognizing it was in a bind, debated whether the chest should concentrate on serving the unemployed or just continue its traditional role of coordinating agencies serving specific needs and specific clients. Solicitation presented even more fundamental problems. Private pleas to the larger donors revealed these usually reliable sources were tempering their generosity with concern over their own security. Still, in the two drives held during 1931, larger-than-ever quotas were almost met in March and exceeded in November. The two funding campaigns took in a total of almost $5 million.

As other established groups such as the Salvation Army and the YMCA continued to help, new agencies emerged. One of the most colorful relief stations was the "White Angel Jungle" on the San Francisco Bay waterfront. Mother Lois Jordan, the self-proclaimed White Angel, served as many as 2,000 men a day with no questions asked. Her soup line, she said, was run entirely on the principles of faith and no red tape, depending entirely on unsolicited contributions of food and money. Mother Jordan provided the press with stories of her faith being rewarded in the nick of time so she could continue serving.[41]

Various organizations and businesses aided the unemployed. The Dairyman's Association, in the midst of the price war, offered free surplus milk to the needy. Policemen and typographers gave donations or designated part of their wages to go to the jobless. And Southern Pacific Railroad employees deducted over $83,000 from their paychecks that the company matched. The $167,000 provided a revolving loan fund for laid-off Southern Pacific employees. Receipts from football games, prize fights, and lavish balls also benefited the needy.

During the Hoover years of the depression the unemployed of San Francisco did little in an organized way to assist one another. As late as 1933 the Bay Area had only four self-help organizations with a total membership of 300. In his study of self-help in California Clark Kerr explains this: "The city [San Francisco] had one of the lowest rates of unemployment of any large city and provided a higher standard of relief."[42]

The higher standard of relief Kerr alludes to was provided in the main by the local government. The city's relief effort rested on the passage of the $2.5 million bond proposal in February. Until the election was held, the mayor and board of supervisors juggled moneys to provide what they could to keep the 1930 work relief program going, but a full month before the vote the *News* reported that, after spending $293,000 the supervisors had scrounged, the city had no money left to aid the jobless. The need for the bonds, as Mayor Rossi said in his annual message, was acute. On 6 February 1931, San Franciscans approved the bond issue by a 7 to 1 margin—a much stronger endorsement than Angelenos gave their issue. The massive relief program got under way immediately.

Rossi appointed Charles M. Wollenberg to oversee the operation. The fifty-eight-year-old superintendent of the Laguna Honda Home for the impoverished, who started his career at the time of the 1906 earthquake and fire, was an experienced social worker. In keeping with the city's standard practice of using private agencies to dispense public charity funds, the bulk of the money was funneled to the needy through the Associated Charities, the relief arm of the community chest. Moreover, the supervisors were willing to surrender direct control of the assistance funds to assure that the most qualified people administered them. The most experienced relief workers, like Wollenberg, headed or were employed in private agencies, so the role of the Associated Charities grew considerably over the course of the depression. It dispensed 315 percent more relief in 1931 than it had in 1929. The relief agency added forty extra staff members, including some of the unemployed themselves, to handle the increasing load. The Eureka Benevolent Society and the Italian Board of Relief also received funds to provide for families. The city remembered single women with less prompting than Los Angeles. The Women's Division of Unemployment Relief received 6.6 percent of the fund to help jobless women.[43]

The first task was to compile a list of the unemployed. During 1931 almost 30,000 people—almost three-fourths of the entire jobless population in San Francisco—placed their names on the list.[44] Unlike Los Angeles, San Francisco sought to assist even migratory workers. Wollenberg pointed out that migrants spent their summer earnings in San Francisco and the city owed them some assistance.

In an age that considered the word *dole* an obscenity, no one thought of providing anything but work relief. From February until July five dollars a day was given to men working on some kind of public works project.

The relief program's needs quickly exceeded both expectations and available funds. The bond issue, intended to last through two winters of unemployment, was almost expended in 1931—in fact, the city had spent well over $2 million of it before the year ended. In spring the Associated Charities and the Salvation Army indicated that unemployment was growing, rather than moderating, with the warmer weather. As money ran low and joblessness climbed, the supervisors instituted a new program in which the relief recipients worked one week to get a three-week supply of food. If necessary, the applicant could obtain a three-day supply of food immediately.

Inevitably, with such a large expenditure of money, the relief effort was not free of problems. The substantial financial establishment of the city helped out by either loaning money interest free or buying the bonds themselves while legal hitches were ironed out. But a host of complaints about relief money being spent unwisely or wrongfully punctuated the spring of 1931. There were reports that some men, after getting the cards that assigned them to a particular job, sold them to others. The head registrar was charged with favoritism in registering the unemployed, and a great argument broke out about expenditures for overhead. Supervisors and trustees of the bond money were upset to learn it paid for park department employees, who served as job foremen. Adolph Uhl, a candidate for mayor, claimed that most of the money went for administration and equipment, rather than to those entitled to relief.

The major debate, however, was over how much money was going to be spent in 1931 and where an additional amount could be found. As in Los Angeles, circumstances pulled budget-makers in two directions. The city's taxpayers, unprepared to absorb an increase in taxes, were arrayed against the unemployed. The financial committee of the board wrestled with the immensely knotty problem of the 1931–32 budget. Finally, the supervisors ended the debate by slicing the work week for 1,100 city employees from six to five days. In this way, the supervisors presented a budget some $155,000 lower than that of the previous fiscal year and still appropriated $350,000 for further relief.[45]

The supervisors, as it turned out, were no closer to a solution. The head of the community chest foresaw a total need of $4.5 million for relief for 1931–32, and competent forecasters predicted a relief bill for the coming winter of between $1.4 million and $2 million.[46] The fact that San Francisco began a program of direct relief, a less costly form of welfare than work relief, indicates how concerned city leaders were about expenditure levels. Only $400,000 of the $2.5 million voted in February was left in August. The only recourse, it seemed, was to squeeze the approved budget to see what came out. Hopes rose and fell as fund after fund was tapped by the supervisors, then plugged by its administrator. The city engineer won back $800,000 worth of Hetch Hetchy project bonds on a legal technicality, while the school board held back $1.1 million, which had been earmarked for relief, when a partially compensatory school bond failed in November. The board ultimately scraped another $350,000 together to make a total of $700,000 for relief with which the city was to face another winter of unemployment. One thing the supervisors seemed entirely unwilling to do at this time was to go back to the people for another unemployment bond. Although San Francisco was still 65 percent under its legal debt limit, the municipal leaders did not believe San Franciscans were prepared to approve another bond sale of such large proportions so soon.[47]

As 1931 came to a close the same problem plagued both California cities. The city fathers had asked the people to approve a large bond issue to aid the unemployed. At the time of the vote—the early spring—most leaders seemed confident that such a generous action would solve the problem, perhaps with something to spare. When instead a shortfall occurred, it did not seem at all propitious to take a second chance on testing community concern. That left the cities with the task of finding alternate sources of funds and left the jobless even more hard pressed to survive.

If the San Francisco supervisors were unwilling to seek help from the citizenry, they were prepared to call on those over whom they had some control. Once again the city employees were thrown into the breach. Early in September the *San Francisco News* reported that the board was considering cutting employees' work time back to a five-day week with five days' pay.[48] Ten days later city workers magnanimously pledged to sacrifice one day's pay a month to be donated to the relief of the unemployed. The board expected $1 million for the jobless from this source —just about enough, along with the $700,000 already appropriated, to match projected needs for the next fiscal year. Although it was not evaluated as such publicly, even in the *Labor Clarion*, the city's employees bought wage and even job security with their contribution, and the unemployed benefited from what was obviously a little municipal blackmail.

The arrival of transients was also a concern in the Bay Area. Anywhere from 600 to 1,000 men a day flocked into the Golden State seeking better economic conditions and a warmer climate.[49] San Francisco officials did not feel any stronger sense of responsibility toward these transients than did their counterparts in Los Angeles since there were already more than enough unemployed permanent residents to absorb available relief money. Pressed by cities and counties all over the state, California erected work camps for the unemployed transients in November 1931. By July 1932 the state had spent $210,000 of forestry and highway funds to subsidize the camps and would spend $400,000 more the next winter. Men who registered with the various relief agencies in the Bay Area went to the foothills of the Sierras to improve roads, remove fire hazards, and clear breaks and trails. Most of the men were laborers, although professionals and college graduates were among their number. They lived in barracks and were provided with food and clothing. According to San Francisco Community Chest leaders, the state labor camps removed a significant burden from their shoulders. Local governments had to provide only the cost of transportation, medical exams, emergency hospitalization, and burial expenses if necessary. Moreover, the prospect of being sent to one of the camps cut down on the number of transients entering northern California, although the number of potential workers continued to exceed the camps' capacity.[50]

San Francisco received little state and federal aid. A summer statewide hearing on the unemployment situation, which Governor Rolph authorized, yielded the news that local governments needed more money, and more state funds were appropriated, both for highways and to help local programs. San Francisco was the distribution point for the veterans' bonus in Northern California. The Bay Area hoped for a $10 million infusion of federal funds from this source.

San Francisco at the end of 1931 was struggling. Proportionately the city and county of San Francisco was much more generous than its southern counterpart. Still, neither city had sufficient resources to keep up with the need and faced 1932 without outside assistance.

The response to the depression in Seattle was unique among the cities along the West Coast. Although it included all of the expected elements of community chest, private charities, and city and county public works, the Seattle model included the unemployed as a part of the administration of relief. As a result Seattle's program best reflected the sense of Hoover's ideas about cooperative individualism. In the northwest city the merging of a group composed of the unemployed with the city's relief effort embodied the spirit of voluntary cooperative self-help that the president hoped would mitigate the woes of the depression. This response exemplified and was intended to preserve the American values of individualism and mutual concern. There is no record that Hoover knew his specific recommendations were being played out in Seattle, and no evidence indicates that anyone in Seattle consciously modeled their responses on Hoover's ideal of cooperative individualism. Nonetheless, the story of Seattle in the Hoover years of the depression is a case study through which the efficacy of the president's hopes and values can be evaluated especially well.

For the first half of 1931, Seattle allowed private agencies to play the major role in relief operations. Statistics for the whole of 1931 reveal a distribution of relief responsibility very different from that of San Francisco and an even less vigorous public response than in Los Angeles. While total private expenditures on all charity items in Seattle and King County rose from $181,000 in 1930 to $288,000 in 1931, an increase of approximately 60 percent, city and county funds designated for relief rose only 24 percent, from $429,700 in 1930 to $522,800.[51] The city and county administrators clearly continued to count on private charity and the duty many felt to take in under their own roof relatives hit by hard times.

And private assistance was forthcoming. The Seattle Community Fund raised $813,000 for 1931–32, and King County added $83,000 to the fund's budget in 1931.[52] Besides the community fund, the *Seattle Times*' Christmas fund and the Sunshine Club donated goods to the needy. Sears Roebuck matched employee contributions to aid over 700 families, while labor unions took up a collection to provide a soup kitchen for their unemployed members.

In 1931 the state of Washington contributed an extra $200,000 in state highway appropriations. This was the last of the little it provided for unemployment aid during the Hoover years. As conditions became desperate, Governor Roland Hartley clung to his belief that the state government should not interfere in local affairs. Far more than President Hoover, Hartley worried that "More and more the government . . . is interfering with private business, destroying self-reliance and individual independence."[53] The cities of Washington could expect no aid from the state government as long as Hartley sat in the governor's chair.

In the first half of 1931, Seattle's major public response to unemployment continued to be municipal works projects. But even these were carried out on a far more limited scale than in the California cities. At the beginning of 1931 there were no bond elections in sight. Instead, Mayor Robert Harlin warned that since public funds were inadequate, it was critical that the private sector help out.[54]

The veterans' loan bill stirred the greatest enthusiasm in Seattle. The veterans' bonus at least temporarily stimulated the money flow. Merchants reported that business was better, and many veterans paid off debts.

Neither private charity nor what few public works the state and local government provided nor a bonus loan could touch many jobless in any significant way. Those most tightly held in the grip of the depression responded in their own way, out of sheer necessity. In October 1931 a haphazard shanty town arose on the tide flats of Elliott Bay near downtown Seattle. These scrap lumber, cardboard, and tin shacks were constructed mainly by unskilled laborers who could not find jobs in their usual endeavors—logging, fishing, agriculture, or mining.[55] They named their town Hooverville in honor of the man whom many of them blamed for their plight. At first the Public Health Office declared it an eyesore and a menace to health and burned the shacks. After setting the torch to Hooverville twice, the city gave in to the persistence of the men and let it stand as a monument to the depression until 1941.

All the residents of Hooverville were male. They were usually over forty and mainly foreign-born whites.[56] They had come to the edge of Puget Sound because they were dissatisfied with taking charity. As long as the economic conditions endured, men continued to settle in the waterfront community, surviving by their own wiles and with the frequent aid of benevolent businessmen. Hooverville, as well as a monument to the depression, was a manifestation of the pluck, independence, and individualism held in such high esteem by the man whose name the community had taken.

Another group of men, not as desperate as the residents of Hooverville but nevertheless searching for a solution to their problems, responded to the depression more actively. On an evening in July 1931 about forty unemployed men met together in West Seattle seeking a way to alleviate their condition. By the end of the meeting, they resolved to work out a plan for unemployment relief for the coming winter, present their needs to city authorities, and make a survey of unemployment in Seattle. To implement this program, they formed a group called the Unemployed Citizens' League (UCL), which was to have a major impact on Seattle's program of relief for the next sixteen months.

The idea for organizing the unemployed in such a manner originated in informal conversations between Hulet Wells and Carl Brannin. They quickly incorporated J. F. Cronin and C. W. Gilbreath into the leadership. Though the emergent group seemed tailored to Hoover's concept of locally financed self-help, the four men were not the kind of people Hoover envisioned as the leaders of a new American individualism. Wells and Brannin were both socialists and played major roles in publishing the weekly radical newspaper the *Vanguard*, which became the unofficial spokesman of the UCL. Brannin, whom a contemporary described as "definitely Marxian," was the head of the Seattle Labor College. Wells had an interesting and long career in Seattle's left-wing community: he had been a Socialist candidate for mayor, the head of the Seattle Labor Council, a postal worker, and an attorney. On the eve of World War I he had issued a circular calling for resistance to conscription. He received a two-year sentence for conspiring against the joint resolution of Congress declaring war. The Industrial Workers of the World (IWW) later actively sought his release. Gilbreath, who had been in the trucking business, was now also a Labor College leader, and Cronin was a sixty-nine-year-old unemployed building contractor, former newspaper reporter, and onetime member of the Knights of Labor. Despite the strong socialist tinge of this leadership, the UCL itself in its first year of existence was not a particularly left-leaning organization—even when judged by the criteria of the time.

The league grew at a phenomenal rate. Twice as many unemployed turned out for the second evening of meetings, and soon every neighborhood in the city with a sizable number of men out of work had a local branch. At its peak, the UCL could boast of between 40,000 and 50,000 members.[57] The state of Washington had earned a reputation for radicalism by the late 1930s. The UCL was surely a cooperative endeavor, and the leadership openly advocated a reorganization of the economic structure. But the origins of the league were found in the individualism and independence normally associated with the West. The rank and file of the UCL was composed of rather conservative skilled and common laborers. These men joined together simply to help themselves. Wells himself despaired that the UCL was not encouraging "for those who look to mass intelligence for social betterment."[58]

But the crucial fact was that people were endeavoring to overcome their problems substantially without the aid of existing institutions. According to the constitution ultimately drawn up for the Unemployed Citizens' League, the first objective was employment, primarily through public works, the second was self-help, then came unemployment insurance, and finally, if necessary, direct relief.[59]

Among these goals, self-help inspired the most interesting and imaginative responses. Because the organization was one of the first of its kind, the UCL had no pattern to follow. With the spontaneity that characterized its formation, the league threw itself into self-help projects. Beginning with wood cutting on land donated for that purpose, various UCL locals extended their activities to picking unwanted fruit in the Yakima Valley and fishing in Puget Sound. The league set up commissaries where the wood and food could be distributed and created a barter economy. In return for these goods able-bodied members chopped the wood, repaired shoes, tailored, and performed other services on behalf of their fellow jobless. With a minimum of contributions UCL members took advantage of available manpower and skills to aid each other through rough times. Another service UCL members sometimes provided was a bulwark against eviction. Usually through negotiation, the league could stave off an ouster. If necessary, however, UCL members would simply move the evicted friends and furniture back in.

The Unemployed Citizens' League, and the part it soon played in Seattle's relief effort, are the unique elements in the story of the Hoover years on the West Coast, although self-help was not restricted to Seattle. In 1932 a similar movement grew in Southern California. The unemployed in Muncie planted subsistence gardens, Coloradans set up a barter economy, and self-help grew out of the Mormon Church in Utah. But in Seattle by the end of 1931 the UCL was already a force in the city. City councilmen and mayoral candidates came to meet with and speak to its members. As it worked out the UCL would not be courted only for the votes it could muster. Seattle had been slow establishing relief, and the UCL was ahead of private and public agencies, new or old, in coping with the conditions of the depression. Once the city of Seattle organized to provide assistance, it discovered that the UCL possessed the most experienced hands and greatest efficiency.

In the late summer of 1931, with the peak of the unemployment cycle only a few months away, Seattle officials finally decided that the conventional methods they had depended on to handle the now unconventional economic and social displacement were woefully inadequate. In the latter half of September, Mayor Harlin created the Mayor's Commission on Improved Employment. A full year after Los Angeles and San Francisco established their initial programs, and one-half year after the California cities approved their unemployment bonds, Seattle for the first time instituted a program that specifically addressed the problems of the unemployed.

As head of the committee, the mayor chose I. F. Dix. Dix epitomized the "go-getter" businessman of the time. Born in Brooklyn, Dix, fifty years old, was the general manager of Pacific Telephone and Telegraph. Although he had been in Seattle only two years, having worked in Los Angeles for the previous twenty, Dix was already serving as the chairman of the community fund and was the president of the Seattle Chamber of Commerce. To this full schedule the lean, businesslike man added what was to be his most demanding job. He was the expert business leader who could guide the local relief effort most efficiently, and, according to the Hoover philosophy, most successfully. Besides Dix, the group was composed of two men representing labor, an American Legion executive, a minister, and three other businessmen.

The Dix Commission, as it came to be called, was primarily an organizing committee designed to work with and through already established public and private agencies. Because the commission limited itself to coordination, Seattle's response continued to lag a year behind that of the rest of the West Coast.

Although the commission's goals were to stimulate and encourage commerce in the Seattle area, its first order of business was to register the unemployed. In one month 5,000 families had registered for aid and employment.[60] Soon five regional depots opened to receive donations of food and clothing and distribute them to the deserving needy, after a proper investigation. James F. Pollard, the general manager of Seattle Natural Gas, was in charge of the single men's division, while former mayor Bertha K. Landes headed the women's relief operation. For both men and women the commission sought to provide food and shelter for some minimal amount of work.

Throughout October and November many suggestions, estimates, and proposals were discussed in the city council chambers. The severity of the problems, mounting as the fall of 1931 went on, brought forth a greater willingness on the part of city leaders to provide funding for a more direct and energetic program. The council intended to establish a special emergency fund to finance the mayor's commission, and council members advocated $140,000 to $1 million be apportioned, reserved, or raised through a bond election for a variety of projects. According to the Dix Commission $35,000 per month would be needed to furnish adequate work relief.[61] As in Los Angeles, there was a hot debate on wage scales. The mayor, a former union leader, recommended that $4.50 per day be paid to unemployed working on city projects. Harlin asserted this wage would stimulate efficiency and provide workers with an adequate living.[62] Naturally, the UCL heartily endorsed this plan. Several councilmen, looking toward the taxpayers and a tight budget, proposed a scale of $1.50 to $3.00 (based on how many dependents the man had to support). Despite the Dix Commission's approval of the sliding scale, the labor wing of the council persuaded enough of their cohorts to push through the $4.50 wage. Finally, the city council caught up with their counterparts in the other cities and passed an emergency measure of $1 million.

From this appropriation the Mayor's Commission on Improved Employment created the District Relief Organization (DRO). Dix showed his desire to work through existing agencies by placing the DRO, which was to become the principal relief arm of the municipal government, under the authority of the community fund. Once again the pattern of mingling public and private administration emerged as city moneys passed through the community fund to the DRO, which was administered in conjunction with private charities.

But in Seattle, this cooperative activity went much further than the other cities, since the self-help group of the unemployed took the lead role for a time in relief administration. Claiming that the UCL was better organized and could do more than his agency alone, Dix made the league the basis of DRO operations during the last months of 1931 and early weeks of 1932. Besides the five district depots, the DRO had three to seven UCL commissaries in each district from which it could dispense relief.

Using the unemployed to administer relief to themselves was a practical, if unusual, approach to public relief. First, many of the jobless were given a stake in society. At a time when their pride was shattered, they could function usefully as administrators, rather than be passive recipients. Second, relief itself became work relief. Many unemployed persons volunteered their services to help in the commissaries. This at least created a feeling that work was accomplished in return for relief. There was also one important disadvantage to this method. The unemployed checked eligibility of relief applicants. Even if those entrusted with this task were scrupulously honest, criticism of this procedure was inevitable; in fact, accusations of fraud were a factor leading to the ultimate failure of the system. As much through circumstance as from principle, the Seattle approach to relief, by combining the private with the public sector, upheld the Hoover ethic of individualism and ideal of preserving personal pride more than any other city's program.

The dual nature of the District Relief Organization engendered a chaotic structure. The manager of the entire operation was Charles Ernst. His UCL counterpart was C. W. Gilbreath, who was designated "central contact man." Although Ernst was responsible for every phase of operation, the DRO depended on the cooperation of Gilbreath who determined UCL policy and the extent of UCL cooperation in the relief effort. This bifurcated organization pervaded the whole program and, although harmonious relations usually prevailed, it was a definite threat to efficiency.

According to Ernst a "typical" DRO budget for one month called for $155,000. Out of this sum, administration and operation costs took $8,000, leaving $147,000 for relief.[63] The DRO furnished both work relief and direct relief in the form of money and food. To be eligible a person had to be unemployed, a resident of King County for at least six months, and receive aid from no other source.

The DRO performed a number of services for the unemployed. Its primary function, of course, was to distribute food to the needy. To assure the recipients of a balanced and nutritious diet the Department of Home Economics at the University of Washington drew up a list of foodstuffs to be included in the distribution. The DRO and the Dix Commission provided other services, such as free transportation to a mass meeting of the unemployed in early 1932. Several people were able to keep their electricity because of entreaties by the commission and the UCL to Seattle City Light, the municipal utility. The DRO did not neglect the UCL tradition of self-help. It encouraged people to continue exchanging the fruits of their skills in sewing, shoe repair, gardening, carpentry, food canning, and wood cutting. From time to time, the city supplied such essentials as seeds, cans, sugar, or transportation to support the self-help projects.

By December 1931, when the entire project was getting under way, $150,000 had already been spent. Most of this put over 3,000 men to work. Ten thousand men had registered, and Dix expected 12,000 to be signed up by the end of the month.[64] As the year closed, the city of Seattle was moving toward alleviating the plight of the unemployed.

Seattle responded to unemployment later than the other cities, conceivably because the economy drifted downward at a slower pace, but also, perhaps, because of an elemental conservatism among the elected officials of the city. When they did respond the city's leaders demonstrated a genuine desire to preserve as much of the individualism of the citizens as possible. As Seattle tried to integrate far more thoroughly a public with a private response, one of its motives was a Hoover-like desire to confine to the greatest extent possible the power of the government —even local government—and allow private citizens as great a role as possible in looking after themselves. This is not to overlook the city leadership's pragmatism —the Unemployed Citizens' League was running and available. But Seattle's response was more than a matter of convenience. The spirit of individualism, so evident in America during the first third of the twentieth century, was demonstrated in each of the cities, but nowhere more clearly than in Seattle.

The year 1931 found Portland going about the business of unemployment relief in the more conventional manner of Los Angeles and San Francisco. As in 1930, private and local efforts provided the mainstay of relief, but the state of Oregon continued to be of more assistance than California and Washington.

Among the private organizations responding to the crisis was, of course, the Portland Community Chest. The chest had served 4,000 people in 1930. This number jumped to 10,000 in 1931.[65] Although it did not become an integral part of the public relief effort, the community chest did more than merely expand its already existing services. In fall 1931 the agency took responsibility for helping single men in the city. After passing the ever-present work test—in Portland at the wood lot—resident single men could obtain room and board and transients received food and shelter for three days.

The greater burden of relief took its familiar toll on the Portland Community Chest. Before the fiscal year 1931 was out, chest officials had to borrow to carry on their work. Throughout the year a few vocal critics complained about red tape and mismanagement. Others, however, believed investing greater powers in the chest was a solution to the city's private relief problems.

The fall 1931 fund-raising campaign was difficult. To provide for its added burdens charity leaders proposed a budget of $900,000. This was cut to $686,156 and an extra $100,000 for a special fund to assist the unemployed. One hundred fifty thousand dollars more than the previous year's pared-down goal, it was as hard to fulfill. By the end of the drive, the fund raisers reported that Portlanders had contributed more than ever before but that the chest was still $42,000 short of its goal. Campaign workers, however, believed this amount was "in the cards," and the next day announced that the goal was oversubscribed. The *Journal*, viewing the fund drive optimistically, in the spirit of the era, editorialized, "Portland can report to President Hoover and his organization for relief 'We are doing our bit. We as a community have assumed the responsibility for this community.'"[66] To a degree this was true. As in the other cities the community chest drive had reached or exceeded its goal. In a most difficult economic environment people had dug deeply to assist their fellow citizens. The problem in Portland, as elsewhere, was that the sacrifices were not commensurate with the needs.

Other private efforts, under the same pressures, fared worse. The Red Cross drive collected only about half of its goal. The Pisgah Home for the aged, facing a 40 percent increase in its load, complained that it could not send anyone to the county poor farm because that public facility was already overcrowded and had a waiting list.[67] Problems of inefficiency and mismanagement afflicted charity organizations. Several retail merchants said they "found conditions which did not speak well for the institution" at Grandma's Kitchen, the soup line that sold tickets to those merchants to use in handling transients.[68] The Sunshine Division, a Christmas charity coordinated by the city police, came in for criticism, especially from those who sought to consolidate the holiday season charities. The City Club complained that the Sunshine Division's efforts were substandard, duplicated others, had become a year-round project, and represented an inappropriate use of public funds.[69] Out of these tensions and criticisms emerged a kind of supercoordinating body. Sorting these claims and overlaps, the Planning Commission of the Council of Social Agencies, which included the community chest, the Public Welfare Bureau, and several charity organizations, assumed oversight of many private charity operations and worked to avoid duplications. Among the four West Coast cities this centralized coordinating agency, in authority even over the community chest, represented a unique effort to rationalize the dispensing of private charity.

Many private organizations not normally engaged in relief work helped the unemployed. The Kiwanis Club assisted the Pisgah Home, and set up an employment bureau. The Women's Clubs of Portland canned food to distribute to the needy. There was the usual array of charity football games, variety shows, boxing and wrestling matches, and turkey raffles to benefit the jobless. The PTA, on a scale far smaller than Los Angeles, provided a double graham cracker and an apple to hungry children at school—after the child had earned his snack by performing a prescribed task. Churches assisted too. The Portland Council of Churches encouraged its affiliates to work through the Planning Commission to assure their charity efforts were carried out well. The Seventh Day Adventists established a lunch room for the unemployed, and Baptists took a collection to establish a relief fund. In a telling message, though, R. W. Anderson, a newly installed Methodist Episcopal minister, called for more to help the distressed than sermons and devotions on Sunday mornings.[70]

Once again in Portland, as in Los Angeles and San Francisco, public employees were paragons of generosity. City employees contributed one day's pay out of the month for a six-month total of $75,000, and the county employees added contributions of $15,000. State employees gave $1,000 to the Sunshine Division in Portland.[71]

The unemployed were also given the opportunity, or a push, to help themselves. The *Oregonian* continued to solicit for the citywide fix-up, clean-up campaign designed to solve the job problem privately and piecemeal. Some jobless set themselves up as apple vendors. Apple stands appeared on downtown sidewalks—until the city, influenced by retail grocers who felt the competition, banned them. Blacks came together to form an economic organization to help themselves, and several veterans, after meeting in a soup line, discussed their plight and formed a self-help group. Several Hoovervilles, complete with scrap lumber and stove pipe shanties, sprung up around the city. About 315 residents found shelter in Sullivan's Gulch. (Today a freeway named for T. H. Banfield, one of the leaders of the relief effort, passes through the site.)

All was not sweet charity in Portland. On 1 January 1931 the police declared a 6 P.M. curfew in the skid row area, arresting anyone on the streets who was jobless. A soup kitchen called for the patrol wagon when the line got too long. Police arrested a jobless man when he took a second slice of bread. A landlord murdered a tenant when he tried to run out on his rent payment of eighty cents. And, of course, racketeers claimed what they could. Men collected job cards, permissions to work on city projects, and sold them for a profit. A charity racket soliciting for Christmas trees for the needy raked off 60 percent for overhead.

Early in 1931 Portland's leaders realized that, like the other cities, its public and private attempts to cope with the depression had failed. The county's public welfare budget would be overspent by two-thirds. The $300,000 that the city and county had budgeted in late 1930 provided several thousand man hours of work during the winter. But these funds ran out in March. The Civic Emergency Committee (CEC), the group of private citizens overseeing work relief in the area, called for a ballot on $2 million worth of bonds—almost as much as San Francisco had approved. The city would receive $1 million and the county would use the other half if the bond were approved. The state legislature approved placing the issue on the ballot in April. There is no evidence that any major opinion-maker opposed the relief measure, and the voters approved the bonds overwhelmingly. The final vote for the city's portion was 23,387 for and 9,933 against. In the county 25,442 approved and 11,464 voted against the issue.[72]

Relief work had been suspended at the end of March when funds ran out. To restart it the city loaned the CEC $30,000 against the sale of the bonds. The county, however, refused to do the same and that work languished until June. The CEC sought to make the relief process more efficient and accountable. Accordingly, everyone had to reregister for the relief work. The men picked to work a particular rotation assembled on Monday morning at a city storage facility, received their instructions, and were assigned to a foreman. Anywhere from 1,000 to 2,000 might be at work in any given week. To accommodate all of those needing work, men were assigned to a six-day work week every six or seven weeks. A year later, when the funds had been exhausted, over 266,000 man-days of work had been completed. The problem was that over 16,000 men were still registered and in need of help.[73]

Although CEC leaders strove for efficiency and fairness, their efforts generated controversy. The wage scale, as usual, was an issue. The CEC stuck with $4 per day. In comparison, the work relief wage on highway work was $3 a day, and in discussions around the state suggestions for a fair rate ranged downward as far as $1.50 per day. Portland's pay, however, was seventy-five cents under the regular city scale, and forty cents less than the prevailing wage. The $4 wage was common on the West Coast, but it was below standard in Portland.

Discrimination against single men was also a problem. Like other cities, Portland gave work relief preference to heads of families; single veterans apparently had first been given jobs, then excluded. Their exclusion raised a furor, especially among the United Veterans Employment League. Finally, the city appropriated $5,000 explicitly for relief jobs for veterans.

There was also controversy throughout the year over how much overhead should be spent on projects. City Commissioner Barbur wanted a 25 percent overhead payment made to the city for supervising work relief, but CEC head T. H. Banfield suggested Portland should provide supervision out of its own budget, without having to tap relief funds. Banfield argued that the city would have carried out many of the projects under normal conditions, so it had an obligation to pay for equipment and foremen. The latter position won out, and the city spent only about 4 percent of its relief appropriations on overhead during 1931–32.[74]

There were other day-to-day matters to deal with, such as unauthorized use of a truck or falsification of documents, but a concern over efficiency provides insight into some of the personnel problems of administering work relief. County Roadmaster George Buck wrote, "a large percentage of them [relief workers] conscientiously worked to the best of their ability," but he also noted some difficulties. Clearly annoying to Buck were the young men he described as having the gift of gab who stood around telling others how little they should do. Men too old to render vigorous road work and those who had never done manual labor before did not meet Buck's standards.[75] This may have been the case on other work relief projects throughout the nation.

The state of Oregon continued to demonstrate not only a keen consciousness of the problems but also a willingness to contribute to a solution. In August, Governor Julius Meier, declaring that "the time is now at hand for some definite action in the way of relief," called together a group to discuss the problem. The focus of the conference was highway construction for work relief, because the Highway Commission was the only state agency that could spend more money without a bond levy. The state had already spent $3 million of state and federal funds on highway construction by August, and the governor called for $1 million more to furnish 12,000 jobs. The legislature appropriated the money early in 1932. The state government continued to act in partnership with the local government in providing relief.[76]

The capitalist cycle had failed to swing upward during 1931. Instead, the economy had grown much worse. The three cities that had appropriated an extra measure for relief in 1930, did so again in the spring of 1931. Seattle seemed to lag six months to one year behind the others in responding. When the city finally did respond, it did so in an original way. While Seattle adapted citizen self-help to meet its problems, the other cities opted for more prosaic, but temporarily effective, solutions—bond issues and work relief. In each case the local governments bore the burden themselves, although the state of Oregon lent some assistance to Portland.

As 1931 came to a close the four cities found themselves even worse off than they had been at the end of 1930. The depression had deepened further, and support funds were exhausted or nearly so. The public demonstrated an openhandedness as they met the campaign goals of the community chests in 1931, and voters showed their generosity as they approved bond issues, but a repeat performance was unlikely in 1932. As the depression wore on and affected more and more people there were fewer to contribute, more who felt their security threatened by anything but a tax break, and more who needed assistance. In 1931 the cities had made an unprecedented effort to provide work and at least a minimal living standard for their citizens. Across the nation, public relief expense rose from $60 million in 1929 to $256 million in 1932. In the year of the crash public funds accounted for 34 percent of all relief. By 1932 the public share of relief was over 67 percent.[77] The attempt was being made to respond to the crisis, but the pressures were too much to withstand. Political infighting and questions of efficiency and honesty plagued the effort. But, most of all, the cities lacked both the will and the resources for the task. Nineteen thirty-two, the last year the cities would be on their own, would be a difficult time.

Voters made some political changes in San Francisco and Seattle in 1931 that did little to modify the responses of those governments but did change the structure of the government in one case and the administrative personnel in the other. In 1931 San Francisco voters went to the polls twice. At the first election they modified the structure of their city and county government; at the second they retained most of the old hands to run it. San Francisco's new charter, which the voters approved in March, went into effect in 1932. According to its supporters, it provided for a more efficient government by giving the mayor power similar to that of a city manager and by transforming the board of supervisors into a legislative rather than an executive body. A crucial provision prohibited deficit spending. In a time of increased need this requirement for an accurate accounting in all departments and no overruns was a potential handicap to relief efforts.

The other election, held in November 1931, saw Adolph Uhl, a backer of the charter and a strong advocate of efficiency and, above all, economy in government, challenge Angelo Rossi for the now more powerful position of mayor. Rossi stood on a platform of immediate and adequate relief and alleviation of the property owners' tax burden through a city levy on corporations. Uhl proposed turning over the entire matter of relief to the state—forcing Governor Rolph to assume the burden by abandoning responsibility on the local level if necessary. Receiving the endorsement of both labor and business (although there was surely a strong wave of support for the thrifty and businesslike Uhl among the business community), Rossi won the election by 7,000 votes or 52 percent of the vote.

In Seattle, Mayor Frank Edwards removed the popular J. D. Ross as the head of Seattle City Light. Within two months the Citizens' Municipal Utilities Protection League, supported by the *Post-Intelligencer* and *Seattle Star*, had successfully circulated recall petitions. In July the voters recalled Edwards and the city council voted to seat Robert Harlin as the new mayor. Harlin, a Republican, had been the president of a United Mine Workers' local and the secretary of the Washington State Federation of Labor before being elected to the city council. The recall did not significantly affect Seattle's relief program, but it did propel the young attorney who led the campaign against Edwards, Marion Zioncheck, to a seat in Congress in 1932.

SIX

Reaching Bottom

1932

Although the citizens of the four cities could not know it, in the winter of 1932–33 the depression cycle would reach bottom. At the beginning of the year, the optimists and not a few of the realists refused to admit that the depression could get worse. Toward the end of the year, the pessimists and many of their realist friends were wondering if it would ever stop getting worse.

Conditions throughout the nation were bleak. Muncie's industrial index had dropped 40 points (about 40 percent) from 1926. Estimates of unemployment in Milwaukee and Cleveland, and surely throughout urban America, ranged from 25 to over 35 percent, with the latter figure probably more accurate.[1]

Business and unemployment on the West Coast were as grim as anywhere. The Federal Reserve reported that major Pacific Coast financial and business indicators stayed the same or declined during 1932. The Bank of America business index, in which one hundred was "normal," dropped from 70.5 in January to 58.6 by November.[2] By mid-1932 the California employment index was at 35 for sawmills, 36 for canning, and 59 for petroleum, (1926=100).[3] Southern California led the nation in bankruptcies. In Seattle bank clearings were off 30 percent, and auto sales lagged 20 percent behind 1931. Some Portland businessmen thought they had spotted a bit of an upturn, but February bank clearings, down $30 million, and building permits for the month, off 70 percent, were not stuff of an upturn.[4]

By the end of 1932, bank deposits had slid to their lowest levels, although they had not decreased at such a precipitous rate as the previous year. In Los Angeles deposits fell to $879 million by the end of the year—a 39 percent decrease from what they had been in January 1929 and 5.5 percent less than the beginning of the year. In San Francisco depositors had 5 percent fewer dollars in the bank at the end of 1932, and Seattle deposits registered a 6 percent decline, a drop of almost $13 million over the year.[5] Figures are not available for Portland, but the city was surely tending in the same direction. Deposits at the United States National Bank, the city's largest, dropped $10 million from December 1931 to June 1932, and Meier and Frank Department Store had to loan money to the fourth largest bank in Portland, American National, to keep it liquid.[6] Liquidity was surely the problem by 1932—not just for individual banks but for the entire society. The economic system did not have enough energy—circulating dollars —to run well, and through 1932 the supply continued to dwindle.

News of the condition of the banks on the West Coast was mixed but on the whole not very heartening. In California 49 banks closed from January 1930 through June 1932, exceeding the total number of closures in the state between 1910 and 1929. Probably the brightest news came from San Francisco. No banks closed their doors in 1932, and deposits of Bank of America actually rose.[7] The reopening of Hibernia Bank in Portland was one other bit of upbeat news on the West Coast. Two financial institutions in Seattle and three more in Los Angeles closed their doors. Two of the latter were unable to reimburse their depositors entirely.

Construction figures were dismal. Building in Los Angeles had come to a virtual standstill. Permits for 1932 were down almost $24 million from the previous year and were off over 56 percent from the peak of the boom in 1926. In 1923 almost 83,000 residences had been built in Los Angeles. In 1932 contractors erected only 5,400 houses. Even the construction of Hoover Dam offered little opportunity. A friend advised a prospective laborer to stay away from the area. Because it provided many jobs, he counseled, there would be a large number of men at the site seeking them. It was probably the highest concentration of unemployment in the country, he warned. In San Francisco during the first six months of 1932 real estate sales were already lagging $10.3 million behind 1930 transactions, and building was down 20 percent from its peak in the 1920s. Although newspapers might have crowed over new manufacturing plants opening, building permits in Seattle plunged $32 million from 1928 to 1933, a 94 percent decrease. The story was the same in Oregon, where construction expenditures decreased 38 percent from 1931 to 1932, to $28.7 million.[8]

There were other clear indicators of the depression's severity. Department store sales declined about 38 percent from 1929 to 1932 in the two California cities.[9] In a deflationary atmosphere one would expect the cost of living to go down, and it did—by 25 percent in San Francisco and Los Angeles over three years, 1929-32.[10] The decrease in the cost of living was little solace to those who were unemployed or endured deep wage cuts. From scattered evidence it appears payroll declines along the West Coast over the three-year period far outran the drop in the cost of living. Pay levels decreased around 40 to 55 percent, and inevitably in some industries it was worse.[11] In 1932 the long-debated wage cuts in the building industries finally occurred in San Francisco, Seattle, and Portland. In the Northwest they were as deep as 20 percent. Faculty at the University of Washington and University of California at Los Angeles endured salary reductions, and city workers saw less in their pay envelopes in Portland and Los Angeles.

The major industries undergirding the economy of the West Coast were in desperate shape. By 1932 oil production in Southern California had dropped 44 percent to 95 million barrels from an already depressed 137 million barrels in 1930. Washington farmers could get only $.36 per bushel for wheat that had brought $1.36 in 1925. The lumber industry was moribund. In the Northwest it functioned at 20 percent of capacity at times and never produced at more than 50 percent during the year. Lumbermen could get no bank loans and began omitting their tax payments.[12] After a few problems in the first year of depression, one important regional industry began a welcome resurgence. The movies, hard hit by both sound and economic fury, stabilized about 1932 and became one of the most reliable employers in the Los Angeles area. After a four-year low of 74 films in production, the film industry put out 153 in 1932.[13] Tourism also provided a lift to the economies of Seattle and Los Angeles in 1932. Seattle anticipated Rotarians spending $1 million at their international convention held in the city in 1932. But Los Angeles had garnered the economic plum. Preparation for the Olympics helped sustain to some degree the flagging construction industry. In 1932 Los Angeles received 384,000 out-of-state visitors who poured $44 million dollars into the economy and provided for a short time employment for hundreds. Had the Olympics not occurred it would have been a dismal summer. Even with the influx of visitors for the Games, tourism in Los Angeles was down 18,000, causing a $100,000 decline in the tourist trade.[14]

By 1932, as the nadir of the depression was being reached, several key indexes reveal the rate of decline was moderating. People living in 1932, most without statistics at their fingertips, did not make such a subtle differentiation. They knew that for the third consecutive year things were worse and as bad as they could ever remember. President Hoover may have been correct as he claimed that the nation's economy was on the verge of a cyclical upswing in fall 1932 and was responding to his patience. Evidence on the West Coast perhaps lends some credence to the claim. Maybe a slowing in the rate of decline was a step to an ultimate turnaround. For the people of the time and for the purposes of interpretation, however, the difference in the economy between 1929 and 1932 is what counts. The four cities in 1932 were responding to the economic devastation that was occurring.

Almost all of those expressing enduring optimism had finally been converted or had passed from the scene in 1932. The optimists now were of the chin-up, it-cannot-get-worse, persevere-through-trial variety. The *San Francisco News* captured this spirit in its editorial campaign, "Look at the Doughnut—Instead of the Hole." The *News*, for example, encouraged its readers to ignore the "hole" of 12 percent unemployed—an estimate probably too small by half—and concentrate on the doughnut of 273,562 still working.[15] Some inevitably continued to compare their community's plight with that of other cities, proclaiming how much worse economic conditions were in the East. The *Los Angeles Illustrated News* carried the comparative approach a step further, headlining excerpts from the book of Job, "Here's Job's Depression Story: Buck Up All You 1932 Sufferers!"[16]

San Franciscans seemed to be the most positive. If there was a dyed-in-the-wool optimist still alive and well it was Bank of America's A. P. Giannini, who assured a friend in July that the depression had passed.[17] His fellow citizens were not so sanguine, but some still suggested that the trials of yesterday had laid a good, solid foundation for better days ahead.

Assurances could not be made in a vacuum. The problems of 1932 called for ideas, not just cyclical momentum laced with hope. The Hearst $5 billion federal prosperity loan still found a good deal of support. Back-to-the-land movements continued to draw attention, particularly in the two Northwest cities, and the *Los Angeles Daily News* advanced a similar proposal. The plan, the community land chest, would move the unemployed onto donated land. Instead of contributing money to the community chest, the editor suggested, citizens with idle land could donate that property to produce ongoing aid for the needy. Other, less common approaches were suggested. In Portland one individual hoped for a modification of the Sherman Antitrust Act as it applied to lumber. A lottery, technocracy, a barter economy based on credit units, inflation—the suggestion of a United States senator—and prayer all found favor with letter writers and editorialists.

A group of Los Angeles businessmen formed an ominously named, but relatively tame, group to fight the depression. The Minute Men, among other things, proclaimed themselves in opposition to crime, bonded indebtedness, loss of securities and money to fraud, bribery of the judiciary, unemployment, special privileges for special interest groups, and crafty politicians.[18] They sought to fight their battles primarily in the political arena. The history, especially the political history, of Los Angeles through the rest of the depression era would suggest the Minute Men were only partly successful in meeting their stated goals—and faltered notably on their last objective.

Spreading the work continued to be a common idea. Many condemned two-job households, while others supported the five-day week or job sharing. For some the latter meant workers should split evenly a normal work week. At least two Portlanders were ready to reach beyond the local authorities for help. John Latourette, an attorney, and Aaron Frank, a leading official of the Civic Emergency Committee, both suggested some kind of federal augmentation of local relief.[19] Others in Portland were not ready for that step but strongly endorsed the efforts of the state.

By 1932 the public had switched from proffering economic solutions to evaluating the relief programs and offering suggestions for their improvement. One of the great concerns was how much labor recipients of relief should provide in return for assistance. The concern was two-pronged. As Worth Caldwell, the executive director of Portland's Civic Emergency Committee said, the work "preserves the morale and self-respect of the registrants, who exchange their labor for [relief money], rather than . . . accept pure relief."[20] Many Angelenos pointed out the other advantage. Work relief kept professional beggars and moochers off the welfare roles and out of the taxpayers' pocketbooks. Proclaiming that there should be no joy rides for the jobless, one correspondent to the Los Angeles County Board of Supervisors put it as an ultimatum: "Give the unemployed picks and shovels and get into the back yard and plant potatoes . . . and if the worst comes keep a pig."[21] Another letter writer suggested that those unemployed who declined to labor should be sent to a work colony where they would have to till the soil to support themselves. Such work colonies, of course, had been established in California for out-of-state transients. Oregonians apparently admired the work camps. The Statewide Relief Council suggested they be established, at least in part, to discourage those fleeing a similar welcome in California.

Still others wrote to the Los Angeles supervisors about welfare cheating and county expenditures. Several recommended closer investigation of recipients.

George Hildebrand complained that food orders were made out to chain food stores and the money funneled to the East Coast. His postscript probably revealed his real frame of mind: "Would it be possible that you could get me a nice fat county job to help tide me over? I hope to try for one in the next election." In a similar vein a medical doctor called for salary cuts for all categories of county employees but three: members of the board of supervisors, nurses, and medical interns.[22]

Citizens and officials unanimously opposed the dole and upheld the principle that the able-bodied should work for their stipends. The other major piece of advice residents offered their local officials was where to do the work. Unsurprisingly the advice was consistent: "In my neighborhood" or "On my favorite project" became a familiar admonition to city councilmen and county supervisors.

From the reactions of those who sought to help, from those who felt uneasy about the situation, and from the jobless themselves it is clear that the perception of unemployment had changed. It was no longer transitory, and it afflicted decent, upstanding people who always before could hold a job. In San Francisco, St. Patrick's Shelter for Men reported in July that 6 percent of its relief recipients were college graduates. The percentage increased the rest of the year. More clerks and skilled laborers were looking for work in San Francisco and Oakland than jobless semiskilled and unskilled. In 1929 the unskilled made up 38.4 percent of the unemployed and the skilled 26.1 percent. The figure changed dramatically in 1932: 34.3 percent of those out of work were skilled and 24.3 percent were unskilled.[23] The story was the same all along the coast.

As the problem worsened, the days became tense for some. A Portland school-teacher, despondent over his inability to obtain a job, poisoned himself. A teacher in Los Angeles who was unable to find work asked to be put in jail on a vagrancy charge. A municipal court judge, who handled ten to twenty eviction cases daily, appealed to the Los Angeles County Board of Supervisors to assist those evicted to find land to farm. Unable to pay its utilities, a family ineligible for relief because it possessed title to a house cooked donated food over a backyard bonfire. In San Francisco a printer told the Associated Charities that he had searched for a job without success for two years and did not have enough food to last the week. According to the *Portland Advocate*, the newspaper of the black community, a drive was on in Portland to dismiss Negroes to help take up the slack for whites in the job market.[24]

These stories represent the tragedies of thousands out of work in the four cities. It is difficult, as always for the Hoover years, to find reliable statistics to verify just how many thousands were suffering. At a time when figures were desperately needed for decision-making, the attempts to calculate unemployment levels were not sophisticated and the estimates were unreliable. The California Unemployment Commission, which traveled throughout the state in 1932 gathering information, estimated that as many as 700,000 were unemployed statewide, affecting 1.6 million (i.e., the unemployed and their dependents). The largest concentration of the unemployed, 49.2 percent or 344,000, resided in the Los Angeles area and 86,100 were in San Francisco. Citing a number some 100,000 less, the *Times* maintained in May 1932 that the unemployment rate in Los Angeles County was 20 percent. Relief statistics for Los Angeles for 1932 point to unemployment closer to 30 than 20 percent.[25] County cases were up 55 percent in the 1931–32 fiscal year, and the Municipal Service Bureau of the city served 42 percent more homeless men than in 1931.[26]

The State Unemployment Commission suggested a high unemployment rate for San Francisco, perhaps as much as 32 percent. Given the rest of the economic evidence, this would seem too high, or else even an estimate of 30 percent for Los Angeles is too conservative. From monthly statistics in the Bay Area it does appear employment continued to decline in San Francisco, but at an uneven rate. The California Labor Department indicated that the 1932 state jobless rate was consistently higher than 1931, but during four months, mainly through the summer, the picture improved from one month to another. By December the growth of unemployment had moderated.[27]

Trustworthy figures for the two Northwest cities are even more difficult to obtain. In Seattle the intuitive estimates of a county councilman and the Unemployed Citizens' League ranged from 40,000 to 55,000 unemployed.[28] Such a figure would put unemployment at a minimum of 25 percent, upward to 33 percent, which does not seem unlikely.

Estimates of the number of jobless in Portland were between 27,000 and 30,000. The Oregon State Relief Council believed 25 percent of all Oregonians were without jobs in 1932.[29] If the percentage was accurate, the estimates of unemployed Portlanders might have been low. Calculations of the jobless rate in 1930 went as high as 30,000, and others suggested a 25 percent rate of joblessness at that time. The rates were surely higher two years later. From the figures available, joblessness was the lot of one-quarter to one-third of those gainfully employed in 1929, and, combining the always difficult task of identifying the unemployed with an unsophisticated information gathering system, even those figures may be understated.

The unemployment situation had become chronic, and many must have believed that marches by the unemployed had become a permanent fixture of society as well. Several marches in Los Angeles ended in confrontations with the Red Squad and arrests. In the other cities officials met the parades with mounting irritation but a minimum of violence. Interestingly, in Los Angeles a few citizens and newspapers began to voice their disapproval of police responses in 1932, despite the fact that William Z. Foster, a prominent radical leader, attended one rally. The Municipal League, the *Examiner*, and the *California Eagle* all complained about police brutality and corruption in the police force. The *Examiner*, especially, noted that with so many unemployed it was inappropriate for the police to take action against seemingly every assembly of the jobless.[30]

A small movement among the unemployed must have caused some concern. Unemployed councils, avowedly Communist organizations, began to organize in each city. A Los Angeles branch obtained an appointment to meet with the board of supervisors and would have had a chance to lay out their demands had the

Red Squad not met them first. In Los Angeles and Portland unemployed councils helped forestall evictions and utility cut-offs, and in Oregon they may have had a hand in picketing the governor's relief conference. But this seems to be the limit of radical activity in any of the cities.

The urban centers of the West Coast were still relatively peaceful. Even with the Red Squad active, unemployed councils forming, and any variety of isolated radical rockets going off sporadically throughout the year, the employed and jobless alike were too occupied with providing relief or surviving to turn the situation into a time of ferment and class consciousness. The attention was still on the individual and on individual sustenance.

Vital and demographic statistics that afford a closer view of the day-to-day affairs of average citizens tend to bear out that society, although under stress, was not on the verge of coming apart. Though deeply affected by the economic collapse, people were endeavoring to carry on their lives in as normal a manner as possible. The birth rate, as one might expect, declined steadily during the first three years of the depression. Perhaps more surprisingly, the death rate also declined. Suicides increased at an alarming rate in Los Angeles and Seattle. But while some may have sunk into psychological depression, others found healthy outlets for their frustrations. Los Angeles public library borrowing was up by 1 million in 1932 over the previous year, and the adult use of recreation facilities in Los Angeles rose 40 percent. Society did not get more violent during the 1929–32 period. Homicides were up in the cities, but not by much, and arrest for assault in Los Angeles was actually down. The noticeable change in 1932 crime statistics was in burglary and robbery. In Los Angeles and Seattle these offenses were double what they had been in 1929. But even under enormous pressures, the people as a whole were law abiding, and they treated themselves as well as they could afford. The vast majority seemed not to harbor any particular bitterness toward institutions or their fellow citizens.[31]

It is important to comprehend this attitude to gain a full understanding of the Bonus March. This, the best known national march of the unemployed during the period, originated on the West Coast, specifically in Portland. The Congress had passed a bill in 1924 providing a bonus payment to First World War veterans in 1946. Logically enough, a number of veterans believed they could use the money better in 1932 than fourteen years hence. Members of Congress who agreed proposed a bill to accelerate issuance of the bonus.

In May 1932 a group of Portland veterans decided to go to Washington, D.C., to do what they might to urge passage of the bill. The idea was not a new one. Portland veterans had gone to Washington the preceding year. Senator Frederick Steiwer had received them genially, heard them out, and helped them make their way back home. The warm reception may have encouraged a second trip east.[32] Veterans were already soliciting Portland merchants to support another trek by October 1931, and enthusiasm among veterans was strong by March 1932.[33] Why was Portland the base? Perhaps Oregon was good to its veterans, providing them with a state bonus and other favors.[34] Perhaps such largess encouraged veterans to ask for similar federal assistance.

The marchers announced their intentions on 29 April 1932 and prepared to get under way 10 May. Walter Waters, who was in his mid-thirties, was the leader of the Portland march and the entire so-called Bonus Expeditionary Force (BEF). He had been a sergeant in the Great War, and since the war had held several jobs including a supervisor's position at a fish cannery. In 1932 he was unemployed and penniless. The BEF sent out an advance party to raise funds and clear the way. The main contingent from Portland, reasonably well organized and orderly, rode the "side car Pullmans" (boxcars) or drove in a few rickety automobiles, gathering more and more supporters as they crossed the continent. Ultimately, about 20,000 to 25,000 arrived in Washington.[35] Despite the fact that the march originated in Portland, the local papers did little to cover it, mainly handling it like any national news story. Although the *Journal* published a supportive editorial, no paper made much mention of the march's Oregon roots.

The only other major BEF contingent to receive extensive coverage on the West Coast was a group of over one thousand from Los Angeles. The Southern California group received far more publicity than their northwestern cohorts, who left a month earlier. This band marched or rode in their dilapidated cars and trucks down Broadway, a downtown thoroughfare. The leader of the Southern Californians, Royal Robertson, a navy veteran, kept his group separate from the rest of the BEF, picketing and camping on the capitol grounds. In July Robertson returned to Los Angeles to accept an offer for the film rights to his story, but soon returned to his roofing business.

The story of the events once the BEF arrived in Washington is by now a familiar one. The veterans lost both their cause and their camp with relative peacefulness and orderliness on their part—again, exemplifying attitudes evident on the urban West Coast, and throughout the nation in the early 1930s. After Congress turned down the bonus, the Oregon veterans went once again to Senator Steiwer to seek help getting home. Chief of Police Pelham Glassford informed Steiwer and Congressman Charles Martin that 350 veterans from Portland were stranded in the capital and it would cost just over $11,000 to get them home. Martin cabled the Portland Chamber of Commerce about the need and received a telegram of rejection. Finally, several VFW posts took up collections. These funds and some railroad charity passes got the men home by early August. The Southern California contingent experienced the same problems but held together as an organization for a time after returning. Fifty-five BEF veterans set up a small farming and bartering community in Los Angeles that resembled a Hooverville. For the veterans in the West their peaceful appeal for help died with a whimper.

The contest over budgets and taxes that had already been waged in 1931 in Seattle and San Francisco and had been simmering in all four cities for at least two years emerged fully in 1932. Each city and county moved closer to the limit of its indebtedness in 1931, and financial institutions were even more reluctant to purchase municipal bonds. If the economy was declining at a slower rate, it was still declining, and the number of families and individuals in need of relief was growing, perhaps at an accelerating pace as more who had been laid off earlier were coming to the end of their resources. But in each city relief funds were exhausted or nearly so. Increased taxation, of course, could meet the pressing need. And, on this issue, any sense of cooperative individualism evaporated. Throughout the nation the tax levy was the point of increasing community tension during the Hoover years. In Philadelphia 15,000 demonstrated against tax increases. Chicagoans also protested against state tax hikes, and, when Rochester citizens discovered that their city spent more on relief than comparable cities, they clamored for immediate economies.[36] Taxpayers applied the same pressures in the West.

In Los Angeles those who sought a lighter tax burden won the battle. It was clearly an important contest. Tax delinquencies were running at 11.22 percent in June 1932. Although this was lower than the national average and lower than the delinquency rate in the Northwest, it was 4 percentage points higher than the previous year and it represented $14 million in back taxes.[37] Downtown businessmen and property owners, the chamber of commerce, the realty board, and the 1,500 taypayers who stormed the county board of supervisors sought and got tax relief. This relief came in two forms: budget cuts resulting in a lower city levy and reduction of property assessments. An article for the Municipal Research Bureau made the case for the latter point, claiming city assessments still reflected the inflated boom times of the 1920s and needed to be reduced to come in line with the deflated 1930s. The county assessor agreed. Valuations in the county, which had been lowered each year of the depression, dropped a third time in 1932 almost 20 percent, a reduction of $608 million. Among cities larger than 500,000, Los Angeles was the only one that lowered its assessments during this time.[38]

The other method of decreasing the tax load was to pare the tax levy. Los Angeles did this too, reducing its tax rate from $1.64 per $100 of valuation to $1.53. The county held the line, and city schools and the Metropolitan Water District boosted their rates, effecting a net increase of $.08. Still, with the assessment reduction, the taxpayer's burden was lighter.[39]

The pressures on the city government continued. Water bonds voted in 1930 went begging, and the financial houses lowered their ratings of Los Angeles city utility bonds from AAA to AA.[40] With less tax revenue and no realistic chance to use bonds to supplement city income, there was a serious lack of operating funds. The only method left to city officials to balance the budget was a slash of expenditures. The council recognized this early in 1932, even before it began putting together the 1932–33 fiscal year budget. In February, citing an expected deficit of $650,000 to $700,000, leaders formulated plans to cut 858 city positions. Before they had completed the retrenchment, the council and city department heads examined five-day weeks, salary reductions, and layoffs and came up with a scheme that would incorporate all three. The ultimate solution called for five-day weeks, a sliding scale of wage and salary cuts ranging up to 10 percent for employees at the higher end of the scale (those being paid $400 a month or more), and the elimination of just over 300 jobs.[41]

In summary, the depression presented an increasingly complex problem for the city of Los Angeles. Revenue was down, but the need for municipal assistance to the unemployed was as great as it ever had been. The city budget, which had shown surpluses in 1929 and 1931, was over $11 million in the red by the end of fiscal year 1931–32—a figure that exceeded the worst expectations of early spring.[42] Taxpayers, many just as hard pressed as the city, clamored for relief. The city council followed the lead of its counterparts in San Francisco and Seattle: it opted to meet taxpayers' needs, over and against making a greater commitment to relief for the unemployed. Still the council fell well short of its goal of a balanced budget in a difficult economic situation. The 1932–33 deficit was $6 million.[43]

The county confronted the same crisis and responded in the same way. The county budget remained nearly the same. Salary cuts were made, and expenditures continued lean. Although William Harriman, the superintendent of charities sought $16 million for the Welfare Board, he could obtain only $7 million. Again, the scale tipped in favor of the homeowners, in the form of a constant tax rate on lower assessments and away from those in need of weekly incomes to survive.[44]

The San Francisco Board of Supervisors had already made its budget cuts. By mid-1932 the San Francisco tax delinquency rate, although by far the lowest among the four cities, was on the rise. It reached 3.58 percent versus 2.68 percent for 1931.[45] Both the charter and concerned taxpayers constrained the supervisors as they coped with deficits. The board again sought to cut expenditures rather than raise revenue. They considered several approaches. Revenue-generating bonds would not work. Although the city maintained its excellent credit rating, only San Francisco banks would purchase Hetch Hetchy bonds, and that seemed to be mainly a public service rendered by a fairly stable banking establishment to keep the project moving.

Mayor Rossi and the supervisors then turned to the city employees. A pay slash would be more difficult than before to bring about in San Francisco because a charter amendment was now necessary to cut salaries across the board. Although taxpayer groups circulated an initiative petition for city pay cuts, it did not gain enough valid signatures to be placed on the ballot. As the supervisors discussed pay warrants and a city-sponsored drive to amend the charter, employees and officials reached a compromise. The terms were by now all too familiar. If city employees donated $1.5 million to unemployment relief, the board of supervisors would agree to maintain their wages and salaries. Once again the municipal workers cut their own wages—this time by 3 to 12 percent. But by taking the avenue of voluntary contributions they were keeping open the possibility that the reductions would not be permanent.[46] The board of supervisors thus trimmed the budget. The tax rate dropped from $4.04 per $100 assessed value to $3.96, on top of lower valuations citywide.[47] At the same time the board redirected an important portion of the salary budget toward relief. In December 1932 the *San Francisco Chronicle* proudly noted the *New York Herald Tribune*'s assessment that San Francisco was free from financial crises, since the city had not raised taxes nor had its employees suffered payless paydays.[48] Such a declaration smacked of hyperbole given the voluntary wage reduction, but, of the large cities on the West Coast, San Francisco was best equipped to hold the fiscal line while not abandoning its commitment to the needy.

The pressure for budgetary restraint and lower taxes intensified in Seattle in

1932. In addition to newspaper articles and increased activity by the community clubs, taxpayers were simply not paying their taxes. The delinquency rate, which normally ran higher than the national average, continued to be high as the depression wore on. In 1933 it grew to 28.3 percent, about 2 percent over the national average and some five times higher than San Francisco's rate for the same year. The greatest decline in payment of taxes in 1932 was among the young (under fifty) who had lived in the same precinct four to five years (22.1 percent fewer paid property taxes in 1932 than in 1928 among this group).[49] Moreover, Seattle banks took a hard line against cashing city employee warrants, and Governor Hartley added his advice, that less relief money should be spent. When the council finally approved the new budget in September 1932, fiscal conservatives prevailed. The budget included a pay cut for city employees, a reduction of staff by 195, and a leaner budget by $2.5 million. Seattle pruned the city welfare budget the most, but, according to a newspaper article, this was not as serious as it appeared. When the money was needed, the city could always obtain it by declaring an emergency.[50] King County was under the same pressures and followed suit by reducing its budget $146,000. Wage reductions, cuts in department budgets (especially welfare), staff reductions, and a hope for Reconstruction Finance Corporation assistance all contributed to budget paring.[51]

A greater challenge was in the offing for city and county budget-makers in the state of Washington. In November 1932 state voters approved a tax limit on all counties. This tax ceiling restricted the combined tax assessment (including city, county, and any special taxing districts) to forty mills. In 1933 Seattle and King County would have to depend on outside resources.

Portland shared both the problems and solutions of its West Coast neighbors. Bonded indebtedness was at a worrisome level: Multnomah County and the state were having problems finding major buyers for their bonds even as early as 1931, and tax delinquencies—29 percent in Multnomah County—were an astronomical 38.7 percent statewide.[52] Added to this were the familiar calls for tax relief. The *Portland News-Telegram* declared war on high taxes and Taypayers' Leagues from all over Portland demanded wage cuts for city workers as deep as 25 percent.[53] The city was particularly anxious as officials counted up anticipated revenue trying to figure in the impact of tax delinquencies and interest payments. The result was a small reduction in the budget, which, because of declining property assessments, led to an increase of $.02 per $100 of assessments. The county yielded as well to tax-reduction pressures and lowered its budget for 1933 by almost $200,000, about a 6 percent reduction.[54]

By mid- or late 1932, trends in the decision-making process of 1931 had become firm policy. The anxiety and desperation that many property-owning citizens felt, represented by a national property tax delinquency rate of 26 percent, had overcome the ideals of selfless devotion to others in all but San Francisco. When there was banding together in 1932, it was more often than not homeowners seeking to protect their property from taxes. City and county officials responded to the pressure. All along the West Coast, property valuations were dropping, budgets were shrinking, and tax levies were declining or, at most, rising marginally.

SEVEN

In Time of Their Greatest Need

Local budget reduction was occurring in the face of the greatest sustained need in the history of each city. It was little wonder that 1932 saw the exhaustion of the relief programs of 1931, programs that were supposed to see the cities through their time of crisis. And in 1932 no new ideas, no new programs, and, most important, no new sources of local funds, private or public, appeared. The response of the cities to the Great Depression essentially came to an end, even as the relief burdens grew.

Los Angeles demonstrated convincingly in 1932 that the willingness to be taxed and to give had virtually disappeared. The community chest strove valiantly throughout the year to use its funds to meet the crisis. The chest hired the unemployed to prepare distributions of food. But because the community chest by October 1932 was handling 67 percent more cases than the previous year, without receiving commensurate funding, the jobs and food did not make much of a dent in the need.[1] Community chest leaders revised the budget and sought further assistance. At the beginning of the year administrators cut their own and their staff's salaries 10 percent. Then, in May, the chest asked for $1 million for relief from the Water and Power Commission. The commission had given over $70,000 to charity already but found the million dollar request too much and rejected it. Finally, as they prepared the budgets for 1933, community chest officials cut the contributions to their constituent agencies 22 to 30 percent.

The goal for the fall campaign was $3.4 million, only $100,000 more than the previous year, with almost half—$1.5 million—earmarked for the emergency relief fund. Eighty-seven percent of the fund was designated for some form of relief-oriented assistance. The campaign, which had always extended beyond its deadline, this time ran into the next year. Toward the end of January 1933, campaign leaders announced the final totals. They had received $2.9 million, or 87 percent of what the chest had received in 1932—about 14 percent short of the 1933 goal.[2] The community chest looked beyond an immensely difficult 1932 toward even harder times.

The same pressures virtually overwhelmed other private charity activities. From June 1929 to June 1932 the Municipal Service Bureau's case load had risen 1,050 percent. The Salvation Army's ministry to transients had increased 1,471 percent from 1928 to 1932. The Midnight Mission served 181 percent more people in 1932 than in 1930. Mary Covell, its director, entreated the Los Angeles City Council for help but was rejected.[3] The Catholic Welfare Board closed its doors in the afternoons because it ran out of time and room to help those still outside.

The agency also cut its food allotment by 10 percent to American families and 25 percent to Mexican families. The discrepancy was explained as a difference in dietary standards.[4] The Angelus Temple, which ran one of the most generous soup lines, moved to a work test to cut down on its charity outlay. Another soup kitchen closed after the "no questions asked" policy had used up $20,000 of its proprietor's funds. And a charity activity for women suffered the same fate when community chest contributions to the program ran out.

Smaller organizations and private groups still tried to lend a hand. The American Legion, focusing on veterans, initiated a job aid plan with the goal of creating at least one job in every business concern through prorating the hours of those already employed. The Associated Women's Commission did the same thing for women. The PTA continued its subsidized school lunch program, feeding over 14,000 by June 1932. And the Junior League of Los Angeles proudly announced, "Women of the leisure class are meeting to see what they can do toward helping to relieve the prevailing economic distress."[5] Two charity events gave the jobless the opportunity to assist their fellow citizens in return for a meal or a bit of income. Unemployed men could wash cars for a lunch or dinner. The car owner paid a dollar for the service. A human auction was held in which unemployed people were put on the block to sell their services and consequently receive some degree of assistance.

By 1932 a number of the unemployed in Los Angeles had taken the responsibility to help themselves. A Hooverville sprang up at 85th and Alameda, and by the spring of the year had over 700 residents. Unlike the Seattle settlement, this poverty village admitted families. The Angelus Temple supplied food to the residents, and others donated wood so the inhabitants of the shacks and tents could cook.

The self-help movement started in a big way in 1932. Perhaps taking its cue from the Unemployed Citizens' League in Seattle, which may have been the first depression-spawned group formed in the nation and surely the first on the West Coast, a self-help group formed in the Los Angeles suburb of Compton in March 1932. By December the Los Angeles movement was strong. Within a year there were twenty-three groups in the city and forty-five countywide. Although the self-help groups in Los Angeles never attained as prominent a political place as the UCL, they were an important part of the relief effort. Self-help provided as much as one-third of relief in the area even after the advent of the New Deal.[6] Although the membership of the groups never reached a majority of the unemployed, Los Angeles became a major self-help area. By 1934 as many as 10 percent of those involved in self-help nationwide were in Los Angeles.

Why was Los Angeles such a hotbed for cooperatives? The large amount of perishables in Southern California enabled members to keep one another supplied by working in the orchards and fields and bringing foodstuffs back to headquarters. The large retirement community residing in the Southland probably encouraged cooperative ventures. By the mid-1930s, the cooperators averaged 52.4 years of age. A combination of a particularly strong adherence to the value of self-reliance combined with necessity drew many in. One of the necessities was the awkward status of being an impoverished property owner. A homeowner, no matter how destitute, was often ineligible for relief. The local self-help group was a boon in these cases.[7] Finally, self-help flourished most vigorously in the two cities—Los Angeles and Seattle—that were less energetic in meeting the needs of the unemployed. The cooperative spirit was as much born out of necessity as it was an ideal in Los Angeles and Seattle.

The members of the Los Angeles groups were mainly blue-collar or clerical workers who had not gone beyond grammar school. They were almost all American-born, and there were more Protestants than in the Los Angeles population at large. There were also slightly more Democrats than Republicans among the ranks. Like their counterparts in Seattle, the Angeleno self-helpers gleaned unwanted crops, engaged in clothing manufacture and assorted handicrafts, and helped run the organization. The groups used a barter system that was facilitated by payments in scrip, which happened to be illegal in California and caused problems as some challenged its worth.

The cooperative effort served some useful purposes. Although the level of assistance provided was submarginal, it did provide relief for some, especially older people, who would have been hard pressed to obtain assistance and found it virtually impossible to gain employment. The groups helped preserve at least a modicum of self-respect and in the process siphoned some of the jobless out of the relief system of Los Angeles.

There were distinct drawbacks. Inexperience, inefficiency, and dishonesty plagued the movement. An insufficient foundation of goods thwarted its effort.[8] Some onlookers raised the valid concern that the groups might establish themselves outside the economic framework or become politicized. The latter worry almost materialized when Upton Sinclair successfully sought the self-help groups as a part of his End Poverty In California constituency of 1934. In all, however, self-help in the Southland was benign, and Angelenos could be thankful that so many took it on themselves, partially out of necessity, to help themselves.

On a smaller scale, other jobless people in Los Angeles exercised self-reliance. As many as 1,500 went to the San Gabriel Mountains to pan for gold. Los Angeles homeowners staged a drive to raise $2 million for a fund to forestall eviction. According to the proposal a threatened homeowner could draw as much as $500 at 6 percent to stave off the loss of the home. The announcement that the drive was getting under way was the last evidence of its existence.

Despite a fuller realization that the need existed, Los Angeles city and county leaders remained reluctant or unable to fill it. Early in the year Mayor John Porter acknowledged in a letter to the county board of supervisors, "The emergency is great and it must be met," yet a POUR report estimated the city had $6 million less to provide for assistance than in 1931. By May the community chest and other welfare agencies had depleted their resources, even as POUR estimated 93,000 people were destitute in Los Angeles.[9] The city was in no shape to fill the gap. By spring the council had ascertained that the city was running a large deficit—over $11 million as it turned out—and began to make staffing and pay cuts. Any saving in the area of relief was almost impossible. The city had spent from $13 to $17 dollars per case per month as it dispensed relief—well under the $24.65 average recorded in a twenty-four city survey.[10] Even this tight-fisted response had overmatched its ability, or its will, to supply the needs of its people. Los Angeles would no longer sustain any substantial relief effort.

Within the city government the only hope for additional funds rested with the Board of Water and Power Commissioners. The cash-rich department from time to time transferred part of its excess revenue, which was earmarked for future construction projects, to the city's general fund for charity. In the midst of the city budget crisis chamber of commerce, POUR, and community chest officials came hat in hand to the Water and Power Board to seek $1 million for city relief. At the hearing prominent city leaders hissed the president of the board as he called for a grant of only $50,000 for relief.[11] Ultimately, the Department of Water and Power did distribute $381,500 to the city and private agencies for relief and another $780,000 for street maintenance and direct relief in 1932–33.[12]

As usual it was up to the county to provide the estimated $16.5 million needed to assist the jobless during the year. Relief, already at a high level, increased 60 percent during the winter of 1931, and the 1932–33 load was double that of the previous fiscal year.[13] William Harriman, the superintendent of charities, informed the board in April that the seasonal decline in unemployment was not taking place in 1932, and the chairman of the board of supervisors warned, "We are reaching the danger point. Soon we may be unable to pay county warrants when they are issued."[14] The county then cut pay and instituted a five-day week in response to its deficits.

This eased the strain on the budget somewhat, but it did not fulfill the county's responsibility for relief. At the urging of the regional POUR committee and others, the board of supervisors decided in early June to submit a $12 million bond to the voters. After being assured of its legality, the supervisors laid out its provisions. A work test would be involved, and a social worker would supervise cases where work was not feasible. The bonds would be sold as needed to supply clothes, food, fuel and shelter for the needy. POUR chairman John Austin strongly urged the plan: "This is not a bond issue. This is emergency relief—a war measure."[15] Joseph Scott of the community chest was almost apocalyptic. "This is war," he wrote. "We are fighting starvation and the temptation of men to take the law into their own hands and say 'Stick 'em up'. It's everybody's business unless we want a dictatorship. We can't cover the situation up any longer. The people have got to know the truth . . . We should ask the newspapers to spare more space for this purpose. Let's know something besides Babe Ruth's batting average."[16]

County residents were less enthusiastic. Letters to the editor of the *Daily News* were about evenly divided on the issue. And when Harry J. Bauer, chairman of the Governor's Unemployment Commission and supporter of the levy, informed the supervisors that he was not optimistic about its chances at the polls, the board suddenly withdrew the proposal. Instead, they stated, they would count on the proposed special session of the state legislature to provide the necessary relief funds to the county. If relief was to be provided at sufficient levels it was up to the state.

While the county waited for the state to supply relief money, it passed a less than adequate $7-million welfare budget, approved a few stop-gap public works, and considered a proposal to channel some of the Olympic Games' profits to relief work. In November the state authorized $20 million in relief bonds and permitted the county to borrow $12 million from this fund.

From the beginning, the response of the Los Angeles governments was not generous compared to the other cities. The city responded relatively quickly in 1930 and provided the $5-million relief bond in 1931, but Los Angeles lagged behind other cities of its size in dispensing relief. The county fulfilled its legal obligations and saw its welfare budget swell, but it, too, kept as tight a rein as possible on its expenditures, though its relief programs suffered from inefficiency. By mid-1932 there were no longer sufficient funds in the budgets of either government to sustain the relief effort adequately. Ostensibly, relief needs had exceeded the resources of the local governments. Something more, however, may have been at work. Given the proportionately smaller outlay for the relief effort and the authorization of lower valuations and property taxes, the will of the community gave way before its economic ability did. Although a sense of cooperation and charity was extant in the Southland, anxiety for one's own status—while admonishing self-reliance for others—constricted the relief effort well before it should have run out of funds. The response of Los Angeles never fulfilled President Hoover's expectations of Americans in the face of adversity.

As it had throughout the depression, San Francisco was more prepared in 1932 to provide private and public assistance than Los Angeles. Even as private relief expenditures continued to rise, the city and county government of San Francisco assumed almost total responsibility for relief. The public portion of contributions to Associated Charities rose from 8.5 percent in 1929 to 84 percent in 1932, as the government spent almost 900 percent more on relief than it did the year of the crash. This translated into $3.8 million of aid distributed in work or direct relief.[17]

Private agencies raised money at a fairly constant rate despite the prevailing economic conditions. In 1932 contributions to charity dipped $65,000 to $646,000 —a total still $100,000 higher than in 1929. The goal for the December chest drive was $2.5 million, a figure that included other customary services as well as relief. When the collections fell $700,000 short the campaign was extended three days. At the end of that time the chest lowered its goal to $2.35 million. Three days later the revised figure finally had been collected. No wonder, then, that there was strong support among the members of the community chest executive council for abandoning their new depression-created responsibilities and turning them over to the city. The private sector had tried, but by 1932 in San Francisco charity was itself a victim of the depression.

San Francisco businessmen and industrial leaders continued to push for familiar remedies for the depression. In February the junior chamber of commerce established the first of several work-creating commissions formed during the year. These groups used several strategies to create a better job market. As in the 1930 paint-up fix-up campaign, they asked householders to employ people in odd jobs. But the economy of 1932 called for a considerably bolder plan. The slogan of a drive, which businessmen from the Twelfth Federal Reserve District instituted, was "Job Security through Job Sharing." This was a catchy phrase for prorating work hours to spread employment. The slogan helped bring home the nature and the necessity of the program. If the employee was not prepared to sacrifice a few hours for the sake of others (job sharing), he could not be entirely confident that he would continue to work for his company (job security). There is no record of how many jobs were shared, and thus stabilized, in the 2,000 firms that enlisted in the drive by the end of the year.[18]

Dire predictions that jobless white-collar workers who had used up their savings would flood the city's relief rolls were coming true. At the same time, San Francisco was plunged into a budget crisis. In April the city ran out of relief money. Since the new charter made deficit spending illegal, the board had to borrow from an unlikely source—the community chest.[19] No further money would be available until the next fiscal year, which began 1 July 1932, so San Francisco's relief effort limped into a new fiscal year, leaning unsteadily on the community chest loan and the continuing contributions of the city employees.

By June many San Franciscans knew that relief money for the next year would be inadequate. Even in a horribly depressed market, a bond sale offered the only solution. A group of thirty-five members of charitable and labor groups called on the mayor and the board of supervisors in late June advocating a $6.5 million bond issue. Mayor Rossi, stating a fact more than a principle, echoed President Hoover's sentiments saying the burden of relief rested on the people—the state and federal governments could not be depended on to help. Therefore, the board unanimously approved a bond issue and, after the state supreme court approved its legality, placed it on the ballot. Every San Francisco daily newspaper and the *Labor Clarion* promoted the bonds. The papers pointed out that if the issue did not pass, many tenants whom landlords carried because of the nature of the city's relief program, would be evicted and taxes would soar. The bonds should be approved, urged the editor of the *Call-Bulletin*, simply "in the name of humanity. . . ."[20] Unlike Los Angeles, San Francisco went through with its election, and the people demonstrated their humanity on 30 August 1932 by endorsing the $6.5 million issue 135,000 to 18,700.[21]

The board of supervisors quickly implemented a program to use this money, for by September it was already needed. Fortunately, the right set of circumstances existed for raising money through bond sales. The city's credit rating was impeccable. Several of the comparatively healthy banks were able and, in the face of crisis, willing to purchase much of the first issue.

By June 1933, the end of the fiscal year, two-thirds of the bond money had been spent. Because it was well financed during this period and because its administrators were now experienced, the San Francisco program was at its best during the last year of the Hoover administration. What was the nature of the program? How was it run? What were the problems involved? The testimony of Charles Wollenberg, who continued to administer assistance, and others provides a description of one of the better coordinated relief efforts in the country. By June 1932, although administrators were encouraging relatives to help their needy relations, at times as many as 58,000 individuals drew unemployment relief—a 600 percent increase from 1929.[22] A family was eligible for relief if it had been in the city a year or more and made less than a prescribed income. Often a person owning encumbered property was admitted to the relief rolls, but if public aid would facilitate a property purchase it was withheld. Most of the qualified family heads received four weeks of food for five and one-half days' work. Single men were given food and two days of shelter, often in poor surroundings, and then asked to move on. Single women worked three days to get a ration of three weeks' food.[23] Workshops provided opportunities to labor on and sell goods. In some cases families simply received direct relief.

The effort was the target of complaints about inequities in the distribution of relief, the monotony of the relief diet, the heavy load carried by administrators, and the cursory checking of eligibility. The most consistent and valid criticism was probably the practice that Wollenberg himself called "buncoing the landlord." Because there was not enough money to help the unemployed pay their rent, the relief program would help out only if the landlord threatened eviction. If renters did lose their residence, they received a month's rent for a new place. In this way, many generous landlords who permitted their renters to fall several months behind on their payments often ended up helping foot the relief bill.

From 1930 to 1932, the reactions of San Franciscans to the depression were considerably more charitable than Angelenos'. Bay City voters approved $9 million in bonds to aid the unemployed—a laudable act and an amount in excess of the larger city of Los Angeles. The city employees showed a good deal of willingness to help, yielding to prodding with significantly little murmuring, and the city leaders showed a consummate skill in shuffling the budget to gain relief dollars. From the accounts of Wollenberg and a special commission that studied the program, a suddenly massive job of relief was administered fairly efficiently. Not a great deal more relief money could have been pried from the people, especially the beleaguered city employees, but with the transbay and Golden Gate bridge construction imminent, San Francisco might have administered sufficient relief on its own for several more years. Through a singular generosity, an alacrity in establishing a relief program (which may have in turn imbued San Franciscans with a greater sense of responsibility for the unemployed), skillful budget balancing, the acquiescence of its employees, the strong financial position of many of its banks, and, not least, the good fortune of an economy sturdier than that of the other three West Coast cities, San Francisco came the closest of the four cities to fulfilling, at least for a time, Herbert Hoover's faith in the ability of a local community to survive and take care of its own.

Seattle's response was unique. But it plunged Seattle into turmoil that the other cities did not encounter. The community fund was still functioning, and private ideas for assistance continued to percolate. From 1928–29 to 1933–34 contributions to the Seattle Community Fund had decreased 24 percent, as compared to a national decline of 9 percent. The goal for the fall 1932 community fund drive was $140,000 less than in 1931, and Seattleites failed to meet even this by the scheduled end of the campaign. The record of other private assistance was similarly poor. The PTA involved itself in child welfare and the chamber of commerce promoted a regionwide job sharing campaign, but the city and King County bore the responsibility for the welfare of its citizens. As 1931 came to an end, the city took meaningful steps in carrying out its role.

Almost immediately, however, any optimism that the program might meet the relief need all but vanished. Unemployment figures in the city steadily worsened, and the first weeks of 1932 saw the city transfer partial responsibility for maintaining relief to King County because it no longer had sufficient resources to provide full support for the District Relief Organization (DRO). As early as January, the county passed $125,000 through the Community Fund to the DRO. The organization of the relief program remained essentially the same as the county began to assume increasing authority.

King County soon found itself in the same straits as the city. In May 1932 the county commissioners voted $417,000 for relief and announced they had run out of funds. County officials then followed what seemed to be their only recourse and approved a bond issue. The commissioners planned to submit the $200,000 relief bond to the voters on a special September ballot, but by law the date had to be set back to the November election. Since pressing needs called for urgent action, the county took a test case to the state supreme court to establish whether the commissioners could exceed the county's legal debt limit. The court ruled swiftly and humanely. In their June decision the justices declared that it was the county's duty to aid the unemployed, and they authorized King County to appropriate the $200,000 without a special vote of the people. Because the voters would restrict the tax assessment to 40 mills in November, this was the last significant contribution to relief from local funds. A state income tax, approved at the same time as the assessment limitation, was supposed to offset this restriction on taxing authority, but it was declared unconstitutional by the state supreme court.

In May a tired I. F. Dix stepped down as head of the mayor's commission to devote more time to the telephone business and to regain his health. In July the city gave up its remaining power over the local relief program, though it continued to provide some funds. This was a logical step now that the county had court approval to go beyond its debt limit. With the county heading up the effort to aid the unemployed, the King County Emergency Relief Organization replaced the DRO.

The court decision and the reshuffling of responsibilities, however, could not solve, even temporarily, other serious problems that the relief effort was facing. Most Seattleites, even the conservative elements of the population, accepted the Unemployed Citizens' League as a necessary, even useful, organization spawned by the economic conditions. There had been no notable outcries when the UCL became the foundation for the District Relief Organization. In such a group, however, existed the seeds of social disruption. This was an important factor that Hoover should have anticipated when he encouraged self-help at the local level.

The unemployed—the have-nots—organized themselves into a relatively efficient group. The very nature and function of the group prepared the way for the UCL to turn itself into a socialistic organization. Moreover, the leadership's political stance was left of center, although Wells, Brannin, Gilbreath, and the rest were probably not sure themselves just where they fit. Their unofficial organ specialized in radical rhetoric. The *Vanguard*, or the *Unemployed Citizen* as it was called part of the time, espoused political and industrial action, industrial unionism, and a modified Marxism. Such unmistakable left-leaning invited city and county officials, along with a number of citizens, to keep a close watch on the UCL.

During 1932 two things happened to the league that severely damaged its credibility, destroyed its usefulness in providing relief, and, in turn, deprived the UCL of its power in the community. Externally its problem was graft. At least the accusation was leveled that the UCL was mismanaging relief funds. More critical to its stability and more disastrous to its ongoing role in Seattle were the UCL's internal divisions. Arthur Hillman, a sociology professor at the University of Washington, studied the UCL in 1934. He concluded that certain league members, dissatisfied with the relative mildness of the trade unionists, progressives, and socialists who were the original organizers, forced these men out of the leadership and replaced them with more radical individuals of their own choosing.[24]

From the content of the *Unemployed Citizen*, however, it is hard to see how many of the jobless could have found much fault with the radical tone of the views that the original leaders expressed. The divisions within the UCL were probably the result of a power struggle more than an ideological contest. Members of the IWW and the Communist party, who were scattered throughout the organization, saw in the league a field ripe for harvest and were determined to reap its fruits.

In mid-1932 members of a local branch of the UCL began to acquire control of the league. Composed of Wobblies and supported by Communists, the Capitol Hill Gang consisted predominantly of single men who had been pushing for more militancy among their fellow unemployed. Several times they aggressively forestalled evictions of families. In August 1932 this faction assumed leadership of the UCL. The significance of this change in leadership was demonstrated in a new UCL constitution. Although the first objective of the organization continued to be the unification of the jobless to fight unemployment, the ultimate goal, according to the constitution, was to achieve public ownership of all business and industry to put an end to the intolerable exploitation of the workers. Ultimately, the unemployed were to combine to overthrow the capitalist system.[25]

As the league's brand of cooperative individualism became threatening, businesses withdrew their support from the self-help program. Popular reaction was negative, and many of the unemployed were alienated by the UCL's growing radicalism. In November the former UCL leaders formed a new group called the Economic Security League. It never achieved the size, power, or significance of the original organization.

The struggle within the UCL continued. After the Wobblies eliminated the socialists and union men, the Communists asserted their power. In a Machiavellian ploy, they allied themselves with the more conservative UCL members to oust the IWW men. Ultimately, William Dobbins, a Communist, became chairman of the league. By this time the organization's effectiveness as a voice of the self-help movement among the unemployed was over. During the IWW days of the summer of 1932, the group staged an essentially fruitless march to see Governor Hartley in Olympia. In February 1933 the UCL held a sit-in at the County–City Building in Seattle without significant results. Members again went to Olympia in March and were ignominiously turned away when "vigilantes" met them at the outskirts of town.

The Unemployed Citizens' League was the closest thing to a militant response to the depression in any of the cities. This organization of the unemployed, however, helped the jobless and had an impact on the city only as long as it remained nonmilitant. Rather than opposing the power structure, it cooperated with it. Rather than demanding relief, it furnished a method by which the unemployed could aid themselves. When it radicalized and attacked the status quo, it lost its power. Clearly jobless Seattleites joined the UCL not to express themselves in a united way against the system but to satisfy a need for which the government and community initially felt no responsibility.

The spirit of cooperative individualism, which the UCL and its activities represented, owed its demise to local relief funding problems, internal strife, and the leftward turn of the league, but local politics played an important part as well. In fact, the league's high point in both notoriety and power came on the eve of its decline. In March 1932, before radical elements seized control of the UCL, the league made its first and last significant foray into Seattle politics. The most important contest in that election was the mayoral race. The three major candidates were the incumbent Robert Harlin, former mayor Frank Edwards, who had been ousted in the earlier recall election, and John Dore, a criminal attorney. Edwards hoped for support from conservatives and some factions of labor, while Harlin advertised himself simply as "A Safe Pilot in a Troubled Sea." Dore, a Democrat, was the most interesting candidate in the field. A flamboyant speaker, called by some a demagogue, Dore campaigned for greater economy and lower property taxes, thus endearing himself to beleaguered taxpayers. He was also able to cast himself as the friend of Seattle's liberal community. Most significantly, Dore won UCL endorsement with promises of jobs.[26]

In addition to Dore, the UCL supported Frank Fitts and Roy Misener for city council spots. The conservative *Seattle Times* labeled these three men radicals. If they accepted such an evaluation, *Times* readers woke up on 9 March 1932, to find themselves under a radical government. Seattle gave Dore the largest margin of victory accorded a mayor up to that time, and the UCL-endorsed councilmen did almost as well.[27]

The Unemployed Citizens' League quickly claimed a share of the credit for the victories. Dore, Fitts, and Misener all acknowledged the importance of UCL support. The two councilmen estimated that the league's approval might have made a difference of 20,000 votes, and Fitts generously gave the league credit for 60,000 votes in the general election. Many community leaders, although not I. F. Dix, acknowledged that the organization of the unemployed was a significant political force. The important thing, no matter how much political clout the UCL claimed, was that the group had entered politics. Up to this time, the UCL concerned itself with feeding and aiding the unemployed on its own or in tandem with local government. This March election, however, was the highwater mark of organized political activity among the unemployed. They never again exerted their influence so strongly.[28]

Although the UCL and liberal Seattleites had endorsed Dore, the new mayor quickly dismayed his supporters. In the campaign he promised to cut the wages of only the highest paid members of the municipal bureaucracy. In June, however, he quickly antagonized six councilmen and supporters by calling for across-the-board pay slashes. The editor of the *Seattle Star*, once an adamant Dore supporter, now assailed the mayor for attempting to destroy the city's wage scale. When the councilmen opposed Dore's demands, he called them "public enemies" and the "six sillies." For two months the city council and the mayor wrangled bitterly over salary cuts for city employees. While the council sought a reduced work week, Dore continued to call for a 10 percent slash in wages.[29]

To the chagrin of Dore's campaign supporters, the bankers soon came in on the mayor's side. The city had been giving its employees pay warrants, which had to be cashed at banks. From time to time, especially when they thought the municipal government was practicing unsound finance, the banks would stop cashing the warrants. With such powerful backing, the mayor got his economy message across. Despite city council resistance, Dore circulated a petition among city employees. By signing, the workers agreed to accept voluntarily a wage reduction. Their alternative, they were told, was dismissal as an "economy measure." Caught between the banks, which would not honor their pay warrants, and the mayor, few employees hesitated to sign. Later in the year the mayor and the banks coaxed and coerced the council into another boon for the taxpayer—a lower budget. The split between the mayor and his jobless supporters continued to widen. By October he was labeling them radicals and communists.[30]

To close political observers such as George Starr, chairman of the Democratic State Central Committee, Dore's turnabout was not surprising. According to Starr, "Campaign promises did not mean anything to Dore, and once elected he was determined to go his own way."[31]

Because the UCL had become a success in relief administration and politics and because it moved steadily left in 1932, neither the conservative mayor nor the county commissioners, who were in charge of administering relief, now sanctioned the role the league was playing. Dore, along with several others, recommended that paid checkers be placed at the commissaries to watch over the administration of relief. When charges of extravagance and mismanagement arose, the UCL called for a county inspection to stop the rumors. In June an unpaid observer selected by the county was placed at each commissary to watch for fraud. With this step the crisis seemingly passed. County Commissioner Donald Evans said there was no reason to change the operation as long as it was well run.[32]

But the calm was short-lived. Anxious county commissioners, monitoring the turmoil within the UCL throughout the summer of 1932, readied for action. In September, league members at the Ballard District commissary complained that meat from Frye's Packing Company, which was distributed at the commissaries, was inferior and—possibly more significant—that the nonunion company was unfair to labor. The controversy was settled, but it led to the county's reappraisal of relief administration. At the end of the month, the commissioners decided that a more permanent system should be created, and they replaced the UCL workers with paid managers. League members, of course, objected strongly and refused to cooperate. In numerous cases the new managers were unable to obtain the lists of relief recipients from their UCL predecessors. The county was obliged to set up several new depots when relief workers would not accept the authority of the new managers at the old ones. Justifying the takeover, Commissioner John Earley claimed that the UCL had padded the lists of relief recipients and had been lax in its record keeping.[33]

By the end of 1932 the Unemployed Citizens' League had declined drastically. Without its position in the relief operation, its political clout dwindled. In November 1932 the league made one last attempt to recoup its power by supporting John C. Stevenson and Louis Nash for county commissioners, assuming that the two would reinstate the UCL in the relief program. Although they were elected and replaced the paid managers with jobless people, the two new commissioners refused to make UCL membership a qualification for the position. The league had lost its power.

Once again a local approach to relief came up short, but it did not collapse. In fact, in some ways it went forward in a more vigorous, or at least better funded, manner than before. In the same general election that sealed the fate of the UCL, Seattle voters approved $3 million in relief bonds. The relief effort, thus underwritten, would continue effectively but in a more conventional manner. The case of Seattle and the UCL is important because in that city the ideals of the president were brought into practice. Citizens independently formed a self-help organization in order to avoid public relief. Local authorities, not the state or federal government, provided the financial undergirding for the grass roots effort. Although the support Hoover expected from wealthy private sources was notably absent, a business expert—I. F. Dix, the qualified technician—set up and initially ran the operation. The UCL appears to have been the kind of group Hoover envisioned, and its relationship with local government seemed to represent cooperative individualism. Because so many elements were present that Hoover would have endorsed, it is important to analyze why the enterprise failed.

More than anything the severity of the economic crisis defeated Seattle's attempt at self-help, just as it overwhelmed the more standard efforts of Los Angeles and Portland and heavily burdened San Francisco. The relatively meager resources of the UCL could not hold out in the face of overwhelming problems, and the funds of the city and the county were almost depleted. Had the federal government not stepped in, the $3 million bond issue would have been exhausted in fairly short order. Moreover, the cooperative ideal itself—at least as it was manifested in Seattle—was afflicted with problems Hoover did not anticipate. Several factors would probably have doomed the Seattle effort even under less trying conditions. First, the internal organization of the UCL changed in ways unacceptable to city and county leaders. Most were reluctant to support or defend a relief program manned by members of a radical organization. Second, charges of graft and waste leveled at the UCL had a ring of truth and were never satisfactorily answered. Third, politicians had reason to fear the growing power of the UCL as a political machine. After the league demonstrated its influence in the mayoral election, no candidate could afford to ignore it. The county commissioners, therefore, decided to remove the UCL from the relief program, reducing its visibility and destroying its power base. Finally, once it became clear that the economic crisis and its problems would not soon pass, the commissioners established a permanent relief organization directly under their control.[34]

It is difficult to judge the relative importance of one factor over another. Each played its part in the league's downfall. Frank Foisie, a member of a committee that studied unemployment relief for the Washington State Legislature in 1932, wrote that the UCL was replaced because of a substantial increase in fraud and the county's fear—shared by some citizens—of the league's growing political power. Unless UCL opponents had fabricated the lists containing fraudulent entries, the UCL-administered program was not an entirely honest operation. Moreover, since both the mayor and the county administrators had reason to fear the UCL's political power, especially after the radicals took control of the organization, they must have been eager to limit league influence. Furthermore, the commissioners, uneasy at the unemployed administering relief to themselves, would logically have seized any opportunity to put the program under their supervision.[35]

Hoover, in many ways more idealist than politician, was reluctant to admit that local solutions, even augmented with federal aid, were proving ineffective. He did not perceive that his ideal of cooperative individualism was fraught with serious political pitfalls. A self-help organization composed of unemployed people was a likely, even easy, target for militants who could guide it in a far different direction than the capitalist democracy of which Hoover would approve. Hoover's ideal, it appears, was a somewhat simplistic one. As it worked itself out spontaneously in Seattle, cooperative individualism encountered a variety of significant problems. Neither local government nor the UCL would overcome these problems or the larger one of the failure of the national economy.

In Portland, 1932 held less drama than it had in Seattle. Private welfare again fell short and the public assistance program ran out of money. The Portland Community Chest went through the same gyrations its counterparts endured in the other three cities. In 1931, Portland citizens had exceeded a record goal. In 1932 both the level of generosity and economic wherewithall declined. Community chest officials set the goal at $787,296 for the fall campaign, about $100,000 over the 1931 basic target. Of this, $150,000 was to go to a special relief fund—an increase of $50,000 over the previous year. Even after the familiar extension of solicitation the drive fell short by almost $180,000. The campaign raised less in 1932 than in 1931, and 21,000 fewer people pledged.[36]

The community chest was under more than economic pressure in 1932. Probably because it was running in the red and pressing for more funds some citizens strongly suspected some gross inefficiencies or mismanagement. In 1933 the *Western World*, a leftist Portland newspaper, leveled specific charges, including lack of oversight of its constituent agencies, pledges forced on employees by their employers, and a general lack of accountability.[37] Although other newspapers defended the chest's operations, such allegations were telling and had been made in other cities. The community chest in Portland, or anywhere else for that matter, had not been created to be a relief agency. It was a charitable organization established to serve the whole community, not just the unemployed. But under crushing need it had to adapt as well as it could. By 1932 its best was not good enough.

In 1932 one of the major private efforts to combat unemployment was a throwback to 1930. Grandly labeled the "Portland Plan," it aimed at sharing what work was available. The six-hour day, home improvement, business expansions, public works, and "Buy Oregon" were all features of the program. Similar strategies were advocated in many cities well before anyone had heard of the Portland Plan. Ultimately, Portlanders pledged $10 million worth of work. This support had no major impact on the numbers of the unemployed, but, as one newspaper commented, at least things were astir.[38] The age of ballyhoo and optimism had not yet passed.

The various charity and service groups struggled to carry out their responsibilities in Portland. These efforts were commonplace, except in terms of greater volume. The Sunshine Division distributed 1,200 Christmas baskets, the Salvation Army provided 22,000 meals by the end of June, and several groups butchered animals or canned produce for the needy.

The unemployed formed two self-help groups: the Unemployed Citizens' League (unrelated to the Seattle group) and the Civic Emergency Federation. Neither had the impact of self-help groups in Los Angeles or Seattle, but their action indicated a widespread belief among the unemployed that local and national relief efforts were inadequate. They also demonstrated the willingness of individuals, even in 1932, to devise their own solutions to problems rather than rely on authorities. The preamble to the constitution of the Unemployed Citizens' League indicated that its formation was a response to the community's failure to provide:

> Through no fault of their own, useful and productive citizens, workers, are and have been for some time denied access to the means of production thereby being deprived of the bare necessities of life.
>
> Realizing the eventual, if not imminent failure and exhaustion, and withall the total inadequacy of existing relief measures we therefore create and organize the Oregon Plan, Unemployed Citizens' League of Portland and Multnomah County, and call upon all unemployed citizens to join with us to secure for our families the means of life, compatible with American standards by self-help, cooperative methods, mutual aid and by any and all lawful means within our power.[39]

The motto of the group was "If You Would Find God, Serve Man," but the policy statement printed above the constitution may have given some pause. It read, "From each according to his ability, to each according to his need."[40] Despite the communist credo, the organization remained in tune with the promise of its preamble to operate on the basis of cooperative individualism. Similar to its Seattle namesake, league members harvested and hauled fruits and vegetables, chopped wood, and exchanged skills as they tried to maintain the American standard of life. All evidence points to an organization made up of people seeking to help themselves—a goal Portlanders admired and assisted.

The Civic Emergency Federation met with the same positive response. It pushed for such commonplace actions as rotation in work and a moratorium on evictions, but it went further than the Unemployed Citizens' League and called for unemployment insurance, old age pensions, and a more progressive tax structure.[41]

Most unemployed Portlanders turned their attention to the local governments, which were still the main source of sustenance. Public relief efforts were severely strained by 1932. Some people complained about inefficiency and misuse of funds, but lack of funds posed the most difficult problem. Public Welfare Bureau cases, which had doubled in 1931, doubled again in 1932.[42] In January and February, relief officials earmarked the remainder of the $2 million raised from the sale of bonds to aid the 1,400 work relief recipients who had registered with the CEC. Finding buyers for the relief bonds became so difficult that the city and county sold the bonds in increments as small as $500 to attract small investors.

By March about $1.3 million in bonds had sold, but it was no secret that the whole relief operation was on the verge of financial collapse. Jobless registrations were growing by hundreds, perhaps even by a thousand each day. Desperate city and county officials appealed to the state highway commission to extend and enlarge its program. The highway commissioner thought expansion too costly.

Multnomah County decided in late March to put a $1 million bond issue and a tax levy of $750,000 before the voters. Portland approved an additional $1 million in relief bonds for the May election, then promptly declared that it could provide no more work until voters approved the bonds. In an attempt to trim the work relief rolls the CEC again began to reregister the entire roster. To help reduce the budget further, city employees agreed to graduated pay cuts of between 3 and 15 percent. Then in mid-April the state supreme court ruled that the submission of the $750,000 levy must await the November election, in effect leaving the county dependent on bond sales for seven months—a difficult prospect indeed.[43] Portland, therefore, placed an additional $400,000 bond issue on the ballot, bringing the total for voters to consider to $2.4 million.

Aaron Frank of the Civic Emergency Committee presented the bond issues to the public in terms that indicated he understood the tax-paying voters' minds. He pointed out that the relief operation was costing them only $.62 per $1,000 of assessed valuation and warned that they might lose their property to violence if the bonds were not approved.[44] Whether such reasoning swayed voters is not clear, but they approved each of the issues by at least a five-to-three margin.[45] Unlike Angelenos, but not as generous as San Franciscans, the people of Portland voted to continue to help their unemployed neighbors.

Almost as soon as the bonds infused new life into the relief effort—city and county work relief had been in abeyance since early spring—the pressures of insufficient resources mounted again. More unemployed registered, and the moneys allotted for the remainder of 1932 fell short by autumn.

Multnomah County went back to the polls once more in November. This time the voters were not so generous. They approved yet another work relief bond for $195,000 but turned down a 1.5 mill levy that could have raised approximately $530,000. Although Portlanders recognized the need for help, they were unwilling to accept a tax increase.[46]

Local officials adamantly demanded that Oregon create more jobs in highway construction and repair for the unemployed. State Highway Commissioner Leslie Scott disagreed. From August 1931 to mid-1932 the highway commission had spent $750,000 on relief employment throughout the state—almost half of it in Multnomah County—but much of the expenditure was over Scott's protests.[47] From the beginning of the year, Scott complained about the inefficiency of the unemployed. It was a violation of his public trust, he said, to use anything but contract labor, which he maintained was twice as efficient as relief workers.[48] Based on this belief, Scott suggested relief workers receive a daily wage of $1.50 rather than the prevailing wage of $3 to $4. This stirred a storm of protest throughout the state, especially among organized labor.

As the ire began to focus on Governor Meier, who quickly affirmed his support for $3 a day, Scott tendered his resignation. The governor accepted it reluctantly, then persuaded Scott to return by reaching agreement to do only contract and machine-aided labor on the highways, thus avoiding the relief wage controversy.[49] The state still used the unemployed on highway construction and repair, but only on Leslie Scott's criteria for efficiency.

The state did take one more step to respond to worsening economic conditions. In June, Governor Meier formed the Statewide Relief Council, which studied the problem. But the council only coordinated relief efforts, discouraged ill-advised ideas, and encouraged formation of county councils to assist the jobless. During the harvest season, the council also placed a labor information office at the Siskiyou Summit along the Oregon–California border. It was equipped with a tent, stove, chair, and cot to entice drivers to stop for a rest and information. The clerk staffing the "office" informed potential laborers that there was no work available in the orchards for the 1932 harvest and asked the people to head back to California to spread the word.[50]

Formerly so active in funding relief remedies, Oregon grew efficiency conscious in 1932 and fell back on a planning committee, a practice more typical of the first year of the depression. Portland regressed too. The Portland Plan, extolled as great and innovative, was little more than a give-a-job drive combined with work rotation—which other cities had long since undertaken. Nonetheless, the people of Portland and Multnomah County passed bond issues by significant margins. Mixing some outmoded approaches with generosity Portland moved through 1932, albeit with increasing difficulty.

The relief efforts of each city reached their limits and were breaking down by the onset of the fourth winter of the depression. This season promised the worst unemployment of the period, with fewer funds and less willingness to provide more. Equally dire or worse conditions existed in other cities. Boston, Philadelphia, and Chicago were insolvent by 1932. Chicago prepared to discharge teachers. Detroit, Cleveland, Cincinnati, and Birmingham were ready to curtail essential health and safety services.[51] The cities, however, were not entirely on their own. In July 1932, the Congress passed the Emergency Relief and Construction Act, which amended earlier legislation creating the Reconstruction Finance Corporation (RFC). The RFC was empowered to distribute over $1 billion for relief and public works. Hoover had vetoed an earlier bill calling for over $2 billion in aid, castigating it as a "raid on the public treasury." The relief money came as a loan, thus disturbing the federal relationship as little as possible. To local governments desperate to sell relief bonds and public work bonds the willingness of the federal government to provide even this much came as a relief. Immediately city and county officials drew up shopping lists for the governor, who could apply for as much as 15 percent of the available funds. Los Angeles, San Francisco, Seattle, and Portland prepared their appeals in less than a week, and the funds they received were essential to the survival of their relief efforts until the New Deal. City leaders in California implored Governor Rolph to ask for $45 million, the maximum allowable under law.

The RFC was a careful custodian of its funds but the two California cities were major recipients of RFC grants. The Department of Water and Power retained Joseph Scott, who nominated Hoover at the Republican Convention, and William G. McAdoo, a leading Democrat, to request $32 million to build power transmission lines from Hoover Dam. After six months of answering questions and waiting, the RFC granted $22.8 million. The RFC also purchased $40 million of bonds from the Municipal Water District for work on the Colorado River Aqueduct, which, as a self-liquidating project, did not fall under a funding limit. The county hoped for a $10 to $18 million loan for direct relief.[52] In February 1933 the RFC provided the county with $1.77 million—$900,000 for work relief and $870,000 for direct assistance—and offered more if the county put 25,000 to work with the money.[53] Relief officials promised to do so and immediately petitioned the federal agency for $4.4 million more. This time the RFC came closer to meeting the hopes, needs, and requests of local officials by granting just over $3.7 million for March and April relief. Although excruciatingly cautious with its funds, the Reconstruction Finance Corporation played an important part in the Los Angeles relief effort during the latter part of the Hoover years.

The same cautiousness on the part of the federal government plagued other cities as well. San Francisco sought help with its bridges but did not press for specific relief funds. In late April, the RFC agreed to buy $61.4 million of Oakland Bay Bridge bonds, but only after legislation, court tests, and a guarantee of state assistance. Even then the RFC bought the bonds at a quarter of a percent discount.[54] Seattle found itself entangled in the same red tape. Seattle City Light and the water department secured loans totaling $3 million but received them only after an audit. A $675,000 loan to the county for relief was also held up pending approval of a repayment plan.[55] Governor Roland Hartley made procuring funds more difficult in Washington. Staunch individualist to the end, Hartley refused to sign the necessary paperwork to draw in federal money, and, as he saw it, interference. It was fitting that Portland gained its funding the easiest of the four cities. As Senate whip, Charles McNary had brought his colleagues into line behind the legislation. Multnomah County received $1.9 million in 1932-33.[56] Though parceled out in increments, it met the community's need.

The general election of 1932, although few realized it then, marked the conclusion of local responsibility for relief. Franklin Roosevelt was the choice of the people of the West Coast metropolises. In Los Angeles the Democratic presidential vote grew 248 percent from 1928 to 1932, as the party ran especially well among new voters. Roosevelt defeated Hoover by a five-to-three margin. In San Francisco, Roosevelt made a major campaign speech on expanding the role of the federal government. The traditionally Democratic city endorsed Roosevelt and his program by a two-thirds majority. In Seattle, where the Democrats' campaign strategy was to "Hang Hoover's hide on every barbed wire fence," Roosevelt received 60 percent of the vote. Hoover polled only 40 percent of the electorate in Portland, where registered Republicans outnumbered Democrats two to one.[57]

Other Democrats also did well. In California, William G. McAdoo, a progressive Democrat, won a U.S. Senate seat by defeating Tallent Tubbs—who had beaten Samuel Shortridge, the incumbent, in the primary. Roosevelt's coattails probably gave the victory to McAdoo, who received only 43 percent of the vote in a three-way race. Bob Shuler, a prohibition advocate, was the third candidate.[58] The 1932 election in California started the Democrats toward political respectability in the state. They dominated the congressional delegation for the first time since 1896, and by 1934 Democratic registration outpaced Republican.

In Washington, Homer T. Bone won the Senate race two to one over Wesley Jones, and Clarence Martin won the governor's race decisively. Bone, a fierce advocate of public power, had switched parties. Martin, from Cheney, Washington, south of Spokane, owed his victory to strong support in eastern Washington. Marion Zioncheck, a third notable winner, went to the House from King County. Zioncheck was a Democratic firebrand who had been a lawyer for the UCL and led the recall of Mayor Edwards.

Portlanders sent Charles Martin to a second term in Congress. Joseph Carson, a Democrat attorney standing for economy in government, succeeded George Baker, who retired. Senator Frederick Steiwer, though a conservative Republican, survived Roosevelt's landslide with relative ease.

A general election in which there is such a distinct shift in party preference is an opportunity to examine the attitudes of the populace. Seattle voter registration books for 1928 and 1932 contain a wealth of information about each voter that reveals much about the city's voting patterns and explains more precisely how different groups reacted to the economic pressures besetting them.[59]

In general Seattleites were more interested in politics in 1932 than in 1928. In

1928, 70.3 percent of those who had registered voted in at least one local or national election. In 1932 this figure jumped to 82.9 percent. The 1932 elections stimulated greater interest, especially among younger citizens. Among voters in their twenties there was a 21 percent increase in voting, while 13.9 percent more thirty to forty-year-old voters went to the polls. People in certain occupational categories voted in greater numbers. Coinciding with the increase in younger voters, 35.4 percent more students cast ballots. More semiskilled laborers (up 16.2 percent), lower-level white-collar workers (salesmen and clerical employees—up 15.8 percent), and professionals (up 15.7 percent) turned out to vote. The smallest increase was among the unskilled—8.4 percent. Primarily the younger and often better educated Seattleite—and, coincidentally, the groups that paid the least attention to voting in 1928—took a greater interest in the 1932 elections. The depression stimulated those who had been complacent in the prosperity of the late twenties.

What were the characteristics of the voting shift toward the Democrats in 1932? Who provided the solid majority for Roosevelt in Seattle? Who switched party allegiance in 1932? Who continued to support their chosen party? These questions might be answered through an analysis of nine sample precincts. Of the precincts selected, two were strongly Republican in both presidential contests, five showed a Democratic majority in 1928 and 1932 (and displayed a variety of Republican percentages), in one a significant shift from a Republican majority to Democrat occurred, and one was fairly representative of the city as a whole.

The strongest factor that determined voting behavior in each precinct was occupation. In the two Republican precincts, managers and professionals predominated. Along with lower-level white-collar workers, they represented 70 to 80 percent of the registered voters in these neighborhoods. In the Democratic precincts blue-collar workers were in the majority. They included skilled, semiskilled, and unskilled workers. The order of dominance of these three categories had little impact on voting patterns.

A closer analysis reveals that the relative size of the blue-collar and white-collar population in each of the Republican precincts had an important effect on the size of the Democratic or Republican percentage in 1932. In the precinct that was heavily white-collar, Hoover lost 15 percent of his majority, as it fell to 60 percent. In the other Republican precinct, which had a higher percentage of blue-collar workers, the Republican vote dropped 23 percentage points to 56 percent.

A similar phenomenon occurred in the Democratic areas. In three of the four Democratic precincts the Republican total fell precipitously in 1932, while the Democrats either gained marginally over the 1928 majority or suffered a small loss in percentage. In the precincts where the white-collar minority was larger —usually represented by salesmen and clerical workers—the 1932 Republican minority was a bit larger than in the more solidly blue-collar precincts.

In Seattle, immigrants were also an important factor. Although not as decisive an influence as occupation, immigrant status (that is, the percentage of first-generation immigrants) in a precinct correlated with the vote. In the two Republican precincts there was a 10 to 12 percent immigrant population, whereas in the more strongly Democratic precincts the proportion was 20 percent or higher.

In 1928, but more so in 1932, Seattle immigrants, most of whom were Scandinavian, were drawn to the Democrats.

In three precincts where voting allegiance fluctuated, different patterns and new variables emerged. In one of these precincts the Democratic majority increased considerably in 1932. The outstanding feature of this precinct was the plight of the taxpayer. In 1928, 81 percent of the registered voters paid their property tax. In 1932 the figure was just over 59 percent. In this predominantly blue-collar area, taxes contributed to a dramatic jump of 27 percentage points in the Democratic vote.

In the other two "swing" precincts, where a Republican majority dissolved into a Democratic win, the largest occupational group was lower-level white-collar workers. It formed a consistent Republican constituency in other precincts but was a politically volatile group in these two neighborhoods. In addition to lower-level white-collar workers, a large number of the blue-collar workers and several people who could be classified as managers lived in these areas. It was in mixed neighborhoods such as these that Franklin Roosevelt made the greatest gains for his party in Seattle. The newest members of the Democratic coalition were most likely salesmen, secretaries, accountants, and possibly small businessmen and the more successful skilled laborers.

Another less prominent trend evident in two of the three swing precincts was a large percentage of housewives. Roosevelt may have added this group to the Democratic coalition of 1932. In the volatile Democratic precinct, one where the Democratic majority increased considerably, and in one of the swing precincts, between 35 percent and 40 percent of the resident voters were housewives. This figure is matched only by the strongest Republican precinct. After voting Republican with the rest of the nation in their first three Presidential elections, homemakers turned for the first time to the Democrats.

In summary, election results in 1928 and 1932 demonstrate both continuity and change. In 1928 Hoover captured most of the white-collar vote. Al Smith, on the other hand, was strong among the working class and many immigrants. In 1932, while many white-collar voters—especially lower-level white-collar workers—cast their ballots for Roosevelt, Hoover continued to be successful among this class as a whole and held on to islands of such voters in blue-collar precincts. Roosevelt drew only a few more blue-collar workers in 1932 than Smith had in 1928 but attracted a significantly larger number of Seattle's lower-level white-collar population.

The analysis might be cast in somewhat different terms. Herbert Hoover in both 1928 and 1932 achieved his greatest success in what could be considered upper middle-class and upper-class neighborhoods. The Democratic presidential candidates found consistent support in lower middle-class and working-class areas. By 1932, Republican support was almost nil in such precincts. The most dramatic change occurred in the middle-class neighborhoods. It was here that one could observe the largest switching of party allegiance. This was the area where the depression made its greatest impact on the politics of Seattle, and possibly on the nation.

Whether one puts it in terms of class or occupation, this analysis substantiates Samuel Lubell's belief that there was an "Al Smith revolution." That is, in Seattle many of the blue-collar workers, whom Franklin Roosevelt had supposedly forged into his new coalition in 1932, had already come into the Democratic fold by 1928, if not earlier. Al Smith had also attracted the immigrant to a great degree, despite that fact that most Seattle immigrants were Scandinavian and Protestant. Roosevelt attracted the lower-level white-collar worker, the middle class, to the Democratic party for the first time in 1932.

The election of 1932 did not, of course, mean immediate change. Cities, counties, and states planned for another winter of depression and could not make many assumptions about what might emerge once the Roosevelt administration took office in March.

The economy was not improving in 1933. A few salient statistics illustrate this. In San Francisco wholesale sales were half of what they had been in 1929; in Seattle sales had declined by two-thirds. In Los Angeles building permits for 1933 were 20 percent of what they had been in 1930. The three largest lumbermills in Portland ceased operations for the winter.[60] The greatest crisis occurred among the banks. Five times as many California banks failed in 1933 as had in the two previous years combined. In January 1933, 160 fewer banks in Washington held almost half as many deposits as in January 1929.[61] The First National Bank of Portland took over Hibernia, which had closed, reopened, but operated with difficulty. On 2 March 1933, two days before the presidential inauguration, the governors of each of the three states declared a bank holiday to keep the whole system on the West Coast from disintegrating. The economy verged on collapse.

The four cities continued their struggles to find relief in the first months of 1933. Los Angeles authorities warned of bankruptcy every time RFC funds ran low. Although San Francisco had its $6.5 million in relief bonds, Mayor Rossi once again looked to city employees as he began a search for additional revenue. Before the New Deal intervened, an election to amend the charter to allow a pay slash for municipal employees was in the works.

Despite the successful November bond elections, officials in Portland and Oregon expressed their desperation by spring because their funds were dwindling rapidly. More disheartening was the sight of Civic Emergency Committee members charging one another with playing politics. By February, Portland planned to issue scrip to pay for work relief. This would mean either that businesses would temporarily underwrite relief operations by accepting the scrip or that the workers would labor for paper until the city had sufficient funds to redeem it. The jobless endorsed the idea. Bankers and heads of utilities did not. The scrip was issued but had little impact.

A new state administration brought a change in Seattle's relief operations. On 11 January 1933 Clarence Martin, a Democrat, became governor of Washington. Under Martin's supervision the legislature quickly passed the McDonald Act, which set up the Washington Emergency Relief Administration. The state assumed responsibility for relief and authorized a $10 million bond to pay for it. This was crucial because the state supreme court struck down the state income tax —a major revenue source—voters had just approved. For a time it appeared the bonds were in jeopardy as well because the $10 million exceeded the debt limit. To gain approval for exceeding the limit, the state had to prove to the court that Washington was in a state of war or needed the funds to repel an invasion or suppress an insurrection. Five of the eight justices voting agreed with the state's attorneys that the people of Washington would not starve to death quietly and approved the bond on the basis that it would avert violence.[62] The McDonald Act not only set the foundation for administering New Deal programs in Washington but also replaced the Seattle and King County relief organization with the King County Welfare Board. This board abolished the commissary system and replaced it with vouchers that the deserving unemployed could use at participating markets.

All of this was done with only token protest from the UCL, even though the new professionally run program sealed its doom. The march on Olympia symbolized the UCL's demise as the marchers turned from the capital without even entering the city.

As self-help declined in Seattle, it emerged as a significant and recognized force in Los Angeles in early 1933. A worried *Los Angeles Times*, fearing that the self-help groups were unemployed councils filled with Reds, sent out a reporter to investigate. He assured *Times* readers that he had found the group, already grown to 177,000 members, to be engaged in a "practical undertaking."[63]

The unemployed in Portland were not as calm as the self-helpers in Los Angeles. Men at a community chest woodyard staged a week-long strike, demanding wages rather than room and board. They returned to work only after being assured their complaints would be heard. Another one-hundred-fifty unemployed, most from Multnomah County, converged on the state capital in Salem asking for a hearing.

Despite major state assistance in Washington, the prospect of bridge building in San Francisco, and a growth of benign self-help in Los Angeles, the urban West Coast was faring poorly by March 1933. These cities clearly needed more federal help to bear their burdens.

EIGHT

No Longer on Their Own

Continuities and Contrasts

Franklin Roosevelt brought a major change in the source of funding and an increase in the amount of funds provided for relief. A whole array of New Deal programs had both a direct and indirect impact on the four cities over the next two years: the Federal Emergency Relief Administration (FERA) and the Civil Works Administration (CWA) furnished relief, the Public Works Administration provided employment, the Civilian Conservation Corps brought young men to work in the West, the Home Owners Loan Corporation helped desperate homeowners, and the National Recovery Administration set prices and opened the door to labor activity, most notably the 1934 dock strikes. Obviously, the New Deal transgressed the tenet of cooperative individualism, which demanded self-reliance, private charity, and, at most, local assistance as a response to need. The Hoover administration had already broken through proscriptions with the RFC, but Roosevelt accepted a far wider responsibility for the federal government as he searched for relief and a cure for the depression.

Still, strong elements of continuity inhered in both the values that governed relief and the shape and operation of the relief programs. The preservation of the work ethic remained a central tenet—work relief was preferred to less costly direct relief. Federal funds bailed out the relief programs, but local officials still ran out of money and regularly, sometimes desperately, appealed to Washington, D.C., for an increase in assistance. The implementation of the CWA in the fall of 1933 matched the rhythms of the Hoover years. The CWA was the extra effort commonly undertaken to absorb the jobless during peak unemployment seasons. The warming of the springtime air always brought a new optimism that the worst was over. Hope emerged that no new relief effort would be needed. It was no different in April 1934. As the seasonal crisis supposedly abated, the president terminated the program. As he looked ahead to the Works Progress Administration in January 1935, Franklin Roosevelt assured the public that federal public works would continue, then signaled his belief in a key tenet of cooperative individualism: "The lessons of history confirmed by the evidence immediately before me, show conclusively that continued dependence upon relief induces a spiritual and moral disintegration fundamentally destructive to the national character. To dole out relief in this way is to administer a narcotic, a subtle destroyer of the human spirit."[1]

As Franklin Roosevelt took office on 4 March 1933, the urban West Coast and the nation had reached the nadir of the depression. It was the third day of the bank holiday on the Pacific Coast. In San Francisco—probably the least affected of the four cities—39 percent of those who had been employed in 1930 were out of work. Payrolls in Los Angeles continued their slide, dropping just over 10 percent from 1932. Only half of the Washingtonians who had been at work in 1926 were employed in 1933. In Oregon the lumber industry was at 40 percent of 1929 levels, and individual income had fallen to 55 percent of what it had been in 1929. Of the 59,000 unemployed in the state, 30,000 were registered in Portland. Property tax delinquencies in the West Coast cities, with the exception of San Francisco where the rate was between 4 and 5 percent, demonstrated the breadth of the troubles. Homeowners in Los Angeles were defaulting at the rate of almost 13 percent; 25 percent in Seattle failed to pay property taxes in 1933; and, if the *Oregonian* was correct, there was "virtually a tax strike in Multnomah County." Half of the property owners in the county were in arrears in their tax payments.[2]

The American economy thudded to the bottom in spring 1933. As the New Deal deployed its relief and recovery agencies, the West Coast began to emerge from the depth of depression. In Los Angeles manufacturing employment in 1934 was 12.6 percent above 1932 rates, and building permits increased 117 percent from 1933 to 1935. Thanks to its bridge building projects, San Francisco in 1933 had one of the largest building permit totals in its history—over $56 million. The Bay City lost over $2 million with commercial failures in 1933, but this was 63 percent less than in 1932. In the Northwest, lumber production increased steadily from 1932 to 1936, from 4 million to 8 million board feet. Building climbed in both Seattle and Portland. These were hopeful signs, but unemployment in Seattle still hovered around the 20 percent mark and even increased in 1935.[3]

New Deal strategies first quickly met the economic stasis with all the measures and resources that could be marshalled. In time, as the economy got moving again, New Deal administrators devised programs and operating guidelines that assumed state and local officials would handle their problems with progressively less federal assistance. The primary example of this swift action was the bank holiday. After governors in all three Pacific states had declared bank holidays, the business community in each city considered clearinghouse certificates—a kind of scrip based on the deposits of a group of local banks. Commercial leaders and bankers fretted over the details until the president declared the holiday over. Two institutions in Los Angeles, one in Seattle, and one in Portland remained closed as banks in the West and across the nation opened their doors to a rush of deposits. In Portland, where the scrip plan emerged prior to the bank holiday, the idea of using substitute currency as a credit measure bumbled along into August. Otherwise, the cities seemed little affected by their brush with financial collapse and moved into a year of mild economic upturn seeking sources of relief, which would now include the federal government as the major provider.

Many approaches and attitudes that had guided problem-solvers lingered on.

Private efforts still played some part in relief. Even though federal funds lessened the cities' reliance on the old standby, the community chest, campaigns went forward, with reduced goals, in 1933. Yet again the pledges fell short in each city. The goals were raised in 1934 and again went unmet. Community chest leaders speculated that state and federal relief limited contributors' generosity. The valuable public welfare operations that the member agencies conducted for the aged, the blind, and children seemed less urgent than tending to the jobless.

Individualistic self-sufficiency (perhaps, better said, stubbornness) had not yet passed away. In summer 1933 the *Seattle Post-Intelligencer* reported a widow who pushed a baby buggy through the streets collecting tin foil for resale to provide for her needs. In 1934 a child died in Seattle from eating poisonous weeds in his back yard. Investigators discovered that the family had not eaten in two days —a half-full can of black pepper was the only food in the pantry. The father, a shoemaker who had been unemployed for a year, explained that he did not know how to go about getting on relief.

With the infusion of federal aid the need for self-help activities among the unemployed should have diminished. The movement was waning in Seattle but had just gotten underway in Southern California in 1932. By 1934 estimates of group membership ranged up to 250,000—mostly concentrated in the Southland. In June 1933, 77 percent of the members of California self-help groups were from the Los Angeles area.[4] Through the first part of 1934 the Unemployed Cooperative Relief Association (UCRA), the main coordinating body, was well accepted. Local, state, and federal agencies helped fund self-help efforts—the Federal Emergency Relief Administration contributed $164,600 to Los Angeles groups between October 1933 and December 1934.[5] The self-help elements also helped transform conservative Southern California into the major support base for Upton Sinclair. The groups took a significant part in the 1934 End Poverty In California (EPIC) campaign and gained the radical label for themselves.

Other organizations pushed anything from supplementing relief to restructuring the economy. Perhaps the strongest were the Utopians, a secretive group that espoused the ideal of production for consumption as a substitute for the profit system. Based in Los Angeles, this movement claimed a following of some 500,000 at its height in 1934.[6] Since production for use was a central plank in his EPIC platform, Sinclair found much support among Utopians. Long Beach was the home of Dr. Francis Townsend, progenitor of the Townsend Plan pension for the elderly. Most western politicians, especially those from the Los Angeles area, supported it as an article of faith.

While these and other proposed structural solutions gained currency during the period, most voters opted for less dramatic change. The West had clearly voted for change in 1932. Matters were not so clear at the state level in 1932 and 1933. In California the Democrats, only 20 percent of the electorate in 1930, were on their way to becoming the majority party by 1934.[7] Republicans, however, would continue to dominate Sacramento. James Rolph, then Frank Merriam, who defeated Sinclair in 1934, gave Republicans control of the governor's chair until 1938. The Democrats did not attain a simultaneous majority in both houses of the state legislature until 1958. Rolph's budget for 1933–35 demonstrated his continued fiscal conservatism in the face of depression. It was $24 million less than his 1931–33 budget.[8] Later, Merriam, though somewhat more receptive to the idea that the state government should take a larger responsibility for relief, feared the consequences of a society overly dependent on government aid.

At the municipal level, Mayor Angelo Rossi continued to guide San Francisco into the New Deal years. In the June 1933 city election Los Angeles voters turned out Mayor Porter and installed County Commissioner Frank Shaw, who had parlayed his prominence in the relief program into the mayor's position. Demonstrating that he understood the new relationships, Shaw made frequent trips to Washington, D.C., seeking alliance with Franklin Roosevelt, and requested the FERA to revise upward its unemployment statistics for Los Angeles.[9]

More evident change occurred in Washington with the defeat of Roland Hartley. Unemployment relief was Clarence Martin's top campaign promise. Democrat Martin had already revamped Washington's relief structure by the time federal assistance began to arrive.

In Oregon, Julius Meier served until 1934, when he decided not to run for reelection. Given his progressive position the state probably had a more liberal administration than it would have had under a Democrat. Roosevelt realized this. By 1934 Republicans held fifteen of nineteen Civil Works Administration posts in Multnomah County.[10] As it turned out, Charles Martin, who was elected governor in 1934 as a Roosevelt supporter, became a vocal, conservative opponent of New Deal policy.

Several of the senators from the Pacific Coast were ready, even eager, to work with the Democratic administration. Progressive Republican Hiram Johnson of California endorsed Roosevelt in 1932, and Charles McNary and Frederick Steiwer, Republicans of Oregon, both lobbied Roosevelt for federal hydroelectric projects. McNary occupied the central, but now less significant, position of Republican leader of the Senate. He supported most New Deal legislation and agencies except the Federal Emergency Relief Administration, which he believed extended direct relief too liberally. Mainly McNary defended, to their own party, senators who supported New Deal initiatives as he did. Roosevelt appreciated McNary's willingness to lead the Republicans to the position of bystanders and felt more obligated to see that the Northwest got its dams. Steiwer, perpetually concerned about the expansion of the federal government, nonetheless supported much legislation during the Hundred Days, including the FERA. Later he voted against the Works Progress Administration, maintaining it seemed less like relief and more resembled Tammany Hall buying votes. In Washington State, C. C. Dill and Homer Bone, both progressive Democrats, campaigned for public power. Compelled by the desperate situation, these leaders, Republican and Democrat, holding national, state, or local office cooperated with the new president—even when this meant the creation of a new federal relationship.

Neither the old responses to unemployment nor newer, more radical, schemes had much part in solving the relief problem. At the local level the community chest, self-help, and less traditional solutions made little difference. More important, public sources of assistance, except in Washington, proved less than adequate. The depression continued to narrow the tax base, while it sapped the will of the taxpayer. In Los Angeles property valuations and the tax levy continued to drop through 1935. City taxes for 1934–35 were $2.5 million lower than 1933–34 and $10 million less than 1931–32. Over the three-year period property values and per capita taxes dropped about 35 percent. A report to the city council revealed that Los Angeles had the lowest tax rate for general services of cities over 300,000 population in the United States.[11] The report appeared to be largely self-congratulatory, but it pointed up the fact that a city with a high rate of unemployment—the Los Angeles unemployment rate stood at 16.4 percent, compared to a state average of 13.2 percent—was one of the most fiscally conservative cities in the nation.[12] Depending on the nature of the city's reserve fund, this conservatism was downright penuriousness. One author has suggested the $3 to $6 million stashed away in the city's reserve fund was available for relief and other necessities, but Mayor Porter and a city report maintained the reserve was encumbered. It was merely set aside to keep the city on a cash basis until tax collections came in and for "meeting contingencies as they might arise."[13] Whatever the case, Los Angeles was unwilling to tax or to spend an inordinate amount of its own resources in the first half of the 1930s.

Both the people and the government of San Francisco were more generous, but frugality marked their efforts as well. San Francisco reduced disbursements to the unemployed by $9 million from 1932 to 1933 and then restored $2 million.[14] In 1934 the board of supervisors rescinded the cuts made in city employees' wages. The vote on the bond issue of 1933 probably best measures San Franciscans' willingness to assume a continuing part in the local relief effort. Thirteen issues totaling $35 million were on the ballot. If approved, the Public Works Administration would purchase the bonds and subsidize the projects up to 30 percent. Voters ratified five of the projects, worth $20 million. San Franciscans continued to demonstrate a willingness to solve their problems.

Seattle's budget and finances came under several pressures. The 40 mill tax limit Washington voters approved in 1932 was the most severe. Mayor John Dore continually pushed for a leaner budget. The results, after much wrangling in the city council, were progressively lower tax levies. By 1934, Seattleites paid city taxes at half the rate they had in 1931—a $6 million reduction.[15] Some city council finagling contributed to this. The council upped anticipated revenue from nontax levy sources each year to reduce the taxpayers' burden. Yearly deficits, nearly $800,000 in 1935, were neatly rolled over into the next year's budget.[16] Matters were no better for King County. Property valuations fell until 1935. The county clearly relied on state and federal aid as it slashed the relief budget in 1934 from a preliminary $1.5 million to $0.4 million—a 71.4 percent cut. This kind of hewing at budget figures showed up in the tax levy, which decreased $1.9 million in 1934.[17]

The trend was the same in Portland. Valuations and the city budget decreased from 1931 through 1934. Tax delinquencies averaged over 25 percent during the period.[18] Portland was closer to the brink than the other cities when in August 1933 local banks agreed to help fund city pay checks if Portland promised a balanced budget and an acceptable reimbursement plan.[19] Even though administrators in the other cities might not have had to answer so directly to their bankers, times continued tight for city finances well into the 1930s. But by the mid-1930s city and county budget makers no longer tested the will of their taxpayers, and the search for revenue resources was less frantic.

Two of the three states initially displayed little resolve in assisting the unemployed. California's budget problems paralleled those of the cities. Deficits and the inability to increase revenues led to state warrants in lieu of paychecks by the end of 1933. California, however, assumed a progressively greater responsibility. Voters approved a $20 million employment bond in 1933, and the legislature voted $24 million to assist the unemployable indigent when federal rules required it.

Oregon experienced the greatest difficulties. In mid-1933 Highway Commissioner Leslie Scott had predicted calamity as he guarded highway funds and called for a sales tax. "If you turn down the second proposed sales tax," Scott threatened Oregonians, "you will have to starve." Oregonians preferred anything to a sales tax. By 1934 Governor Julius Meier declared, "Oregon is dead broke."[20] Neither Scott nor Meier exaggerated much. The state supreme court approved the use of warrants in March 1933, and in the fall Meier summoned a special legislative session to meet federal demands on the state to contribute to relief. Legislators had already considered at least ten separate revenue sources in a regular session but could not agree. Finally, in November, Oregon made the sale of liquor a state-operated monopoly and earmarked the profit and taxes of $3 to $4 million to the required matching fund.[21] Despite Meier's doleful statement of 1934, this assured federal funds until the next biennium.

Washington, under Governor Clarence Martin, was on its way to a solution of relief problems before Roosevelt's inauguration, although it did not find the task easier than the other two states. In his inaugural address Martin accepted state responsibility for relief and suggested ways in which that need could be met. He included a call to set aside the rugged individualism of his predecessor.[22] When the state supreme court struck down the income tax, the legislature quickly approved a $10 million state bond for relief and a business and occupation tax to make up for the lost revenue. By August the state marketed the first bonds.

The new federal–state–local relationship was more welcomed than feared. Concerns about meeting needs had long since replaced anxiety over loss of local control. Still there were problems of coordination, of compliance with funding formulas, and of obtaining satisfactory financial assistance. Except in Washington, only the carrot of federal funds could elicit extensive state relief assistance. Throughout the early years of the New Deal Harry Hopkins, head of the Federal Emergency Relief Administration, and others continually reminded, cajoled, and threatened local and state leaders that the continuation of federal relief and construction project funds depended on the states' bearing their responsibility. Some programs required that the states provide a three-quarter share. What impact did increased resources and goading have on relief programs at the local level? Did a new philosophy or strategy of relief emerge? How much authority did local decision-makers retain?

Major elements of the relief structure did not change. The new source of funds, however, meant that the ultimate oversight of programs did. From 1933 to the advent of the Works Progress Administration in 1935 unemployment relief went through three phases. The first, affected by the urgency of the situation, rushed help to the needy and set up the unprecedented relationships. The Reconstruction Finance Corporation and the Federal Emergency Relief Administration provided federal funds and guided state emergency relief administrations in this phase. The provision of direct relief with some work relief continued until November 1933 when the Roosevelt administration realized that the Public Works Administration was not planning and funding construction projects as rapidly as necessary. The government instituted the Civilian Works Administration (CWA) to provide more work relief in the slack winter season—by now a classic depression response. Early in 1934, President Roosevelt announced the CWA would terminate in March, the end of the period of low employment. This caught a number of local officials off guard. For a brief period it was unclear how relief would be conducted or whether federal aid would be as extensive as it was during the CWA days. April 1934 to May 1935, the third phase of early relief, was a time of anxiety for local officials. Each month the federal government granted a relief stipend to each state based on the administration's sense of current need and an assessment of how well the state had carried its share of the relief responsibility in previous months. Much of the time the recipients judged the grant insufficient. Finally, in spring 1935, Congress created the Works Progress Administration (WPA), which helped rationalize the process by providing purely work relief (unlike the FERA) based on carefully planned projects (unlike the CWA).

Statistics provide a sense of the impact of federal help on local efforts. They also furnish a background against which the three phases of relief may be examined to determine the extent of continuity and change from the Hoover years to the early Roosevelt years. On the West Coast the federal share of relief from 1933 to 1935 was at least 64 percent. Among the three states, Oregon depended most on federal assistance. The national government provided 87.6 percent of the state's relief in 1933–34. Over the three-year period federal funds for all projects and programs flowed into cities, counties, or states at the following levels:[23]

Time Period	Recipient	Amount of Federal Relief (millions)	Federal % of All Relief
July 1933–Dec. 1935	City of Los Angeles	$65.1	65.0
July 1933–Dec. 1935	City & County of S.F.	16.8	63.9
Jan. 1933–Apr. 1935	King County, Wash.	10.0 (est.)	66.0 (est.)
1933–34	State of Oregon	13.4	87.6
1933–34	Multnomah County, Ore.	9.1	92.0

The states and communities, however, did not simply abandon their responsibility, allowing federal assistance to fill the sizable shortfall in relief. The national government assumed a major role so quickly because local authorities faced a need they could not fill. Further, because the national administration pressed local leaders hard to take a large part in providing relief, cities and counties could not drop their responsibility entirely.

In the first phase of the relief effort the main goal was to provide for the needy in the most efficient, rapid manner possible. Fragmentary figures indicate that relief rolls were shrinking in 1933 until the fall, but the numbers seeking help remained high. One study estimated Los Angeles unemployment at 41.6 percent but San Francisco's at 11.5 percent. After major cuts in King County relief rosters during the summer of 1933, over 45,000 remained on relief.[24]

For the first two months of the new administration, the RFC continued to be the source of federal funds. When, in early May, Congress set up the Federal Emergency Relief Administration, the legislation shifted the mandate for relief from the counties to the federal government:

> That the Congress hereby declares that the present economic depression has created a serious emergency, due to widespread unemployment and increasing inadequacy of State and local relief funds, resulting in the existing or threatened deprivation of a considerable number of families and individuals of the necessities of life, and making it imperative that the Federal Government cooperate more effectively with the several States . . . in furnishing relief to their needy and distressed people.[25]

The word *cooperate* indicates the principle of local authority had not been entirely abandoned. Ideally, each state was to receive one dollar in federal funds for every three dollars it spent on relief. More realistically, Congress prescribed that half of the FERA appropriation could be dispensed without restriction.

With federal assistance came a new structure of supervision. Each state created a relief body. The State Emergency Relief Administration (SERA) in California and Washington and the State Relief Commission (SRC) in Oregon were to oversee the process. States took unemployment relief out of the hands of private groups like the community chest and gave it to the state relief agency. This body, in turn, supervised county efforts. Washington, for example, established county welfare boards headed by a majority of SERA appointees. As a result, the local community still administered relief, but the state relief office determined the amount of money that would go to any county. This shift in authority sometimes engendered friction between state and local administrators, but centralization of relief usually made the welfare program more efficient.

The form of relief changed little. Recipients probably rarely noticed the shift in the source of funds. All four communities supplied food and fuel. Los Angeles used FERA funds to provide shelter; Seattle opted against housing, preferring to find new accommodations for anyone who was evicted. The states still ruled on eligibility. In Washington, for example, only the destitute gained help, so investigators questioned applicants about their savings, loans, insurance policies, and the ability of relatives to provide support. Direct relief and work relief continued to be the mainstays of the programs, although self-help still played a small part. In California the federal government provided grants to cooperatives. In Washington subsistence farming in Seattle and fruit picking in the countryside continued until August 1933, when the director of the King County Board of Relief declared the end of public support for self-help. Two King County commissioners protested the decision, but the ruling, along with the shutdown of the commissary system in February, meant the end of any UCL influence in the relief effort.

Though the source of funds changed, the funding crunch continued in 1933. The appeals of desperate administrators for more relief money were reminiscent of the regular shortfalls of the Hoover years. The rule that the federal government would grant one-third of the amount the state had provided for relief over the past month or two was at the heart of the difficulty. In 1933 if a state reduced its relief expenditure, it was not a sign of better times and decreased need. Instead it meant that the unemployed were receiving inadequate relief from the state and, in the months to come, could expect less help from the federal government. The problem fed on itself. The less a state spent, the less it got. On the West Coast, however, this matching provision was more of a guideline than a regulation. Harry Hopkins or his regional representative would threaten a reduced grant—or even suspension of federal money—if the state had failed to supply relief at the rate it had promised. After some tension, the FERA would announce that assistance would be forthcoming. Despite its threats, the federal government picked up 76 percent of the relief bill in Washington and 89 percent of Oregon's tab in 1933.[26]

Even with this generous outlay, state administrators found their new relationship with the federal government burdensome. In Washington Charles Ernst, the former Seattle DRO chief who had become the SERA director, pleaded with Hopkins in mid-summer to provide federal help in excess of the federal guidelines that demanded states provide matching funds. Hopkins refused. Ernst appealed, asking that the April through June period be used as the basis for funding rather than the January through March quarter since Washington had spent more on relief in the later period. Hopkins remained adamant. Finally, after denying all expenditure for a month, Hopkins relented, allowing Washington an extra measure of FERA funds in return for a promise that the state would sell relief bonds to raise its fair share.[27]

In Oregon traditional political battles were renewed over the search for sufficient funds to qualify for federal help. The *Oregon Voter*, a periodical publication devoted to state politics, suggested the rest of Oregon might let Portland, with its high relief load, find its own matching funds. The editor thought a 10 percent sales tax might do it—a facetious suggestion in a state hidebound in opposition to any sales tax.[28]

California's $20 million relief bond permitted it to meet its obligations more readily. The state legislature passed the bond in April, the voters endorsed it in June, and the bond money began to flow into the counties by October 1933. Technically this money was only a loan to the counties, to be repaid through local motor vehicle fuel tax collections, but it was a boon to the relief effort. Los Angeles County received $12.3 million and San Francisco got $2 million before the bond was exhausted in September 1934.[29]

Another basic difficulty remained constant in 1933 and 1934. Inefficiency and corruption did not disappear with federal assistance. The most serious case of malfeasance may have occurred in Seattle, where Benjamin Hayes, the King County relief director, was indicted for embezzlement. Hayes and J. H. Morris, a county welfare officer, were found guilty of receiving kickbacks from county purchases of firewood.

In Los Angeles a study charged that a lack of systematic investigation and tardiness in completing paperwork were crippling the relief effort. Workers replied that the relief load was too large to handle in an orderly fashion.[30] Transferring all relief responsibility to the County Welfare Bureau and away from the county Department of Employment Stabilization—the agency that Councilman Frank Shaw established clearly for his own political benefit—solved a number of problems.[31]

In 1934 it seemed possible that accusations emanating in Los Angeles would send most of the regional leadership of the CWA to jail. Pierce Williams, the FERA regional director; R. C. Branion, California head; and ten others were indicted in April 1934 on several counts including conspiracy to defraud the government. The main complaints grew out of the fact the CWA in Los Angeles paid several thousand men for doing no work for a week or two. Because no tools were available, the administrators could not send the men out to labor but paid them from CWA funds nonetheless. The case created sensational headlines for over seven months and, undoubtedly, reenforced the stereotype of the CWA held by many. Finally, most of the cases were dismissed. Only three local supervisors were convicted for taking bribes—for selecting certain trucks and drivers for hire.[32]

A lapse in judgment by Los Angeles work relief foremen resulted in tragedy. In October 1933 relief workers helped fight a major fire in Griffith Park. Twenty-nine lost their lives as the wind shifted and fire swept over them. Experienced fire fighters would not have been caught in the hazardous position.[33]

In addition to these serious problems, numerous smaller controversies arose. As in the Hoover years, Adolph Uhl in San Francisco pressed for reduced expenditures for all city services, including relief. Investigators discovered individuals with bank accounts in excess of $1,000 taking relief in the Bay City. In Seattle the deputy prosecutor claimed the price of relief meals was 30 percent higher than what he could find in cafes near his office. More funds and larger programs surely brought problems, but corruption and inefficiency probably were reduced by the professional administration that developed as part of federal supervision. Nonetheless, officials often seemed overmatched and less than efficient in both the early New Deal and the Hoover years. There were always those who sought personal gain at the expense of the programs for the needy.

As the winter of 1933–34 approached, unemployment once again threatened to overwhelm the existing relief system. Local provisions in the four cities constantly fell short of the matching requirement, and relief resources may have been inadequate even with federal funds. During the Hoover years, the cities had always attempted to expand their resources in the fall and winter to care for the added numbers of seasonally unemployed. Congress, facing the same seasonal decline, created the CWA in November to provide only work relief. Superseding all other work relief, it aimed at putting as many people to work as quickly as possible on any projects available. Raymond Wilcox, the state CWA administrator in Oregon, made the goal clear as he announced, "There must be speed, speed, and yet more speed. This program is designed for relief. It must be relief."[34] A report on CWA projects in Portland pointed out: "The money allotted to each project is used to the best advantage. Not only to relieve the unemployment situation, by paying a fair wage to all workers, but also gives to the city those projects most desirable to public needs [sic]."[35]

The new program had an immediate impact. Fifteen thousand were at work in King County by mid-December. A portion of the 10,000 expected to be at work in Portland were on the job by the first week of December. Ultimately, the CWA employed over 17,000 in San Francisco and 58,000 in Los Angeles.[36] Because it took men, and some women, off the relief rolls, most officials could agree with the director of Portland's Public Employment Bureau who extolled the CWA as, "This magnificent movement."[37] The projects were surely short term and mundane—digging, painting, clearing brush, repairing streets—but men were at work. During the winter of 1933–34 each city relaxed a bit in the hope that the relief problem had become more manageable. And because the solution was work relief, the outcome was more palatable.

But problems remained. The Los Angeles Times, critical of the work ethic of CWA reliefers, complained that supervision was lax, wheelbarrows and shovels tended to be half full; and many men saw the work more as a right than an opportunity. A reporter quoted one worker as saying, "Why should I tear my shirt? We had it comin' to us."[38]

While reports of shirkers cropped up elsewhere, an even more serious problem was inefficiency at the administrative level. The CWA program was not that much different from previous work relief programs, but it was carried out on a larger scale and implemented with haste. Charges of favoritism in hiring, problems of drawing workers from the general population rather than from relief roles, and the inability to fill positions with qualified men plagued CWA operations in each city. Despite a host of allegations, charges, and rumors of corruption, the firewood fraud in Seattle and the truck-hiring kickbacks in Los Angeles were the only major proven cases of criminal negligence.

Actually, the major problem with the CWA was its duration. Local administrators were surprised when the Roosevelt administration announced in early 1934 that the CWA would be phased out in March. An energy-sapping cycle of desperation, discovery of sufficient funds, depletion of those funds, and desperation had been going on for four years. The cycle had turned again. Relief administrators once more were unsure about the source of support for their programs after March 1934.[39] CWA officials in Washington, D.C., eased some of the stress by extending the deadline to the first of May and assuring that some unfinished projects would continue under the FERA's work division. The gradual winding down made matters only marginally easier. The CWA had not absorbed all able-bodied men from the relief rolls, and those lists expanded as CWA projects concluded. As CWA funds dwindled, federal assistance did not increase correspondingly to help the state emergency relief administrations. In the face of announcements of 17,000 workers laid off government projects in Los Angeles, 3,000 in Seattle, and 5,000 in Portland, there was puzzlement about when federal spending might shift to help the SERAs and whether federal help would ever approach the levels of the previous year.

In the difficult period of March and April 1934, state relief administrations reorganized to promote more centralized state control and greater efficiency. Officials in California and the state of Washington announced they were restructuring for continued unemployment. The reconstituted organizations—the SERAs in California and Oregon and the Washington Emergency Relief Administration—took complete charge of all emergency relief and instructed the counties to administer relief only to those physically and mentally unable to work. For the first time since the depression began the counties resumed their traditional roles of assisting only the incapacitated. Despite federal assistance pouring into the states for a year or more, this was the first major modification in the structure of relief. The FERA had set aside private agencies, but now an administrative division was made between ongoing welfare and emergency relief. Federal support had made possible a permanent institution of long-term "emergency" relief, the SERA. In California, the SERA took control of all state and federal money. Although the state organizations supplied a good deal of direct relief, they were committed to work relief. White-collar as well as blue-collar jobs were available to the unemployed. Washington supported a writers' project. In Oregon, the SERA replaced the CWA and carried on many of its unfinished projects. Portland, for example, made no discernible change in the organization, reports, or the design of the relief projects begun under CWA supervision when the SERA stepped in.

Formidable challenges faced the new agencies. In Los Angeles relief lists and costs grew by over half from July 1934 to January 1935. Until the city and county finally took responsibility for only the unemployable, San Francisco fought state centralization. Mayor Rossi in particular complained about losing direct contact with Washington, D.C., and charged SERA with wasteful administrative duplication. During the summer, the city's demand for greater control over relief led to a crisis. The federal government refused to grant any relief funds until San Francisco allowed a nonpartisan, nonpolitical citizens' board to oversee the relief program. With its own funds running out, the board of supervisors acceded, allowing the SERA to administer relief projects, while San Francisco provided relief to those unable to work.[40] In Oregon and Washington relief officials had to weather investigations that seemed mainly political in motivation. The Oregon Democratic Central Committee called the relief effort badly managed and prone to favoritism and nepotism. The report castigated the administrators, a majority of whom were Republican, as immature and inexperienced.[41] In Washington a panel of investigators concluded, "there is substantial evidence of conspiracy between the Washington Emergency Relief Administration and various social service organizations to continue this relief set-up for the purpose of furthering their own interest."[42] Nothing beyond the reports came out of the investigations.

The problem from the onset of the depression had been insufficient funds. It was still true in 1934. A Washington FERA Works Division report lamented that the amount of work relief fell short during the period between the end of the CWA and the advent of the WPA.[43] King County could supply neither rent nor medical assistance, although the federal government mandated both. Harry Hopkins threatened Oregon in early summer with termination of federal funds if the state failed to provide its share. He did not follow through, and the state received money throughout the year. By the summer of 1934 both California cities encountered severe fiscal problems. Federal and local contributions were the mainstays of the relief program for much of 1934, but by August these sources were insufficient. Local authorities pressed the state legislature to help. The legislature responded with a $24 million bond issue to be given—not loaned— for relief beginning in March 1935. Although the wait must have seemed interminable, it was fortunate that funds were available in March. Early in 1935 Congress held up a $4.88 billion appropriation for the WPA. This, combined with implementation delays, produced a two-month gap in federal funding from March to May. California released the state bond money at an opportune time.

As President Roosevelt noted when he recommended a massive federal public works program in January 1935, the purpose of the WPA was to move the federal government out of the relief business. No longer would the federal government "dole" out relief, "that narcotic" and "subtle destroyer of the human spirit." The president, whom Hoover and others of like mind accused of weakening the moral fiber of America, remained as committed to the work ethic ideal as his predecessor. It is ironic that, if anything, Roosevelt, by pragmatically altering the federal relationship to provide more adequate relief to the unemployed, did more than Hoover to save elements of traditional values. Once a system of federally underwritten work relief was in place, those who could would work. Direct relief would be cut to such a level that private and local agencies could resume their historic task of serving the unemployable. That the ideal of cooperative individualism could not and did not work out to the fullest is important, but the ideal still informed the restructured operation of relief.

The first two years of the New Deal saw the provision of assistance at the local level evolve. In the early going the RFC and the FERA rushed funding to local authorities. Private agencies returned to their original roles of providing help to their specific clientele, and control over public relief became more centralized at the state level. The CWA represented a hurried response to the needs of the first winter of the New Deal. Decision-making power slid out of the hands of local officials, but the form and conduct of the program was little different from earlier winter work relief programs in the western cities. With the conclusion of the CWA, tendencies toward institutionalizing what continued to be referred to as emergency relief became stronger. By 1934 the SERA had taken full responsibility for coordinating direct relief and work relief, while county welfare returned to aiding invalids and the infirm. The Works Progress Administration was the final step in the transformation of relief. In theory, the WPA was a great expansion of public works, making the federal government a more important employer in the economy. But the federal government was not actually out of the relief business, as Roosevelt suggested. It was getting out of only the direct relief business. Washington, D.C., supplied work relief in a national program, while the states assumed responsibility for direct relief—and Roosevelt's Hoover-like concern for the national individual ethos could be assuaged. To a degree the strategy worked. The WPA and improving economic conditions reduced the numbers of jobless. But state welfare officials in the West continued to complain into 1936 that, as under Hoover, the efforts fell short.

Similarities existed between Hoover-era relief and New Deal relief at the local level: the structure was much the same, the periodic shortfalls in funding and scrambles to come up with new funding were similar; and, despite the obvious shift in the source of funding, the philosophic opposition to direct relief—especially a federal dole—remained.

But the Roosevelt administration was able and willing to do more than fund local relief. Even as Harold Ickes of the Public Works Administration (PWA) was, in the eyes of westerners, living up to his reputation of curmudgeon, the PWA furthered or initiated several undertakings. Each city identified projects eligible for PWA loans and grants. The attitude in Portland seemed typical. A board of education member warned that "Ye Federal Gift Shoppe" may not be open long, so the board should get its wishes in soon. The *Oregonian* noted during a later round of applications that Portland was including in its request "every type of project it could think of or had been under consideration for the past twenty years."[44] The result of such thinking was predictable. Portland began its deliberations by considering $63 million in plans. Only slightly more modestly, Los Angeles and San Francisco prepared requests for $23 million each. Seattle asked for $10 million.[45] The PWA hardly fulfilled such hopes, but through 1933 and 1934 public works money constantly flowed into the four cities for highways, buildings, sewers, and various other projects.

This money exceeded anything local or state work relief directors dreamed of during the Hoover years, but the difference lay in funding for major projects. What made progressive Republicans in the Northwest progressive was their commitment to public power. In a campaign speech in Portland in 1932, Franklin Roosevelt strongly endorsed this ideal. With Northwest federal office holders— especially Charles McNary, Frederick Steiwer, and Charles Martin from Oregon and C. C. Dill from Washington—lobbying him, Roosevelt authorized major hydroelectric dams on the Columbia River at Bonneville, near Portland, and Grand Coulee, in eastern Washington. Harold Ickes groused about the Northwest getting more than its fair share of PWA expenditures, but this was a tremendous boost to employment in the two states, which far exceeded any program of the Hoover years. By the end of 1933 the two Northwest states had received $43 million from the PWA, including $35 million for the two dams.[46] The Reconstruction Finance Corporation, another source of major public works in the West, helped get construction started on the bridges across San Francisco Bay and provided funds for Hoover Dam on the Colorado River. It continued to underwrite these projects well into the New Deal.

The newly unleashed spending power of the federal government furnished relief in other areas. The Federal Transient Service assumed responsibility for the homeless from the private charities that had been providing assistance. Until it ceased operation in 1935, the Transient Service took a good deal of economic and psychological pressure off the communities. For example, it was only after the Transient Service had ceased that Los Angeles erected its infamous bum blockade at state entry points.

The impact of the Civilian Conservation Corps (CCC) was a little different in the West than in other parts of the nation. The CCC drew young men out of western cities, but it was the arrival of corps recruits that westerners most noticed. Some saw a bonanza in the addition of paid consumers entering the local economies. Others feared the young men might stay in the region and become a relief burden when they left the CCC. After the first groups arrived, CCC members had little impact on the economy, the communities, or the consciousness of westerners.

The Home Owners' Loan Corporation (HOLC) eased anxieties by refinancing mortgages. Five hundred people applied the first day in Portland. The HOLC loaned some $37 million to over 20,000 homeowners in Washington by 1936.[47] The federal government also offered aid to self-help groups, to working women, to young men and women on relief seeking higher education, and to those who wanted to get back to the land and set up a farm. These programs not only provided a major infusion of funds but also touched more lives—and surely changed more lives—than would have seemed possible in the Hoover years.

The National Recovery Administration (NRA) was the major attempt at restoring the national economic balance. This move to manage, or at least guide, the economy had no parallel in the Hoover years. Initially, West Coast chambers of commerce welcomed NRA planning enthusiastically. They sponsored rallies and declared themselves conduits of information. California created a similar California Recovery Administration to boost the economy. In Los Angeles, Seattle, and Portland, the NRA was given credit for economic improvement.

From newspaper reports, radicalism and anything the middle class perceived as incidence of radical activity remained constant from the early 1930s into 1934. Officials in each of the four cities believed Communists operated in their communities. In Los Angeles the Unemployed Cooperative Relief Association was believed to be a Communist organization. Thirty-five organizations had registered as Communist in San Francisco. Seattle's UCL, with a membership of only 1,000 by 1934, was Communist-led, and Portland hired an infiltrator to control radicalism. The demonstrations and riots that occurred during the first two years of the New Deal were similar to those that had taken place earlier. Relief workers went on strike against low wages and for cash instead of food vouchers for their work; friends, neighbors, and sympathizers gathered to oppose evictions; "Communists" importuned city councils for more relief or unemployment insurance; and various groups staged hunger marches on May Day and other occasions.

But it was the NRA, which proved a double-edged sword, that led to violence on the West Coast. Under Section 7(a) of the National Recovery Act, which provided for collective bargaining, San Francisco dock workers selected the International Longshoremens' Association as their representative. In March 1934, when organized dock workers threatened a strike along the West Coast, President Roosevelt pushed the union and management into arbitration. This put off a walk-out for two months. By May the disagreements were not resolved, and the longshoremen went on strike all along the coast. In general the strike revolved around how much power 7(a) gave the union. Specifically, the issue at stake was control of the hiring halls. Before it was over, the walkout turned violent in all four cities. Strikebreakers, police attacks, and riots came and went during the early summer of 1934. In San Francisco the AF of L staged a brief general strike across the city. Finally, after lost lives and lost business the strike was settled at the end of July. The two parties agreed on a standardized wage scale and work week, management rehired the strikers and agreed to joint administration of the hiring halls. The latter probably meant essentially union control. That the federal government assisted workingmen to find their voice was a distinct change in each of the cities.

By the end of the second year of the New Deal, many things had changed or were changing on the West Coast. There was continuity as well, and some things settled back into old patterns. The federal government was a fixture of the relief effort, but the WPA was not the final solution. Large numbers of unemployed remained to be served. Much more money and many more programs helped those in need, but the allegiance to work relief, not direct relief, still bespoke an earlier ethic. In sum, the New Deal had indeed brought changes to the West, yet, just as surely, subtle but significant elements of the past remained.

Epilogue

What is to be made, then, of the early years of the depression in urban America? What ideals guided the local response? What factors controlled it? How did the depression, and coping with it, change attitudes and values at the grass roots? The case studies of the four largest West Coast cities suggest answers to these questions. The history of the urban West Coast during the Hoover years, moreover, is in general—and often specifically—the account of the urban nation during these trying years. The stories of Los Angeles, San Francisco, Seattle, and Portland represent well the history of the rest of the nation, and the generalizations that derive from the study of the four cities apply not only to them, but tell the story, at least in its main contours, of cities large and small throughout the United States.

The Hoover years of the Great Depression were a tremendously trying time for everyone in America. Old values were tested and found wanting. The resources of the local governments were exhausted by 1933. Americans not only wanted, but also desperately needed, a new political economy—at least they perceived a need for major modifications to the old federal relationships. Although most Americans came to this conclusion in 1932 and, hoping for something different, elected Franklin Roosevelt, few in 1929 or 1930 would have seriously considered the kinds of changes the New Deal brought about.

In the first year after the crash scarcely anyone on the West Coast believed their city was in a severe economic slump, much less entering a depression. But the depression was affecting the country, even the supposedly geographically insulated West, earlier than most residents cared to acknowledge. Moreover, at its full fury, the depression hit even harder in the West and throughout the nation than many historians thought. The unemployment rate in all four cities was probably closer to one-third than one-quarter by 1932, and in Seattle and Portland the rate must have been even higher.

The citizens, both employed and unemployed, at first acted with remarkable fortitude, almost stolidly. The unemployed spoke up but did not riot. The exception of Los Angeles owes as much or more to the Red Squad than the militancy of the jobless. The same kinds of people marched and demonstrated in the other three cities, but violence flared only when authorities used force.

The reason for both the relative serenity among the jobless and a lack of vigor among local leaders in responding to the needs of their people can be traced to their long-held values regarding the individual and the role of public institutions in American society. Herbert Hoover matched the outlook of the nation—certainly the West Coast—as he called for cooperative individualism. The sense of individual responsibility and the well-inculcated ideal of self-reliance left the jobless without an external focus for their frustrations, spawned the Unemployed Citizens' League, placed boundaries around the scope of the relief response, and kept the inadequacy of relief efforts from generating turmoil and rage. The sense of responsibility and neighborliness moved people to oversubscribe the community chest in 1931 and approve in 1932 large bond issues in San Francisco, Portland, and Seattle.

The combined public and private responses of 1930, and 1931 particularly, also illustrate the principles of cooperative individualism. Each of the four cities did little to meet the needs of its citizens until late 1930 (1931 for Seattle). Besides a confidence in the capitalist cycle, the belief that people were responsible for their own welfare helps explain this. Even if a remarkable level of unemployment was discerned, it was not yet time to respond, most believed, because people could and should take care of themselves. Once a relief effort got under way it was, wherever possible, in the form of work relief, not a dole. Administrators were concerned that direct relief would destroy an individual's self-worth and thereby threaten a basic American value. The dependence on private approaches through 1931 demonstrates a continuing unwillingness and unreadiness for public intervention. The unreadiness was because of a long-time loyalty to self-reliance in each city. The Midnight Mission, the community chest, Grandma's Kitchen, or the White Angel Jungle seemed more prepared than even the county public welfare bureaus to undertake unemployment assistance. Buy now, give-a-job, the five-day week, and, as late as 1932, the Portland Plan provide further evidence of communities desperately hoping that the economic body could heal itself, that citizens of good will cooperating together would overcome the ills of the business cycle. The Unemployed Citizens' League, of course, was the height of this allegiance to the old values, but both politics and the enormity of the economic problems disrupted what may have been America's preeminent experiment in cooperative individualism.

In 1931 the cities became serious about rendering assistance. Although approaches in Los Angeles, San Francisco, and Portland did not change much qualitatively, city leaders worked a good deal harder to match the needs. The work test was still essential. Bonds, rather than budget money, which would bring higher taxes, were still the key. Money had to be dispensed, but businesslike efficiency and conservation of the funds were still important. To insure proper stewardship a civic emergency committee or a district relief organization, replete with business leaders who had volunteered their time in an hour of need, oversaw the administration of funds. Necessity tested the parameters of the old values, but the values remained intact.

In the final full year local governments were on their own, values eroded simply because they were not working, and, if Seattle and Philadelphia are good examples, they were crumbling more swiftly where most strongly adhered to. Cooperation gave way to anxiety in 1932. Tax revolts, which had been rumbling for at least a year, burst forth with full force. Homeowners, even though they understood the need for increased taxation was greater than ever, were more fearful than ever of losing their homes and called for lower city budgets and consequently lower levies. The politicians listened. Local governments slashed budgets, reduced levies, and relief was placed in a more tenuous position than ever. Elected officials encouraged or simply coerced their employees into taking pay cuts as city and county budgets continued to be exceeded because of relief responsibilities. Under pressure to cut taxes or at least not raise them, local officials could not sustain the relief effort. Despite growing tax delinquencies, cities in 1933 almost surely could have raised funds to continue at least minimally adequate relief work, but the political reality was such that the good will of the people had run out. Beset by their own needs the people of the cities simply would not permit more taxes, even to relieve the unemployed from distress.

The depression strained the value of cooperative individualism beyond the breaking point. People still may have paid lip service to it, but they were not willing to honor its principles in action when such honor might pose a danger to their well-being. Righteousness about a bedrock value was changing into self-righteousness.

Even more evident was the pressure of the depression on urban institutions. Civic leaders tried to respond humanely and adequately but conditions overmatched their determination and abilities in each city, although not thoroughly in San Francisco. The public welfare commissions, community chests, and the different traditional sources of private charity were, by 1932, under burdens they could not carry. The depression spawned innovations—mayors' emergency commissions, systematic work relief programs, and self-help—and crushed them. The responses failed primarily because the problem outstripped all traditional resources, although the playing of politics and administrative ineptitude sometimes hindered efforts dramatically.

This did not mean the old values and ideals, shattered though they may have been, had passed away. The New Deal testified in part to the continuation of traditional ideals and ratified the usefulness of many local relief techniques, if properly funded. Hoover, the ideologue, lost the ideal; Roosevelt, the political pragmatist, seemed willing to sully the purity of the value to save what he could.

The FERA really had nothing to do with ideals. It was simply a response to need. The Civil Works Administration, though, offers proof that concern about the dole and its deleterious effects on individualism was still alive, even if it was now the federal government providing relief. The Public Works Administration and Works Progress Administration were the local mainstay, work relief, writ large. And the WPA, by giving the able-bodied more opportunities to work, made it possible to return a semblance of relief to local authorities. The ideal was to leave local agencies with the responsibility for only those incapacitated and in need. It was not so pat, but Roosevelt and the coffers of the federal government had resuscitated cooperative individualism by making the cooperative part affordable again.

The Hoover years of the depression were a time of great change. The boom of the twenties went bust. American self-confidence, and confidence in the all-knowing businessman, was deflated. People's lives changed, forever. But, at the same time, there was some continuity. Important values about self, work, and societal responsibility were badly bashed, but Americans, even by the grueling winter of 1932–33, had not thrown them over entirely. Institutions faltered and failed. Local governments all but collapsed in 1932 when they could not meet the challenges, but many institutional methods remained intact. As the administration of Herbert Hoover came to a close, as Los Angeles, San Francisco, Seattle, and Portland substantially laid aside their responsibility for responding to the crisis, the locus of power clearly changed. But when the national government took on the responsibility for the social and economic welfare of the American people, its operation was still guided to a large degree by old values and its administration of relief was accomplished in some familiar ways. The change in the political economy was enormous. Local communities had prepared the way for the New Deal by exhausting the wills and financial resources of their citizens, but they had also previewed some of the forms—still molded by a residue of the old values —that relief would take as it became a national rather than a local undertaking.

Appendix
Account of Methods Used in Seattle Voter Study, 1928 and 1932

The Seattle voter study is based on a collection of 1928 and 1932 voter registration books held in the University of Washington Libraries (Manuscripts Division). The registration collection is almost complete for both years. Until 1933 in Seattle, voters had to register every four years, whether they had voted or not. These poll books, then, are an up-to-date representation of the voting public in both years. As a result, many of the changes that occurred during the Hoover years of the depression are reflected in the comparison of the 1928 registrants with those who registered in 1932. This comparison on the precinct level is slightly complicated by the fact that Seattle was redistricted between 1928 and 1932. The Seattle Public Library and the University of Washington Libraries have precinct maps for both years. It is possible to establish from these the precincts from election to election, although, in some cases, this can be only an approximation.

The registration books provide the researcher with much information. The most identifiable and usable variables are sex, age, occupation, place of birth, time of residence in the state, county, and precinct, whether the individual voted, and whether the registrant paid property tax. If the person was a naturalized citizen, the date and place of naturalization are also included.

In some cases the information requires some interpretation. The individual's first name, for example, is the best clue to sex (initials seem to indicate a male), although occupation and handwriting are secondary clues. In a number of cases the registrar recorded a capital "L" when the person did not care to reveal his or her age but was clearly of legal voting age. This missing variable makes a negligible impact on this study. The appropriate state or country was recorded as place of birth. The time of residence appears in years and months. When an individual voted, a check was placed by the name. It is impossible to correlate these checks with a specific election. The number of marks vary from precinct to precinct and have been erased in many cases. Because of this lack of consistency, a person was counted as having voted if at least one check, clear or erased, had been entered by the name.

The most varied entry was occupation. To codify and categorize this, a system was devised based on the *Alphabetical Index of Occupations and Industries* published by the Bureau of the Census.

The following occupational categories were used. Examples from designations used in the poll books are provided in parenthesis:

Professional (doctors, lawyers, teachers, artists, engineers)
Manager (proprietors, small businessmen, bankers)
Clerical, Sales (secretaries, bookkeepers, salesmen)
Skilled (carpenters, electricians, bakers, machinists, machine operators)
Semiskilled (truck drivers, construction workers, apprentices, mechanics)
Unskilled (laborers, longshoremen)
Housewife
Service (barbers, cooks, janitors)
Domestic (housekeepers, laundresses)

Protective (policemen, firemen)
Retired
Student
Agriculture (farmers, farm laborers)

The data was used in two ways: in a comparison of the registered voters in Seattle in 1928 and 1932 and in an analysis of nine sample precincts over both years. The study was based on a sample of 2,070 registered voters from each year. This size sample allows for a 90 percent chance that the true value of a percentage based on the entire sample is within ± 1.8 percent. A random sample of 7 out of every 500 was selected from the 1928 registration books and 6 out of 500 from the 1932 poll books.

The nine precincts were selected on the basis of their unique or identifiable voting behavior in 1928 and 1932 (see following pages of the Appendix for precinct profiles). A 15 percent random sample of registrants was selected from each precinct for each year.

Using the *Statistical Package for the Social Sciences,* the study computed a variety of percentages and correlations for the overall study and the precinct study. The most meaningful results appear in several places in the text.

Profiles of Nine Sample Seattle Precincts—1928, 1932

PRECINCT 9 (9=34 in 1932)[1]
"Strongly Republican"

	1928	*1932*
Republicans[2]	78.4%	56.2%
Democrat[2]	16.9	22.4

OCCUPATION[3]

	1928	1932
Professional	25.8%	29.0%
Manager	7.5	8.7
Clerical, Sales	16.1	20.3
Skilled	4.3	0.0
Semiskilled	1.1	0.0
Unskilled	0.0	0.0
Housewife	25.8	30.4
Service	3.2	1.4
Domestic	0.0	0.0
Protective	1.1	0.0
Retired	1.1	7.2
Student	14.0	2.9
Taxpayers	47.3%	59.4%
Nontaxpayers	52.7	40.6

COMPARISON OF PRIMARY OCCUPATIONS OF MALES[4]

1928		*1932*	
Professional	30.2%	Clerical, Sales	37.0%
Clerical, Sales	25.6	Professional	22.2
Student	18.6	Manager	22.2
Manager	14.0	Retired	11.1
Retired	2.3	Student	7.4

1. Seattle was redistricted between 1928 and 1932.
2. This figure is based on the total number of ballots cast in the presidential election. Some did not cast a vote for president.
3. Based on the entire sample.
4. From the registration books it is difficult to determine employment patterns in any given household. Males were considered the "principal wage earners" of most middle-class households (and this probably held true in many lower-class households as well). The evidence points to a strong bias toward keeping men on the job while letting women go as the depression grew. Finally, in most of the nine sample precincts *housewives*, an economically neutral category, overbalances the income-earning designations. The presentation of male occupations, then, provides a useful perspective on the economic contours of most of the precincts.

PRECINCT 118 (118=177 in 1932)
"Strongly Democratic"

	1928	1932
Republican	34.1%	5.4%
Democrat	56.9	61.0

OCCUPATION

	1928	1932
Professional	0.0%	0.0%
Manager	10.9	2.2
Clerical, Sales	6.5	13.0
Skilled	15.2	28.3
Semiskilled	17.4	15.2
Unskilled	17.4	10.9
Housewife	23.9	21.7
Service	2.2	8.7
Domestic	2.2	0.0
Protective	0.0	0.0
Retired	2.2	0.0
Student	0.0	0.0
Taxpayers	52.2%	26.1%
Nontaxpayers	47.8	73.9

COMPARISON OF PRIMARY OCCUPATIONS OF MALES

1928		1932	
Semiskilled	25.8%	Skilled	41.9%
Unskilled	25.8	Semiskilled	22.6
Skilled	22.6	Unskilled	16.1

PRECINCT 168 (168=249 in 1932)
"Democratic with Large Republican Minority"

	1928	*1932*
Republican	35.0%	25.6%
Democrat	51.3	51.6

OCCUPATION

	1928	*1932*
Professional	8.0%	19.6%
Manager	4.0	6.5
Clerical, Sales	30.0	28.3
Skilled	6.0	8.7
Semiskilled	14.0	8.7
Unskilled	4.0	6.5
Housewife	24.0	10.9
Service	6.0	4.3
Domestic	0.0	2.2
Protective	0.0	0.0
Retired	2.0	4.3
Student	0.0	0.0
Taxpayers	32.0%	21.7%
Nontaxpayers	68.0	78.3

COMPARISON OF PRIMARY OCCUPATIONS OF MALES

1928		*1932*	
Clerical, Sales	40.7%	Clerical, Sales	20.8%
Semiskilled	22.2	Skilled	16.7
Skilled	11.1	Professional	16.7
Unskilled	7.4	Manager	12.5
Professional	3.7	Semiskilled	12.5
Manager	3.7	Unskilled	12.5

PRECINCT 196 (196=284 in 1932)
"Average Swing"*

	1928	1932
Republican	55.2%	21.9%
Democrat	39.1	46.5

OCCUPATION

	1928	1932
Professional	6.7%	14.8%
Manager	11.1	9.8
Clerical, Sales	22.2	18.0
Skilled	6.7	6.6
Semiskilled	8.9	6.6
Unskilled	0.0	1.6
Housewife	37.8	36.1
Service	6.7	1.6
Domestic	0.0	0.0
Protective	0.0	3.3
Retired	0.0	1.6
Student	0.0	0.0
Taxpayers	51.1%	50.8%
Nontaxpayers	48.9	49.2

COMPARISON OF PRIMARY OCCUPATIONS OF MALES

1928		1932	
Clerical, Sales	34.8%	Clerical, Sales	28.6%
Manager	21.7	Manager	21.5
Semiskilled	17.4	Skilled	14.3
Skilled	13.0	Professional	10.7
Professional	4.3	Semiskilled	10.7

*This refers to a precinct that was Republican in 1928 but voted Democrat in 1932. The percentage change in party preference in the presidential election approximates that of the entire city of Seattle.

PRECINCT 201 (201 = 289, 290 in 1932)
"Strongly Republican"

	1928	*1932*
Republican	74.9%	60.1%
Democrat	21.4	24.5

OCCUPATION

	1928	*1932*
Professional	6.9%	9.8%
Manager	21.8	17.9
Clerical, Sales	18.8	22.0
Skilled	3.0	3.3
Semiskilled	2.0	2.4
Unskilled	1.0	0.8
Housewife	39.6	36.3
Service	1.0	2.4
Domestic	0.0	0.0
Protective	0.0	0.0
Retired	2.0	1.6
Student	2.0	2.4
Agriculture	1.0	0.0
Taxpayers	79.2%	74.0%
Nontaxpayers	20.8	26.0

COMPARISON OF PRIMARY OCCUPATIONS OF MALES

1928		*1932*	
Manager	41.5%	Manager	32.3%
Clerical, Sales	28.3	Clerical, Sales	32.3
Professional	11.3	Professional	15.4

PRECINCT 208 (208=298 in 1932)
"Strongly Democratic"

	1928	*1932*
Republican	33.8%	11.8%
Democrat	54.2	63.6 ˙

OCCUPATION

	1928	*1932*
Professional	12.8%	8.3%
Manager	7.7	8.3
Clerical, Sales	17.9	14.6
Skilled	10.3	10.4
Semiskilled	12.8	18.8
Unskilled	0.0	4.2
Housewife	33.3	20.8
Service	2.6	2.1
Domestic	0.0	0.0
Protective	0.0	6.3
Retired	2.6	4.2
Student	0.0	2.1
Taxpayers	64.1%	47.9%
Nontaxpayers	35.9	52.1

COMPARISON OF PRIMARY OCCUPATIONS OF MALES

1928		*1932*	
Semiskilled	29.4%	Semiskilled	27.3%
Skilled	23.5	Clerical, Sales	18.2
Clerical, Sales	17.6	Manager	12.1
Manager	11.8	Skilled	15.2

PRECINCT 230 (230=320 in 1932)
"Strongly Democratic"

	1928	*1932*
Republican	20.8%	6.9%
Democrat	62.8	43.9

OCCUPATION

	1928	*1932*
Professional	4.5%	3.1%
Manager	4.6	3.1
Clerical, Sales	7.6	1.6
Skilled	16.7	10.9
Semiskilled	4.5	9.4
Unskilled	50.0	45.3
Housewife	1.5	3.9
Service	4.5	11.7
Domestic	1.5	0.0
Protective	0.0	2.3
Retired	4.5	5.5
Student	0.0	0.8
Agriculture	0.0	0.8
Taxpayers	21.2%	13.3%
Nontaxpayers	78.8	86.7

COMPARISON OF PRIMARY OCCUPATIONS OF MALES

1928		*1932*	
Unskilled	52.4%	Unskilled	48.3%
Skilled	17.5	Service	11.7
Service	4.8	Skilled	10.8
Semiskilled	4.8	Semiskilled	9.2

PRECINCT 238 (238=239 in 1932)
"Big Swing"*

	1928	*1932*
Republican	61.4%	20.7%
Democrat	30.9	60.8

OCCUPATION

	1928	1932
Professional	6.1%	8.8%
Manager	10.6	8.8
Clerical, Sales	21.2	24.2
Skilled	9.1	4.4
Semiskilled	15.2	8.8
Unskilled	1.5	5.5
Housewife	27.3	30.8
Service	3.0	4.4
Domestic	0.0	0.0
Protective	0.0	3.3
Retired	1.5	1.1
Student	1.5	0.0
Agriculture	1.5	0.0
Taxpayers	53.0%	53.8%
Nontaxpayers	47.0	46.2

COMPARISON OF PRIMARY OCCUPATIONS OF MALES

1928		*1932*	
Clerical, Sales	25.7%	Clerical, Sales	26.9%
Semiskilled	22.9	Manager	15.4
Skilled	14.3	Professional	13.5
Manager	14.3	Semiskilled	11.5
Professional	8.6	Unskilled	9.6

*This refers to a precinct that was Republican in 1928 but voted Democratic in 1932. The percentage change in party preference in the presidential election was greater than that of the entire city of Seattle.

PRECINCT 265 (265=347 in 1932)
"Strongly Democratic"

	1928	*1932*
Republican	44.1%	10.6%
Democrat	48.3	65.5

OCCUPATION

	1928	*1932*
Professional	6.8%	1.1%
Manager	2.7	4.5
Clerical, Sales	9.5	7.9
Skilled	13.5	15.7
Semiskilled	14.9	22.5
Unskilled	6.8	6.7
Housewife	40.5	36.0
Service	0.0	3.4
Domestic	1.4	0.0
Protective	1.4	0.0
Retired	1.4	1.1
Student	0.0	1.1
Agriculture	1.4	0.0
Taxpayers	81.1%	59.6%
Nontaxpayers	18.9	40.4

COMPARISON OF PRIMARY OCCUPATIONS OF MALES

1928		*1932*	
Skilled	27.0%	Semiskilled	31.4%
Semiskilled	24.3	Skilled	27.5
Unskilled	13.5	Unskilled	11.8
Clerical, Sales	13.5	Clerical, Sales	9.8
Professional	11.8	Professional	2.0

Notes

INTRODUCTION

1. Dixon Wecter, *The Age of the Great Depression* (New York: Macmillan, 1948), p. 19.

2. Quoted in Arnold Rice, ed., *Herbert Hoover, 1874–1964: Chronology, Documents, Bibliographical Aids* (Dobbs Ferry, N.Y.: Oceana Publications, 1971), p. 46.

3. Quoted in Harris Gaylord Warren, *Herbert Hoover and the Great Depression* (New York: Oxford University Press, 1959), p. 193.

4. Quoted in Robert Bremner, *American Philanthropy* (Chicago: University of Chicago Press, 1960), p. 144.

5. As recently as 1980 Jacob Fisher used the term in *The Response of Social Work to the Depression* (Boston: G. K. Hall and Co., 1980), p. 14. In "The Ordeal of Herbert Hoover," (*Yale Review* 52 [1963]: 563–83) Carl Degler argued effectively that Hoover made a significant response for the time and that his efforts made way for the New Deal by helping to break down the old ideological framework. More recently David Burner, *Herbert Hoover: A Public Life* (New York: Alfred Knopf, 1979) and Joan Hoff Wilson, *Herbert Hoover: Forgotten Progressive* (Boston: Little, Brown and Co., 1975) have explored Hoover and his framework extensively. Both evaluate Hoover as bound by his ideology but convincingly reject "do nothing" as a valid description of his presidency. Martin L. Fausold, in *The Presidency of Herbert C. Hoover* (Lawrence: University of Kansas Press, 1985), writes vigorously against the notion that the Hoover presidency was passive.

6. Warren, *Herbert Hoover*, p. 119.

7. Herbert Hoover, *The Memoirs of Herbert Hoover*, 3 vols. (New York: Macmillan, 1952), 3: 90–94.

8. Bremner, *American Philanthropy*, p. 150.

9. This analysis is best presented in Degler, "Ordeal of Herbert Hoover."

10. Among city biographies are Blake McKelvey, *Rochester: An Emerging Metropolis, 1925–1961* (Rochester, N.Y.: Christopher Press, 1961) and Bayrd Still, *Milwaukee: The History of a City* (Madison: State Historical Society of Wisconsin, 1948). Particularly helpful dissertations include John F. Bauman, "The City, the Depression, and Relief: The Philadelphia Experience, 1929–1933" (Ph.D. diss., Rutgers, The State University, 1969); James J. Hannah, "Urban Reaction to the Great Depression in the United States, 1929–1933" (Ph.D. diss., University of California at Berkeley, 1956); and David Maurer, "Public Relief Programs and Politics in Ohio, 1929–1939" (Ph.D. diss., Ohio State University, 1962). Robert Lynd and Helen Lynd, in *Middletown in Transition: A Study in Cultural Conflicts* (New York: Harcourt, Brace and Company, 1937), provide as good insight as any historian. From Bernard Sternsher, ed., *Hitting Home: The Great Depression in Town and Country* (Chicago: Quadrangle Books, 1970) are the following pertinent articles: David M. Katzman, "Ann Arbor: Depression City," and Bonnie Fox Schwartz, "Unemployment Relief in Philadelphia, 1930–1932: A Study of the Depression's Impact on Voluntarism." See also Charles Trout, *Boston, the Great Depression, and the New Deal* (New York: Oxford University Press, 1977).

11. Herbert Hoover, *American Individualism* (Garden City, N.Y.: n.p., 1922), pp. 66 (quotation), 26–31, 44–45; Burner, *Herbert Hoover*, pp. 265–67.

12. Wilson in *Herbert Hoover: Forgotten Progressive* and Albert U. Romasco in *The Poverty of Abundance: Hoover, the Nation, the Depression* (New York: Oxford University Press, 1965) both use the phrase to describe Hoover's belief about the nature of the corporate economy. The phrase is also apt for Hoover's ideal for the American citizen and will be used in that context throughout the work.

13. William R. Brock in *Welfare, Democracy, and the New Deal* (Cambridge: Cambridge University Press, 1988) points out the positive effects of the centralization of the relief effort under professional, experienced social workers—first at the state and then at the federal level. Brock also presents useful thoughts about the impact of traditional values on the administration of local relief.

14. See Philip Neff and Anita Weifenbach, *Business Cycles in Selected Industrial Areas* (Berkeley and Los Angeles: University of California Press, 1949) and Earl Pomeroy, *The Pacific Slope: A History of California, Oregon, Washington, Idaho, Utah, and Nevada* (Seattle: University of Washington Press, 1965).

15. James Patterson, "The New Deal in the West," *Pacific Historical Review* 38 (August 1969): 327.

ONE. PRELUDE

1. Los Angeles Chamber of Commerce, *Population Census of 1930*, p. 1; Royce D. Delmatier, Clarence McIntosh, and Earl G. Walters, *The Rumble of California Politics, 1848–1970* (New York: John Wiley and Sons, 1970), p. 220.

2. Jacqueline Rorabeck Kasun, *Some Social Aspects of Business Cycles in the Los Angeles Area, 1920–1950* (Los Angeles: The Haynes Foundation, 1954), pp. 14–15

3. Frank L. Kidner, *California Business Cycles* (Berkeley and Los Angeles: University of California Press, 1946), p. 24; Kasun, *Some Social Aspects of Business Cycles*, p. 9; Los Angeles, Office of the Mayor, Community Analysis Bureau, *The Economic Development of Southern California, 1920–1976*, 2 vols. (1976), 2: viii.

4. Robert M. Fogelson, *The Fragmented Metropolis: Los Angeles, 1850–1930* (Cambridge, Mass.: Harvard University Press, 1967), p. 119. San Francisco's shipping exceeded Los Angeles's in value.

5. Los Angeles County, Board of Supervisors, *Los Angeles County California* (Los Angeles: n.p., [1938?]), n.p.; *Los Angeles Times*, 9 October 1929.

6. This study focuses exclusively on the City and County of San Francisco, a politically unified entity. As a result statistics and descriptions of events are confined to the city and county limits.

7. U.S. Department of Commerce, Bureau of the Census, *Fifteenth Census of the United States, Metropolitan Districts: Population and Area* (Washington, D.C.: Government Printing Office, 1933), p. 203; San Francisco Chamber of Commerce, Research Department, *San Francisco: Economic Survey: 1932*, p. 23.

8. Ibid; San Francisco Chamber of Commerce, *San Francisco Business*, 14 May 1930; San Francisco Chamber of Commerce, Research Department, *Annual Survey of Business Conditions in San Francisco, 1933*, p. 10.

9. Seattle Chamber of Commerce, *Seattle Business*, 16 July 1931; Day and Zimmerman, Inc., "Survey of the Industrial Activities and Resources and of the Proposed Establishment of an Industrial District in Portland Oregon," mimeographed (Philadelphia, 1930), p. 2.

10. Edgar I. Stewart, *Washington: Northwest Frontier*, 2 vols. (New York: Lewis Historical Publishing Co., 1957), 2:286; Arthur Hillman, *The Unemployed Citizens' League of Seattle*, University of Washington Publications in the Social Sciences, vol. 5, no. 3 (Seattle: University of Washington Press, 1934), p. 20; E. Kimbark MacColl, *The Growth of a City: Power and Politics in Portland, Oregon, 1915 to 1950* (Portland: The Georgian Press, 1979), p. 519.

11. Washington State Grange, *Proceedings of the Forty-second Annual Session* (Seattle: Central Printing, 1930), p. 10; *Seattle Post-Intelligencer*, 6 May 1930; Leonard Leader, "Los Angeles and the Great Depression" (Ph.D. diss., University of California at Los Angeles, 1972), p. 3; W. H. Olin, "Seattle Makes Forward Strides in Industry," *Union Pacific Magazine*, April 1930, p. 10; Day and Zimmerman, Inc., "Survey of the Industrial Activities," report 145.

12. San Francisco Chamber of Commerce, Research Department, *San Francisco Economic Survey: 1932*, p. 20; Los Angeles Stock Exchange, *Report of the President* (1930), p. 12; Seattle Chamber of Commerce, Industrial Department, "Industrial Report of Seattle and the Puget Sound District," Typewritten (1930), p. 52; Day and Zimmerman, Inc., "Survey of the Industrial Activities in Portland," report 149.

13. *Los Angeles Saturday Night, 150th Birthday of Los Angeles: Fiesta and Pre-Olympiad* (Los Angeles: Los Angeles *Saturday Night* [1931]); California, State Chamber of Commerce, Research Department, *Economic Survey Report*, series 1929–1930, no. 28; E. Myles Cooper and William Goldman, "A Preliminary Estimate of Non-Agricultural Unemployment in California, 1930 to 1939," mimeographed (State Relief Administration of California, 1939), p. 8; *Portland Daily Journal of Commerce*, 31 December 1929 and 8 February 1930.

14. John F. Bauman, "The City, the Depression, and Relief: The Philadelphia Experience, 1929–1933" (Ph.D. diss., Rutgers, The State University, 1969), p. 30; Blake McKelvey, *Rochester: An Emerging Metropolis, 1925–1961* (Rochester, N.Y.: Christopher Press, 1961), p. 59; Charles Trout, *Boston, the Great Depression, and the New Deal* (New York: Oxford University Press, 1977), p. 59; James J. Hannah, "Urban Reaction to the Great Depression in the United States, 1929–1933," (Ph.D. diss., University of California at Berkeley, 1956), p. 78.

15. U.S. Federal Reserve Bank of San Francisco, *Monthly Review of Business Conditions* (November 1929), pp. 82–83.

16. Day and Zimmerman, Inc., "Study of Rail and Water Terminal Facilities and Feasibility of Unification at Portland, Oregon," mimeographed (Philadelphia, 1930), p. 19a: Security First National Bank of Los Angeles, *Monthly Summary: Business Conditions in the Pacific Southwest* (February 1930), p. 6; Louis B. Perry and Richard S. Perry, *A History of the Los Angeles Labor Movement, 1911–1941* (Berkeley and Los Angeles: University of California Press, 1963), pp. 230–31; Seattle Chamber of Commerce, "Industrial Report of Seattle and the Puget Sound District," mimeographed (1930), n.p.; *San Francisco Examiner*, 21 December 1929.

17. James C. Findley, "The Economic Boom of the 'Twenties in Los Angeles" (Ph.D. diss., University of California at Los Angeles, 1958), p. 413. This work provides a full description of the growing pains of Los Angeles during the 1920s. Security First National Bank of Los Angeles, Research Department, *Monthly Summary of Business Conditions in Southern California* 13 (November 1934): 1–2.

18. San Francisco, Supervisors Board, Committee for the Survey of Unemployment Relief Administration, *Report* (1933), p. 29; San Francisco Chamber of Commerce, Research Department, *Survey of Business Conditions in San Francisco*, mimeographed (1934).

19. *West Coast Lumber Facts* (Portland: West Coast Lumberman's Association, 1941), n.p.; U.S. Department of Commerce, Bureau of the Census, *Biennial Census of Manufactures* (Washington, D.C.: Government Printing Office, 1930); Blair Stewart, *Seasonal Employment and Unemployment Compensation in Oregon* (Portland: Reed College, 1937), pp. 9–10; Washington Emergency Relief Administration, "The Washington Apple in the Depression," typescript [1933?], p. 6; Seattle, Public Employment Office, "Annual Report," typewritten (1929), pp. 1–2.

20. Portland, Public Employment Bureau, "Report," typewritten (1930), n.p.

21. Julian Dana, *A. P. Giannini: Giant in the West; A Biography* (New York: Prentice-Hall, 1947), p. 166.

22. Elizabeth F. Derion, *'Twas Many Years Since: 100 Years in the Waverly Area, 1847–1947* (Milwaukie, Oreg.: Author, 1981), p. 97; Hiram Johnson, Jr., to Hiram Johnson, Sr., 9 May 1930, Hiram W. Johnson Papers, Bancroft Library, Berkeley, Calif.; A. J. Mount to H. R. Erkes, 13 November 1929, and H. R. Erkes to A. J. Mount, 12 November 1929, "Biography of a Bank," Source Material Files, Bank of America Archives, San Francisco.

23. A. P. Giannini to W. W. Douglas, 30 October 1929, Amadeo Peter Giannini Papers, Bank of America Archives, San Francisco.

24. G. E. M. Pratt to Wesley Jones, 13 December 1929, quoted in William Stewart Forth, "Wesley Jones" (Ph.D. diss., University of Washington, 1962), p. 754; *Oregonian* (Portland), 24 November 1929.

25. *Los Angeles Examiner*, 3 January 1930; Washington State Chamber of Commerce, *Monthly Bulletin* (March 1930); *Oregonian*, 3 November 1929 and 17 December 1929; *Oregon Daily Journal*, 1 December 1929.

26. Philip Neff and Anita Weifenbach, *Business Cycles in Selected Industrial Areas* (Berkeley and Los Angeles: University of California Press, 1949), pp. 63–69, 107–11, 163–64. Also, in a condensed version, Molly Lewin, *Business Cycles in Los Angeles* (Los Angeles: The Haynes Foundation, 1949), pp. 4–25.

27. Neff and Weifenbach, *Business Cycles*, pp. 108–109.

28. Earl Pomeroy, *The Pacific Slope: A History of California, Oregon, Washington, Idaho, Utah, and Nevada* (Seattle: University of Washington Press), p. 293.

29. Kidner, *California Business Cycles*, p. 56.

30. *Seattle Post-Intelligencer*, 3 January 1930 and 22 July 1930; *San Francisco Examiner*, 3 January 1930; *San Francisco Chronicle*, 3 January 1930; *San Francisco News*, 5 June 1930.

31. Neff and Weifenbach, *Business Cycles*, p. 66.

TWO. THE END OF PROSPERITY

1. *Los Angeles Evening Express, Los Angeles Evening Express Yearbook* (Los Angeles: *Los Angeles Evening Express*, 1931), p. 2; Los Angeles County, Board of Supervisors, *Annual Report* (1930), p. 57.

2. U.S. Federal Reserve Bank of San Francisco, *Monthly Review of Business Conditions* (January 1930), p. 2; *San Francisco Daily Commercial News*, 27 May 1930 and 25 July 1930; *San Francisco Examiner*, 24 May 1930.

3. *San Francisco Examiner*, 19 December 1930; U.S. Federal Reserve Bank of San Francisco, *Monthly Review* (January 1931), pp. 4–6.

4. Washington State Chamber of Commerce, *Monthly Bulletin* (March 1930); Shelby Scates, *Firstbank: The Story of Seattle-First National Bank* (Seattle: Seattle First National Bank, 1970), p. 49.

5. Portland Chamber of Commerce, Research Department, "Portland Retail Trade Area: A Survey," mimeographed (1935), p.1.

6. [California] State Department of Industrial Relations [Report] in J. R. Haynes Collection, University of California at Los Angeles Special Collections, Los Angeles; California, State Employment Commission, *Report and Recommendation* (1932), p. 40.

7. *Seattle Post-Intelligencer*, 12 December 1930; San Francisco Chamber of Commerce, Research Department, *Economic Survey: 1933*, p. 18.

8. San Francisco, Chamber of Commerce, Research Department, *Economic Survey: 1932*, p. 20; John E. Price and Co., *Comparative Statements of Banks in Seattle* (31 December 1930–31 December 1931), passim; *Seattle Post-Intelligencer*, 30 September 1930.

9. Los Angeles Chamber of Commerce, *Southern California Business* (February 1933), p. 20; *Oregon Daily Journal*, 29 September 1930 and 3 January 1931.

10. *Los Angeles Evening Express, Yearbook*, p. 5; Los Angeles Chamber of Commerce, *Southern California Business* (February 1933), p. 20.

11. *San Francisco Examiner*, 26 November 1930.

12. California State Chamber of Commerce, Research Department, *Economic Survey Report*, series 1930–1931, no. 24.

13. *Portland Daily Journal of Commerce*, 2 February 1933; Day and Zimmerman, Inc., "Study of Rail and Water Terminal Facilities and Feasibility of Unification at Portland, Oregon," mimeographed (Philadelphia, 1930), p. 19a.

14. *Seattle Post-Intelligencer*, 1 January 1931.

15. Bayrd Still, *Milwaukee: The History of a City* (Madison: State Historical Society of Wisconsin, 1948), pp. 478–79.

16. Charles Miles and O. B. Sperlin, eds., *Building a State: Washington, 1889–1939*, 3 vols. (Tacoma: Washington State Historical Society, 1940), 3:230.

17. *Seattle Post-Intelligencer*, 16 August 1930.

18. *Seattle Vanguard*, January 1931; Portland Chamber of Commerce, *Commerce*, 3 January 1931.

19. Los Angeles Chamber of Commerce, Research Department, *Los Angeles: "The Magic City"* (Los Angeles: n.p., 1930), p. 20; *Los Angeles Examiner*, 8 February 1930.

20. *Los Angeles Times*, 15 July 1930.

21. *Los Angeles Examiner*, 27 December 1930; Jacqueline Rorabeck Kasun, *Some Social Aspects of Business Cycles in the Los Angeles Area, 1920–1950* (Los Angeles: The Haynes Foundation, 1954), p. 10.

22. Abraham Hoffman, "Stimulus to Repatriation: The 1931 Federal Deportation Drive and the Los Angeles Mexican Community," *Pacific Historical Review* 42 (May 1973): 208.

23. *Oregonian*, 26 September 1930.

24. *San Francisco Examiner*, 3 January 1930; *Oregonian*, 1 January 1930.

25. *Los Angeles Times*, 27 January 1930; *Seattle Post-Intelligencer*, 3 January 1930; *Oregonian*, 22 March 1930; *San Francisco Examiner*, 12 March 1930; *Seattle Daily Journal of Commerce*, 4 August 1930.

26. *Los Angeles Examiner*, 3 September 1930.

27. Los Angeles, Mayor, *Annual Message* (1930), p. 6; Raymond B. Wilcox to Mayor George Baker, 8 March 1930, and L. C. Newlands to the Chamber of Commerce, 13 March 1930, Records of the Portland Chamber of Commerce, University of Oregon Library, Eugene, Oregon (hereafter, PCC); Hiram Johnson, Jr., to Hiram Johnson, Sr., 17 January 1930, Hiram W. Johnson Papers, Bancroft Library, Berkeley, California.

28. *Los Angeles Record*, 7 April 1930; J. Richard Noles, "'Can You Spare a Dime?' Days," *Oregonian*, 11 February 1959, p. 59; *San Francisco News*, 7 March 1930 and 5 May 1930; *Portland News*, 24 July 1930; *Seattle Post-Intelligencer*, 3 January 1930; *Seattle Daily Journal of Commerce*, 20 May 1930.

29. *Los Angeles Times*, 5 February 1930. Two days later the *Times* labeled the story a fraud.

30. Elmer Johnson to R. E. Riley, 18 October 1930 and O. G. Raney to R. E. Riley, 27 October 1930, MS. Series 0201–02, Box 41, Portland Archives and Records Center.

31. John Anson Ford, *Honest Politics My Theme: The Story of a Veteran Public Official's Troubles and Triumphs, An Autobiography* (New York: Vantage Press, 1978), pp. 69–70.

32. John R. Kenny to James Rolph, 11 December 1930, James Rolph Papers, Library of the California Historical Society, San Francisco.

33. Paul Scharrenberg, "Labor after the Depression," *The Commonwealth*, 12 July 1932, p. 128; *Oregonian*, 13 November 1930.

34. *San Francisco Examiner*, 17 October 1930.

35. (Los Angeles) *California Eagle*, 28 March 1930.

36. *Oregon Daily Journal*, 12 March 1930.

37. *Seattle Daily Journal of Commerce*, 19 November 1930; Seattle Chamber of Commerce, *Seattle's Business*, 17 July 1930; *Seattle Post-Intelligencer*, 27 March 1930.

38. San Francisco Chamber of Commerce, *San Francisco Business*, 29 October 1930.

39. *Los Angeles Examiner*, 1 April 1930; The Municipal League of Los Angeles, *Bulletin*, 1 November 1930.

40. *Seattle Post-Intelligencer*, 7 August 1930.

41. John F. Bauman, "The City, the Depression, and Relief: The Philadelphia Experience, 1929–1933" (Ph.D. diss., Rutgers, The State University, 1969), p. 30; Charles Trout, *Boston, the Great Depression, and the New Deal* (New York: Oxford University Press, 1977), p.

59; James J. Hannah, "Urban Reaction to the Great Depression in the United States, 1929–1933" (Ph.D. diss., University of California at Berkeley, 1956), p. 78.

42. *Los Angeles Citizen*, 27 June 1930; *Los Angeles Record*, 14 March 1930; *San Francisco Examiner*, 16 May 1930; *Seattle Vanguard*, February 1930; Lynn Sabin to H. J. Strong, 23 May 1930, and Minutes, Oregon Economic Conference, 11 February 1930, PCC.

43. *Los Angeles Record*, 10 July 1930; *Los Angeles Times*, 20 June 1930; Max Vorspan and Lloyd P. Gartner, *History of the Jews of Los Angeles* (San Marino, Calif.: Huntington Library Publications, 1970), p. 193; U.S. Department of Commerce, Bureau of the Census, *Fifteenth Census of the United States, 1930: Unemployment: Unemployment Returns by Classes for States and Counties, for Urban and Rural Areas, and for Cities with a Population of 10,000 or More* (Washington, D.C.: Government Printing Office, 1933), pp. 25, 40; *Oregonian*, 5 September 1930.

44. Blake McKelvey, *Rochester: An Emerging Metropolis 1925–1961* (Rochester, N.Y.: Christopher Press, 1961), p. 59; James T. Patterson, *America's Struggle against Poverty* (Cambridge, Mass.: Harvard University Press, 1981), p. 17; John Garraty, *Unemployment in History* (New York: Harper and Row, 1978), p. 167.

45. California, State Chamber of Commerce, Research Department, *Economic Survey Report*, series 1930–31, no. 24; Seattle Public Employment Office, "Annual Report," typewritten (1930), p. 2; *Oregonian*, 30 October 1930 and 8 November 1930.

46. Robert Lynd and Helen Lynd, *Middletown in Transition: A Study in Cultural Conflicts* (New York: Harcourt, Brace and Company, 1937), p. 471.

47. International Unemployment Conference to Los Angeles County Board of Supervisors, 19 February 1930, Los Angeles County Board of Supervisors, Executive Office Archives, Record Series 740, Los Angeles (hereafter LABS).

48. Robert Gottlieb and Helen West, *Thinking Big: The Story of the Los Angeles Times, Its Publishers, and Their Influence on Southern California* (New York: G. P. Putnam's Sons, 1977), p. 203.

49. Ibid.

50. Los Angeles, Controller, *Budget Fiscal Year 1930–1931 as Submitted by the Mayor and Adopted by the Council*, p. 3.

51. Leonard Leader, "Los Angeles and the Great Depression" (Ph.D. diss., University of California at Los Angeles, 1972), p. 82.

52. California, State Unemployment Commission, *Report and Recommendations* (1932), pp. 597, 600, 635; Multnomah County, Tax Supervising and Conservation Commission, *Budget Facts and Financial Statistics of Multnomah County* (1930), p. 57.

THREE. TRIED AND FOUND WANTING

1. This section is a summary of a useful analysis of local responses of the period, Joanna Colcord, *Emergency Work Relief: As Carried Out in Twenty-six American Communities, 1930–1931, with Suggestions for Setting Up a Program* (New York: Russell Sage Foundation, 1932), pp. 13–17, 225–40.

2. The material in the preceding two paragraphs is based on several studies of social work and poverty. Most useful have been Edward Berkowitz and Kim McQuaid, *Creating the Welfare State: The Political Economy of Twentieth-Century Reform* (New York: Praeger, 1980); Jacob Fisher, *The Response of Social Work to the Depression* (Boston: G. K. Hall and Co., 1980); John Garraty, *Unemployment in History* (New York: Harper and Row, 1978); James Leiby, *A History of Social Welfare and Social Work in the United States* (New York: Columbia University Press, 1978); James T. Patterson, *America's Struggle against Poverty* (Cambridge, Mass.: Harvard University Press, 1981); and Walter Trattner, *From Poor Law to Welfare State: A History of Social Welfare in America* (New York: Free Press, 1984). The quotations are from Patterson, *America's Struggle against Poverty*, pages 52 and 19.

3. Pauper Act, Statutes of 1901, Act 5814, Section 1, quoted by Edward W. Mattoon, County Council to Los Angeles Board of Supervisors, 8 August 1932, Record Series 40.31, LABS.

4. Helen R. Jeter, "The Administration of Funds for Unemployment Relief by the Los Angeles Department of Charities prior to November 24, 1933," typewritten (Los Angeles: Los Angeles County Emergency Relief Committee, 1933), p. 3.

5. Los Angeles, Mayor, *Annual Message* (1930), p. 54.

6. California, State Unemployment Commission, *Report and Recommendations* (1932), p. 346.

7. "Report of the Midnight Mission" (1931), Record Series 40.31, LABS.

8. *Los Angeles Record*, 27 June 1930.

9. Lawrence D. Pritchard, "The All-City Employee Association of Los Angeles," typewritten (1940), p. 69.

10. *Los Angeles Times*, 1 January 1930 and 18 February 1930.

11. *Los Angeles Times*, 15 October 1930; *Los Angeles Open Forum*, 22 November 1930.

12. *Los Angeles Record*, 24 October 1930.

13. A. C. Price, Assistant Superintendent of Charities to W. H. Holland, 11 July 1930, Record Series 40.31, LABS.

14. Los Angeles, Mayor, *Annual Message* (1930), p. 6.

15. California, State Unemployment Commission, *Abstract of Hearings on Unemployment* (1932), p. 18; Los Angeles County, Board of Supervisors, *Annual Report* (1930), p. 99.

16. H. Brett Melendy and Benjamin F. Gilbert, *The Governors of California: Peter H. Burnett to Edmund G. Brown* (Georgetown, Calif: Talisman Press, 1965), pp. 366–67.

17. U.S. Department of Commerce, Bureau of the Census, *Special Report: Relief Expenditures by Governmental and Private Organizations, 1929 and 1931* (Washington, D.C.: Government Printing Office, 1932), p. 34.

18. *San Francisco News*, 9 June 1930.

19. *San Francisco News*, 17 November 1930.

20. *San Francisco Chronicle*, 30 December 1930.

21. *San Francisco News*, 17 November 1930.

22. *Seattle Times*, 21 September 1930.

23. *Seattle Post-Intelligencer*, 8 October 1930.

24. Seattle Public Employment Office, "Annual Report," typewritten (1930), p. 3.

25. Seattle City Council, Proceedings, Doc. 128840, 10 November 1930; *Seattle Post-Intelligencer*, 11 November 1930.

26. Seattle, Public Employment Office, "Annual Report," typewritten (1929), p. 3; ibid., (1930), p. 2.

27. *Oregonian*, 18 March 1932.

28. *Oregonian*, 10 September 1930; *Oregon Daily Journal*, 27 October 1930.

29. Oregon, *Report of the Committee Appointed by Governor Julius L. Meier to Study Relief Needs of the State of Oregon and to Recommend Plans for Providing Relief Revenue* (1933), p. 5.

30. Resolution, First Oregon Economic Conference (1930), PCC. For a fuller discussion of the influence of progressivism on the Oregon response see, William Mullins, "I'll Wreck the Town If It Will Give Employment," *Pacific Northwest Quarterly* 79 (1988): 109–18.

31. Oregon, Bureau of Labor, *Fourteenth Biennial Report*, p. 6.

32. Oregon, State Highway Commission, "Tenth Biennial Report," mimeographed (1932), p. 24.

33. Multnomah County, Oregon, Auditor, *Annual Report* (1931), p. 39; *Portland Journal*, 6 November 1930 and 3 June 1931.

34. *Oregonian*, 30 October 1930.

35. *Oregonian*, 12 November 1930.

36. *Oregonian*, 4 October 1930 and 24 October 1930.

37. *Oregonian*, 18 November 1930; Austin Moller, "Portland's Civic Emergency Committee: Citizen Involvement in a Time of Crisis: 1930–1933" (unpublished MS at Portland Archives and Records Center, 1980), p. 3.

38. Moller, "Portland's Civic Emergency Committee," pp. 17–18.

39. *Report of the Committee to Study Relief Needs of Oregon*, p. 5.

40. Bonnie Fox Schwartz, "Unemployment Relief in Philadelphia, 1930–1932: A Study of the Depression's Impact on Voluntarism," in *Hitting Home: The Great Depression in Town and Country*, ed., Bernard Sternsher (Chicago: Quadrangle Books, 1970), p. 77; Bayrd Still, *Milwaukee: The History of a City* (Madison: State Historical Society of Wisconsin, 1948), p. 486; David Maurer, "Public Relief Programs and Politics in Ohio, 1929–1939" (Ph.D. diss., Ohio State University, 1962), pp. 10–11; Albert U. Romasco, *The Poverty of Abundance: Hoover, the Nation, the Depression* (New York: Oxford University Press, 1965), p. 170; Trattner, *From Poor Law to Welfare State*, pp. 262–63.

41. Romasco, *Poverty of Abundance*, p. 145.

42. John F. Bauman, "The City, the Depression, and Relief: The Philadelphia Experience, 1929–1933" (Ph.D. diss., Rutgers, The State University, 1969), pp. 89–93; Schwartz, "Unemployment Relief in Philadelphia," pp. 76–79.

43. Romasco, *Poverty of Abundance*, pp. 151–52.

44. Jackson K. Putnam, *Modern California Politics, 1917–1980* (San Francisco: Boyd and Foster Publishing Co., 1980), p. 17; Robert E. Burton, *Democrats of Oregon: Pattern of Minority Politics* (Eugene: University of Oregon, 1970), p. 65; Thor Swanson et al., eds., *Political Life in Washington: Governing the Evergreen State* (Pullman: Washington State University Press, 1985), p. 8.

45. Michael A. Weatherson and Hal Bockin, *Hiram Johnson: A Bio-Bibliography* (New York: Greenwood Press, 1988), pp. 52–53.

46. Steve Neal, *McNary of Oregon: A Political Biography* ([Portland]: Western Imprints, The Press of the Oregon Historical Society, 1985), pp. 116–17, 125, 128; Roger T. Johnson, "Charles L. McNary and the Republican Party during Prosperity and Depression" (Ph.D. diss., University of Wisconsin, 1967), pp. 137, 139.

47. Burton, *Democrats of Oregon*, pp 69–71; Unidentified newspaper clipping, Box 8, Charles Martin Papers, Oregon Historical Society.

48. Melendy and Gilbert, *Governors of California*, p. 372.

FOUR. HITTING HOME

1. This phrase is from Bernard Sternsher, ed., *Hitting Home: The Great Depression in Town and Country* (Chicago: Quadrangle Books, 1970). The book is made up of a series of articles about the Great Depression at the local level. As such, this book is one of the few places, outside of Ph.D. dissertations, that the important story of the local response to the Hoover years of the depression can be found.

2. *Eberle Economic Service Weekly*, 11 January 1932.

3. Los Angeles Chamber of Commerce, Industrial Department, *General Industrial Report of Los Angeles County, California* (1933), n.p.

4. *Eberle Economic Service Weekly*, 11 June 1931.

5. *Portland News-Telegram*, 27 May 1931.

6. Representative Charles Martin to Sam Martin, 29 December 1931, Charles Henry Martin Papers, Oregon Historical Society, Portland.

7. San Francisco Chamber of Commerce, Research Department, *San Francisco Economic Survey: 1933*, p. 18.

8. U.S. Department of Commerce, Bureau of the Census, *Biennial Census of Manufactures: 1933, Washington* (1935), p. 2.

9. U.S. Federal Reserve Bank of San Francisco, *Monthly Review of Business Conditions* (20 January 1931), p. 1.

10. Los Angeles Chamber of Commerce, *Southern California Business* (February 1933), p. 20; San Francisco Chamber of Commerce, Research Department, *San Francisco Economic Survey: 1933*; John E. Price and Co., *Comparative Statements of Banks in Seattle*, (n.p., 1930 and 1931), passim.

11. Marquis James and Bessie Rowland James, *Biography of a Bank: The Story of Bank of America, N.T. and S. A.* (New York: Harper and Brothers, 1954), pp. 314–43.

12. *Seattle Post-Intelligencer*, 16 February 1931, 1 March 1931, 8 July 1931, and 6 August 1931; Banking and Liquidation Files, Boxes 61–76, Washington State Archives, Olympia, Washington.

13. *Oregonian*, 19 December 1931.

14. *Oregon Daily Journal*, 22 December 1931; John C. Ainsworth to D. W. Twohy, 24 December 1931, John C. Ainsworth Papers, University of Oregon Library, Eugene, Oregon; Claude Singer, "The History of United States National Bank and U.S. Bancorp" (unpublished MS, at Oregon Historical Society, 1980), pp. 79–81.

15. Bank of America, Analysis and Research Department, *Bank of America Business Review* (1933), p. 7; *Seattle Daily Journal of Commerce*, 2 January 1932; Los Angeles Chamber of Commerce, Industrial Department, *General Industrial Report* (1933), n.p.; Los Angeles Chamber of Commerce, *Southern California Business* (January 1932), p. 20.

16. U.S. Federal Reserve Bank of San Francisco, *Monthly Review* (January 1932), p. 4; California, Emergency Relief Administration, Division of Research and Surveys, "Economic Trends in California, 1929–1934," mimeographed (n.d.), p. 38.

17. Eleanor Adele Todd, "History of the Milk Wagon Drivers' Union of San Francisco County" (Master's thesis, University of California at Berkeley, 1936), p. 177; *Seattle Times*, 27 September 1931; *Seattle Post-Intelligencer*, 4 December 1931; California Emergency Relief Administration, "Economic Trends," p. 20.

18. Washington State Planning Council, *Employment and Payrolls, Basic Industries of Washington, 1920–1944* (1945), pp. 16–20.

19. *Four L Lumber News*, 10 January 1927, 19 January 1928, 10 January 1929, and 15 March 1932; Los Angeles Stock Exchange, *Report of the President* (1931), p. 17.

20. Robert Lynd and Helen Lynd, *Middletown in Transition: A Study in Cultural Conflicts* (New York: Harcourt, Brace and Company, 1937), pp. 489–90; Los Angeles County Board of Supervisors, "Report on Survey of Unemployment and Public Welfare in Metropolitan Sectors," typewritten (1931), p. 8, Record Series 740, LABS; quoted in Francis W. Schruben, "Kansas during the Great Depression: 1930–1936" (Ph.D. diss., University of California at Los Angeles, 1961), p. 162.

21. Quoted in John D. Weaver, *Los Angeles: The Enormous Village, 1781–1981* (Santa Barbara: Capra Press, 1980), p. 109; *Los Angeles Examiner*, 5 January 1931; Portland Chamber of Commerce, *Commerce* (25 July 1931).

22. Report of Retail Merchants Committee, 30 October 1931, PCC.

23. *Los Angeles Examiner*, 5 January 1931; *San Francisco Chronicle*, 5 January 1931.

24. *San Francisco Examiner*, 5 January 1931; *Seattle Star*, passim, 1930–1931; Weaver, *Los Angeles*, p. 110; *Los Angeles Examiner*, 5 January 1931.

25. Catholic Welfare Bureau of the Archdiocese of Los Angeles, *Report* (1931), p. 9.

26. Hiram Johnson, Jr., to Hiram Johnson, Sr., 12 December 1931, Hiram W. Johnson Papers, Bancroft Library, Berkeley; I. Z. Zellerbach to John Neylan, 20 December 1931, John Francis Neylan Papers, Bancroft Library, Berkeley; *Portland Journal*, 1 November 1931; *Eberle Economic Service Weekly*, 11 January 1932.

27. *Oregon Daily Journal*, 3 November 1931; Memoirs of John R. Quinn (MS, Oral History Program, University of California at Los Angeles, 1966), p. 97; *Seattle Post-*

Intelligencer, 6 January 1931; Los Angeles Public Library, *44th Annual Report* (1932), p. 5; *Los Angeles Examiner*, 27 January 1931.

28. *Seattle Daily Journal of Commerce*, 8 October 1931.

29. *Seattle Times*, 1 June 1931. The editorials in the *Los Angeles Record* started around mid-July.

30. Portland, Public Employment Bureau, "Report," typewritten (1932), n.p.; *Los Angeles Examiner*, 12 December 1931.

31. Angelo Rossi to Los Angeles County Board of Supervisors, 20 November 1931, Record Series 740, LABS; *Los Angeles Times*, 14 November 1931; *San Francisco Labor Clarion*, 15 May 1931, 14 August 1931, and 28 August 1931; *Seattle Vanguard*, October 1930.

32. *Oregon Daily Journal*, 8 September 1931.

33. John Arthur Hogan, "The Decline of Self-help and Growth of Radicalism among Seattle's Organized Unemployed" (Master's thesis, University of Washington, 1934), pp. 68–70; Washington State Grange, *Proceedings of the Forty-third Annual Session* (Seattle: Central Publishing Co., 1931), pp. 59–60.

34. *San Francisco Examiner*, 18 April 1931; Leonard Leader, "Los Angeles and the Great Depression" (Ph.D. diss., University of California at Los Angeles, 1972), p. 9; Bureau of the Census, *Fifteenth Census of the United States: Unemployment* (Washington, D.C.: Government Printing Office, 1933), pp. 364, 373; Seattle, Public Employment Office, "Report," 1931, p. 3; *Seattle Vanguard*, October 1931.

35. Claude Singer, "The History of United States National Bank," p. 75; Portland, Public Employment Bureau, "Report," 1932.

36. Oregon, Emergency Employment Commission, *Unemployment in Oregon* (Salem: n.p., 1931), p. 3.

37. California, State Unemployment Commission, *Abstract of Hearings on Unemployment* (San Francisco: n.p., 1932), p. 19; California, State Unemployment Commission, *Report and Recommendation (1932)*, p. 50; Seattle, Public Employment Office, "Report," 1931, p. 3; *Oregon Daily Journal*, 3 March 1931; Portland Civic Emergency Committee, "Report, 1931–32," mimeographed.

38. Henry Aldrich to Ralph Clyde, 15 May 1931, MS. Series 0201–02, Box 41, Portland Archives and Record Center.

39. *San Francisco Examiner*, 27 December 1931 through 4 January 1932.

40. *Seattle Municipal News*, 14 November 1931.

41. Portland City Council, Minutes, 93 (25 February 1931): 533; *Portland News*, 25 February 1931.

42. *Los Angeles Record*, 4 February 1931.

43. Bank of America, *Business Review* (1931), p. 7; J. L. Jacobs and Co., "Reduction in Public Expenditures, Years 1931–1933 in 46 American Cities" (1933), n.p.; Seattle *Daily Journal of Commerce*, 30 December 1931; Multnomah County, Tax Commission, *Budget Facts* (1933), p. 13.

44. Seattle, Mayor, *Annual Message* (1930), p. 13; Washington, Governor, "Message of Governor Roland H. Hartley to the State Legislature, 22nd Session," 14 January 1931, pp. 5–6, 8–9, 12.

45. The figures on the payment of property taxes derive from a study by the author of Seattle registration books of 1928 and 1932 (See Appendix); *Seattle Post-Intelligencer*, 24 September 1931.

46. "Tax Rate, Unemployment Relief and the $3,500,000 School Bond Issue," *The City* 11 (28 October 1931): 43–44.

47. "San Francisco's 1931–32 Budget," *The City* 11 (28 May 1931): 22; California, State Unemployment Commission, *Report and Recommendations*, p. 600.

48. Los Angeles, Controller, *Budget, Fiscal Year 1931–32*, p. 3.

49. Leader, "Los Angeles and the Great Depression," p. 86.

50. Los Angeles, Controller, "Statement of Bonding Capacity," single sheet (1931).

51. Los Angeles, Controller, *Budget, Fiscal Year 1931–32*, p. 5; California, State Unemployment Commission, *Report and Recommendations*, p. 350.

52. Multnomah County, Tax Commission, *Budget Facts*, pp. 13, 56; Multnomah County, Auditor, *Annual Report* (1932), p. 29.

FIVE. IN SEARCH OF RELIEF

1. *Los Angeles Times*, 3 December 1931.

2. Robert Bremner, *American Philanthropy* (Chicago: University of Chicago Press, 1960), pp. 147–48.

3. California, State Unemployment Commission, *Report and Recommendations* (1932), p. 346.

4. *Los Angeles Record*, 2 February 1931.

5. *California Eagle*, 7 August 1931.

6. *Los Angeles Chronicle*, December 1931.

7. Catholic Welfare Bureau of the Archdiocese of Los Angeles, *Report* (1932), n.p.

8. *Los Angeles Record*, 22 January 1931.

9. George W. Bemis, *Public Relief in Los Angeles County* (Los Angeles: Bureau of Governmental Research, 1938), p. 88.

10. *Los Angeles Times*, 5 January 1931.

11. *Los Angeles Record*, 6 February 1931.

12. Lawrence D. Pritchard, "The All City Employee Association of Los Angeles," typewritten (1940), p. 74.

13. *Los Angeles Times*, 24 February 1931; *Los Angeles Record*, 4 March 1931.

14. Leonard Leader, "Los Angeles and the Great Depression" (Ph.D. diss., University of California at Los Angeles, 1972). p. 61.

15. David Maurer, "Public Relief Programs and Politics in Ohio, 1929–1939" (Ph.D. diss., Ohio State University, 1962), p. 15; Los Angeles County Board of Supervisors, "Report on Survey of Unemployment and Public Welfare in Metropolitan Sectors," typewritten (1931), p. 26, Record Series 740, LABS; James J. Hannah, "Urban Reaction to the Great Depression in the United States, 1929–1933," (Ph.D. diss., University of California at Berkeley, 1956), p. 100.

16. *Los Angeles Times*, 2–7 March 1931.

17. California, State Unemployment Commission, *Report and Recommendations*, p. 345.

18. Leader, "Los Angeles and the Great Depression," p. 53; *Los Angeles Times*, 12 March 1931; Pritchard, "The All City Employees Association," p. 69.

19. California, State Unemployment Commission, *Report and Recommendations*, p. 370.

20. Los Angeles County, Board of Supervisors, *Annual Report* (1932), pp. 142–43.

21. California, State Unemployment Commission, *Report and Recommendations*, p. 51.

22. Los Angeles County, Board of Supervisors, *Annual Report* (1932), p. 141.

23. Louis B. Perry and Richard S. Perry, *A History of the Los Angeles Labor Movement, 1911–1941* (Berkeley and Los Angeles: University of California Press, 1963), p. 227.

24. *Los Angeles Times*, 8 July 1931; William R. Brock, *Welfare, Democracy, and the New Deal* (Cambridge: Cambridge University Press, 1988), pp. 152–53.

25. *Los Angeles Record*, 9 July 1931.

26. Los Angeles Bureau of Budget Efficiency, "Report of the Expenditures of the County Welfare Department for Public Relief," typewritten (1931), Record Series 40.31, LABS, pp. 3–4, 7, 23, 27–29.

27. *Los Angeles Times*, 26 August 1931; *Los Angeles Examiner*, 23 August 1931.

28. *Los Angeles Times*, 30 October 1931.

29. *Los Angeles Times*, 1 March 1931.

30. *Los Angeles Times*, 22 September 1931.

31. Los Angeles County, Board of Supervisors, Minutes, 175 (16 November 1931): 38, LABS.

32. Los Angeles County, Board of Supervisors, *Annual Report* (1932), p. 144; Office of County Counsel to Los Angeles County Board of Supervisors, 24 March 1932, Record Series, 40.10, LABS.

33. *Los Angeles Times*, 4 February 1931. The creation and nature of state work camps is discussed in connection with San Francisco's responses (see below).

34. San Marino City Council to Los Angeles Board of Supervisors, 19 December 1931, Record Series 740, LABS.

35. Francisco E. Balderrama, *"En defensa de la raza*: The Los Angeles Mexican Consulate and *Colonia Mexicana* during the Great Depression"* (Ph.D. diss., University of California at Los Angeles, 1978), pp. 39–40, 48.

36. Ibid., pp. 45, 48, 77; Rafael de la Colina to Los Angeles County Board of Supervisors, 29 September 1931, Record Series, 40.31, LABS.

37. Los Angeles County, Board of Supervisors, *Annual Report* (1932), p. 138.

38. Los Angeles County, Board of Supervisors, *Annual Report* (1931), p. 89; W. H. Holland to Los Angeles County Board of Supervisors, 10 February 1931, Record Series 40.31, LABS.

39. Balderrama, *"En defensa de la raza,"* pp. 44–45.

40. U.S., Works Progress Administration, Division of Social Research, "A Statistical Abstract of Public and Private Assistance in San Francisco, California, 1929 to 1935," mimeographed, p. 27; Emily H. Huntington, *Unemployment Relief in the San Francisco Bay Region: 1929–1934* (Berkeley and Los Angeles: University of California Press, 1934), p. 9.

41. Lois Jordan, *The Work of the White Angel Jungle of the San Francisco Waterfront* (San Francisco: n.p., 1935), passim.

42. Clark Kerr, "Productive Enterprises of the Unemployed, 1931–1938" (Ph.D. diss., University of California at Berkeley, 1939), pp. 75, 337.

43. California, State Unemployment Commission, *Report and Recommendations*, pp. 56, 306, 318.

44. Ibid., pp. 304–305.

45. "San Francisco's 1931–1932 Budget," *The City*, p. 18.

46. *San Francisco Examiner*, 15 August 1931; *San Francisco Chronicle*, 1 December 1931.

47. California, State Unemployment Commission, *Report and Recommendations*, p. 600; "San Francisco's Bonded Debt Status," *The City* 11 (28 October 1931): 30.

48. *San Francisco News*, 11 September 1931.

49. Frances Cahn and Valeska Barry, *Welfare Activities of Federal, State, and Local Governments in California: 1850–1934* (Berkeley and Los Angeles: University of California Press, 1936), p. 222; Rexford S. Black, *Report on the State Labor Camps* (San Francisco: Califonia State Printing Office, 1932), pp. 33–34.

50. Rexford S. Black to Los Angeles County Board of Supervisors, 19 October 1932, Record Series 740, LABS; Black, *Labor Camps*, pp. 45–46.

51. Olive C. Cadbury, "Social Work in Seattle: An Inventory and Appraisal" (typewritten MS, Directed by the Graduate Division of Social Work, University of Washington, 1935), p. 126.

52. Seattle Community Fund, *The Facts about the Community Fund for 1932–1933* (1932), p. 11; Cadbury, "Social Work in Seattle," p. 7.

53. Albert Francis Gunns, "Roland Hill Hartley and the Politics of Washington State" (Master's thesis, University of Washington, 1963), p. 224.

54. *Seattle Municipal News*, 19 September 1931.

55. Donald Francis Roy, "Hooverville: A Study of a Community of Homeless Men in Seattle" (Master's thesis, University of Washington, 1935), pp. 60–61.

56. Ibid., pp. 39, 42–45.

57. Tom Jones Parry, "The Republic of the Penniless," *Atlantic Monthly* 40 (July-Dec. 1932): 449; Murray Morgan, *Skid Road: An Informal Portrait of Seattle* (New York: Viking Press, 1951), p. 230.

58. "Unemployment Relief in Seattle," 30 July 1932, Charles Ernst Papers, University of Washington Library, Seattle; John Arthur Hogan, "The Decline of Self-Help and Growth of Radicalism among Seattle's Organized Unemployed" (Master's thesis, University of Washington, 1934), p. 5.

59. Arthur Hillman, *The Unemployed Citizens' League of Seattle*, University of Washington Publications in the Social Sciences, vol. 5, no. 3 (Seattle: University of Washington Press, 1934), p. 187.

60. Seattle City Council, Proceedings, Doc. 135267, 13 November 1931.

61. Seattle City Council, Proceedings, Doc. 133273, 13 October 1931.

62. Seattle City Council, Proceedings, Doc. 133610, 13 November 1931.

63. "Unemployment Relief in Seattle," 30 July 1932.

64. Seattle City Council, Proceedings, Doc. 133991, 21 December 1931.

65. *Oregon Daily Journal*, 2 January 1932.

66. *Oregon Daily Journal*, 3 November 1931 and 15 November 1931.

67. Pisgah Home Colony to John C. Ainsworth, printed appeal, John C. Ainsworth Papers, University of Oregon Library, Eugene, Oregon.

68. Portland Chamber of Commerce, Retail Merchant Committee, Minutes, 11 September 1931, PCC.

69. *Portland News-Telegram*, 19 November 1931.

70. *Oregonian*, 7 September 1931.

71. *Oregonian*, 16 October 1931; *Oregon Daily Journal*, 19 December 1931.

72. Portland, Department of Public Works, *Civic Emergency Relief Prior to Bond Issue, 18 December 1930–10 April 1931*, B-8, Series 8401–12, Portland Archives and Record Center.

73. Portland Civic Emergency Committee, *Report 1931–32; Oregon Daily Journal*, 30 March 1932.

74. *Oregonian*, 17 July 1931; Portland, Auditor, *Annual Report* (1932), pp. 41, 259.

75. George Buck, County Roadmaster to R. E. Riley, 6 March 1931, Multnomah County Roadmaster Papers, Oregon Historical Society, Portland.

76. *Oregon Daily Journal*, 4 June 1931 and 4 August 1931; *Portland News-Telegram*, 17 November 1931.

77. Los Angeles County Board of Supervisors, "Survey of Unemployment," pp. 11–13, 26; Hannah, "Urban Reaction," p. 100; Jacob Fisher, *The Response of Social Work to the Depression* (Boston: G. K. Hall and Co., 1980), p. 38.

SIX. REACHING BOTTOM

1. Robert Lynd and Helen Lynd, *Middletown in Transition: A Study in Cultural Conflicts* (New York: Harcourt, Brace and Company, 1937), p. 53; Bayrd Still, *Milwaukee: The History of a City* (Madison: State Historical Society of Wisconsin, 1948), p. 485; David Maurer, "Public Relief Programs and Politics in Ohio, 1929–1939" (Ph.D. diss., Ohio State University, 1962), p. 39.

2. U.S. Federal Reserve Bank of San Francisco, *Monthly Review of Business Conditions* (20 January 1933), p. 11; San Francisco Stock Exchange, *Report of the President* (1932), p. 10; Bank of America, *Bank of America Business Review* (1933), p. 1.

3. California, State Unemployment Commission, *Report and Recommendations* (1932), p. 158.

4. *Seattle Daily Journal of Commerce*, 12 December 1932; *Oregon Daily Journal*, 1 March 1932.

5. Los Angeles Chamber of Commerce, *Southern California Business* (February 1933), p. 20; San Francisco, Chamber of Commerce, Research Department, *San Francisco Economic Survey: 1933*, p. 20; Price and Company, *Comparative Statements of Banks in Seattle* (n.p., 1932); Calvin F. Schmid, *Social Trends in Seattle* (Seattle: University of Washington Press, 1944), p. 31.

6. Claude Singer, "The History of United States National Bank and U.S. Bancorp" (unpublished MS, at Oregon Historical Society, 1980), p. 80; E. Kimbark MacColl, *The Growth of a City: Power and Politics in Portland, Oregon 1915 to 1950* (Portland: The Georgian Press, 1979), pp. 403–404.

7. California, State Unemployment Commission, *Report and Recommendations*, p. 41; California, Emergency Relief Administration, Division of Research and Surveys, "Economic Trends in California, 1929–1934," mimeographed n.d., pp. 357–58.

8. Los Angeles Chamber of Commerce, *Southern California Business* (February 1933), p. 20; California, State Unemployment Commission, *Report and Recommendations*, p. 41; Los Angeles, Chamber of Commerce, *Research Reveals the 60 Year Progress of Los Angeles in Twenty-one Aspects* (1948), n.p.; Leonard Leader, "Los Angeles and the Great Depression" (Ph.D. diss., University of California at Los Angeles, 1972), p. 12; Bank of America, *Business Review* (1932), p. 5; "Awards and Decisions: Building Trades–San Francisco," *Monthly Labor Review* 36 (March 1933): 569; Schmid, *Social Trends in Seattle*, pp. 33–34; Oregon, State Planning Council, "A Study of Construction in Oregon: Past Construction Expenditures, Present Allotments for Public Works, and Employment of Construction Workers in Oregon," mimeographed, 1935, Table "C".

9. California, State Unemployment Commission, *Report and Recommendations*, p. 50.

10. California, Emergency Relief Administration, "Economic Trends," p. 18.

11. Ibid., 9, 14; Charles Miles and O. B. Sperlin, eds., *Building a State: Washington, 1889–1939*, 3 vols. (Tacoma: Washington State Historical Society, 1940), 3:291.

12. Security First National Bank of Los Angeles, *Monthly Summary*, February 1933; *Portland Journal of Commerce*, 25 January 1932 and 1 December 1932.

13. *Los Angeles Examiner*, 13 September 1932.

14. *Seattle Post-Intelligencer*, 18 April 1932; *Los Angeles Examiner*, 8 September 1932; Los Angeles, Office of the Mayor, Community Analysis Bureau, *The Economic Development of Southern California, 1920–1976*, 2 vols. (1976), 2:3.

15. *San Francisco News*, 14 March 1932.

16. *Los Angeles Illustrated News*, 30 May 1932.

17. A. P. Giannini to Arthur O. Garrett, 29 July 1932, "Biography of a Bank," Source Material Files, Bank of America Archives, San Francisco.

18. Guy W. Finney, *Angel City in Turmoil: A Story of the Minute Men of Los Angeles in Their War on Civic Corruption, Graft and Privilege* (Los Angeles: American Press, 1945), p. 26.

19. John Latourette to Frederick Steiwer, 12 February 1932, and Aaron Frank to Frederick Steiwer, 7 February 1932, Frederick Steiwer Papers, Oregon Historical Society, Portland.

20. Portland, Civic Emergency Committee, "Report 1931–32."

21. James Robertson to Los Angeles County Board of Supervisors, 8 April 1932, Record Series 740, LABS.

22. Contract Council of Los Angeles to Los Angeles County Board of Supervisors, 19 February 1932; A. W. Brunswig to Board, 18 February 1932; George F. Hildebrand to Board, 12 February 1932; and Dr. M. Morgan Clouth to Board, 2 June 1932, Record Series 740, LABS.

23. St. Patrick's Shelter for Men, *Sixth Annual Report* (San Francisco: n.p., 1933), n.p.; Emily H. Huntington, *Unemployment Relief in the San Francisco Bay Region: 1929–1934* (Berkeley and Los Angeles: University of California Press, 1934), p. 31.

24. *Portland News-Telegram*, 9 February 1932; *Los Angeles Illustrated News*, 15 November 1932 and 22 December 1932; William C. Curtis to Los Angeles County Board of Supervisors, 1 July 1932, Record Series 740, LABS; California, State Unemployment Commission, *Abstract of Hearings on Unemployment* (1932), pp. 117–18, 163–65; *Portland Advocate*, 5 March 1932.

25. California, State Unemployment Commission, *Report and Recommendations*, pp. 13, 39, 192; *Los Angeles Times*, 5 May 1932.

26. Los Angeles County, Board of Supervisors, *Annual Report* (1932), p. 137; Los Angeles, Department of Social Services, Municipal Service Bureau for Homeless Men, *Annual Report* (1932), p. 1.

27. California, State Unemployment Commission, *Report and Recommendations*, p. 40; California, Department of Industrial Relations, Division of Labor Statistics and Law Enforcement, *The California Labor Market Bulletin*, vols. 6 and 7, passim.

28. *Seattle Vanguard*, February 1932; *Washington State Labor News*, 29 July 1932.

29. "Summary of Response to Questionnaire," 25 July 1932, Oregon Statewide Relief Council Collection, University of Oregon Library, Eugene, Oregon; *Oregon Daily Journal*, 9 January 1932; Oregon, Statewide Relief Council, Executive Committee, *Report* (Salem: State Printing Office, 1933), p. 10.

30. Municipal League of Los Angeles, *Bulletin*, 20 February 1932; *Los Angeles Examiner*, 2 November 1932; *California Eagle*, 23 September 1932.

31. Schmid, *Social Trends in Seattle*, p. 198; Los Angeles, Health Department, *Annual Report* (1932), p. 74; Los Angeles Police Department, *Annual Report* (1930, 1931, 1932, 1933), pp. 1–3 in each report; Los Angeles, Public Library, *44th Annual Report of the Board of Library Commissioners of the Los Angeles Public Library* (1932), p. 5; Los Angeles, Department of Playground and Recreation, *Annual Report* (1932), p. 7; Portland, Police Bureau, Detective Division, "Annual Report," typewritten (1930, 1931, 1932); Portland, Bureau of Health, *Annual Report* (1930, 1931, 1932, 1933); Milton Ross Charles, "A Population Analysis of San Francisco" (Master's thesis, Stanford University, 1946), p. 64.

32. Roger Daniels, *The Bonus March: An Episode of the Great Depression* (Westport, Conn.: Greenwood, 1971), pp. 71–72.

33. Retail Merchants Committee, minutes, 23 October 1931, PCC.

34. Daniels, *Bonus March*, p. 73.

35. Ibid., p. 82.

36. Albert U. Romasco in *The Poverty of Abundance: Hoover, the Nation, the Depression* (New York: Oxford University Press, 1965), p. 167; Blake McKelvey, *Rochester: An Emerging Metropolis, 1925–1961* (Rochester, N.Y.: Christopher Press, 1961), p. 65.

37. *Los Angeles Times*, 7 June 1932.

38. Cuthbert Reeves, *The Valuation of Business Lots in Downtown Los Angeles* (Los Angeles: Los Angeles Bureau of Municipal Research, 1932), n.p.; Los Angeles County, *Tax Payers' Guide: Schedule of Tax Rates and Legal Requirements* (1933), p. 16; Leader, "Los Angeles and the Great Depression," p. 77.

39. *Los Angeles Examiner*, 30 August 1932.

40. Leader, "Los Angeles and the Great Depression," p. 83.

41. *Los Angeles Examiner*, 19 February 1932; Burton L. Hunter, "Los Angeles Retrenches: An Administrative History of the Personnel and Salary Curtailments during 1931–32 in the Municipal Government," typewritten (1932), pp. 12–13.

42. Leader, "Los Angeles and the Great Depression," p. 82.

43. Ibid.

44. *Los Angeles Examiner*, 26 August 1932.

45. *San Francisco Chronicle*, 25 January 1932.

46. *San Francisco Examiner*, 19 March 1932; *San Francisco Labor Clarion*, 26 August 1932.

47. San Francisco Chamber of Commerce, Research Department, *San Francisco Economic Survey: 1932*, p. 21.

48. *San Francisco Chronicle*, 19 December 1932.

49. Frederick L. Bird, *Trend of Tax Delinquency, 1930–1941: Cities over 50,000 Population* (New York: Dun and Bradstreet, 1942), p. 25; Seattle voter registration study by the author. (See Appendix.)

50. *Seattle Post-Intelligencer*, 27 September 1932; *Seattle Times*, 3 October 1932.

51. *Seattle Post Intelligencer*, 7 October 1932.

52. *Oregonian*, 8 December 1932, Oregon, Statewide Relief Council Executive Committee, *Report* (Salem, 1930), p. 11.

53. *Portland News-Telegram*, 12 December 1932; *Oregon Daily Journal*, 7 October 1932.

54. Multnomah County, Tax Commission, *Budget Facts* (1933), p. 15; *Portland Journal*, 2 October 1932 and 12 December 1932.

SEVEN. IN TIME OF THEIR GREATEST NEED

1. *Los Angeles Times*, 20 October 1932.

2. *Los Angeles Times*, 11 October 1932, 5–6 December 1932, 26 January 1933.

3. California, State Unemployment Commission, *Report and Recommendations* (1932), p. 51.

4. Leonard Leader, "Los Angeles and the Great Depression" (Ph.D. diss., University of California at Los Angeles, 1972), p. 37.

5. *Los Angeles Times*, 15 May 1932.

6. Constantine Panunzio, *Self-help Cooperatives in Los Angeles*, Publications of the University of California at Los Angeles in Social Sciences, vol. 8, no. 1 (Berkeley and Los Angeles: University of California Press, 1939), pp. 9–11. Much of the information contained in this section is derived from this book.

7. Ibid., pp. 13, 15.

8. Ibid., pp. 109, 112–13.

9. Mayor John Porter to Los Angeles County Board of Supervisors, 12 January 1932, Record Series 740, LABS; *Los Angeles Illustrated News*, 4 February 1932; *Los Angeles Times*, 24 May 1932.

10. Helen R. Jeter, "The Administration of Funds for Unemployment Relief by the Los Angeles Department of Charities prior to November 24, 1933," typewritten (Los Angeles: Los Angeles County Emergency Relief Committee, 1933), p. 21.

11. *Los Angeles Times*, 6 May 1932.

12. Los Angeles, Water and Power Commissioners, Department of Water and Power, *Annual Report* (1932), p. 5; Ibid. (1933), p. 75.

13. *Los Angeles Times*, 26 January 1932; Los Angeles Community Welfare Federation, *Social Service as Administered by Public and Private Agencies*, City School District Publication, no. 263 (Los Angeles: Los Angeles City Schools, 1935), p. 49.

14. William R. Harriman to Los Angeles County Board of Supervisors, 23 April 1932; Record Series 40.31, LABS; *Los Angeles Times*, 6 May 1932.

15. *Los Angeles Times*, 2 June 1932.

16. Ibid.

17. California, State Unemployment Commission, *Report and Recommendations*, p. 50; Emily H. Huntington, *Unemployment Relief in the San Francisco Bay Region: 1929–1934* (Berkeley and Los Angeles: University of California Press, 1934), p. 9; U.S., Works Progress Administration, Division of Social Research, "A Statistical Abstract of Public and Private Assistance in San Francisco, California 1929 to 1935," mimeographed (1936), p. 28.

18. San Francisco, Chamber of Commerce, minutes, 15 December 1932, Greater

San Francisco Chamber of Commerce Papers, California Historical Society, San Francisco.

19. California, State Unemployment Commission, *Report and Recommendations*, p. 309.

20. *San Francisco Call-Bulletin*, 29 August 1932.

21. California, State Unemployment Commission, *Report and Recommendations*, p. 309.

22. Ibid., p. 50; *San Francisco Chronicle*, 7 October 1932.

23. *San Francisco Examiner*, 19 December 1932; San Francisco, Supervisors' Board, Committee for the Survey of Unemployment Relief Administration, *Report* (1933), pp. 54, 56.

24. Arthur Hillman, *The Unemployed Citizens' League of Seattle*, University of Washington Publications in the Social Sciences, vol. 5, no. 3 (Seattle: University of Washington Press, 1934), pp. 204–205.

25. "Constitution of the Unemployed Citizens' League," typewritten, Seattle Public Library, Seattle, n.d.

26. Joseph P. Harris, "Seattle Gayly Elects a New Mayor," *National Municipal Review* 21 (May 1932): 309–10.

27. *Seattle Star*, 27 February 1932; *Seattle Times*, 10 March 1932.

28. Hillman, *Unemployed Citizens' League*, pp. 208–209, 236–38.

29. *Seattle Star*, 25 June 1932; Hillman, *Unemployed Citizens' League*, p. 210.

30. *Seattle Post-Intelligencer*, 25 October 1932.

31. George Starr, interview with the author, 6 February 1974.

32. *Seattle Post-Intelligencer*, 21 May 1932.

33. *Seattle Times*, 26 October 1932.

34. Hillman, *Unemployed Citizens' League*, pp. 217–19.

35. Frank Foise to Joanna Colcord, 31 October 1932, Charles Ernst Papers, University of Washington Library, Seattle.

36. Portland Chamber of Commerce, *Commerce*, 5 November 1932.

37. *Portland Western World* [Lem Dever and Roy E. Metcalf, eds.], *Portland Community Chest Racket* (Portland: Western World, 1933), p. 9.

38. *Oregon Daily Journal*, 29 January 1932; 5 May 1932; *Portland News-Telegram*, 25 March 1932.

39. Oregon Plan Unemployed Citizens' League of Portland and Multnomah County, "Constitution," typewritten (1932), Miscellaneous Collection, Multnomah County, Board of County Commissioners, Portland.

40. Ibid.

41. "The Civic Emergency Federation," December 1932 (pamphlet), Miscellaneous Collection, Multnomah County, Board of County Commissioners, Portland.

42. "Free Employment," Mayor's Office Papers, MS. Series 0201–02, Portland Archives and Record Center.

43. *Oregon Daily Journal*, 19 April 1932.

44. *St. John's Review* (Portland), 4 May 1932.

45. *Oregon Daily Journal*, 29 May 1932.

46. Board of Multnomah County Commissioners to Governor Julius L. Meier, 19 December 1932, Miscellaneous Collection, Multnomah County, Board of County Commissioners, Portland.

47. Ibid.; Oregon Bureau of Labor, *Fifteenth Biennial Report and Industrial Directory of the Bureau of Labor and State Welfare Commission of the State of Oregon from October 1, 1930 to September 30, 1932* (1933), p. 4.

48. Oregon, State Highway Department, "Tenth Biennial Report," mimeographed [1932], p. 24.

49. *Portland News-Telegram*, 6 September 1932.

50. "Functions of Executive Committee Governor's Statewide Relief Council," 23 June

1932, Paul Maris to George Montgomery, 8 November 1932, Oregon, Statewide Relief Council, Executive Committee Collection, University of Oregon Library, Eugene, Oregon.

51. James J. Hannah, "Urban Reaction to the Great Depression in the United States, 1929–1933" (Ph.D. diss., University of California at Berkeley, 1956), pp. 132–33; Charles Trout, *Boston, the Great Depression, and the New Deal* (New York: Oxford University Press, 1977), pp. 90, 95, 120–21; Albert U. Romasco, *The Poverty of Abundance: Hoover, the Nation, the Depression* (New York: Oxford University Press, 1965), pp. 167–68.

52. *Los Angeles Examiner*, 26 August 1932; *Los Angeles Times*, 29 August 1932.

53. *Los Angeles Illustrated News*, 4 February 1933; *Los Angeles Times*, 4 February 1933.

54. Rose Marie Shiely Rinne, "The San Francisco–Oakland Bay Bridge: Its History and Economic Development" (Master's thesis, University of California at Berkeley, 1936), pp. 109, 111.

55. *Seattle Post-Intelligencer*, 28 September 1932 and 11 December 1932.

56. *Portland News-Telegram*, 5 December 1932; Oregon, State Public Welfare Commission, "Statement Showing Expenditures by Program by Years of Federal–State and County Funds for the Years 1932–1947," mimeographed, n.d., p. 1.

57. Michael Paul Rogin and John Shover, *Political Change in California: Critical Elections and Social Movements, 1890–1966* (Westport, Conn.: Greenwood, 1970), pp. 120, 124; Leader, "Los Angeles and the Great Depression," p. 246; *San Francisco Examiner*, 9 November 1932; George Starr, interview with the author; *Seattle Post-Intelligencer*, 23 November 1932; *Oregon Daily Journal*, 11 December 1932.

58. *San Francisco Examiner*, 10 November 1932.

59. This derives from the Seattle voter study by the author.

60. U.S., Department of Commerce, Bureau of the Census, *Census of American Business, 1933: Wholesale Distribution*, vol. 7, *Mountain and Pacific States* (1935), pp. 88, 122; Philip Neff and Anita Weifenbach, *Business Cycles in Selected Industrial Areas* (Berkeley and Los Angeles: University of California Press, 1949), p. 8; Security First National Bank of Los Angeles, "Index of Business Activity in Southern California," printed sheets [1933], n.p.; E. Kimbark MacColl, *The Growth of a City: Power and Politics in Portland, Oregon, 1915 to 1950* (Portland: Georgian Press, 1979), p. 453.

61. Neff and Weifenbach, *Business Cycles in Los Angeles*, p. 16; Shelby Scates, *Firstbank: The Story of Seattle First National Bank* (Seattle: Seattle First National Bank, 1970), p. 57.

62. *Seattle Post-Intelligencer*, 8 April 1933; Edgar I. Stewart, *Washington: Northwest Frontier*, p. 299.

63. *Los Angeles Times*, 10 February 1933.

EIGHT. NO LONGER ON THEIR OWN

1. Quoted in California, State Relief Administration, *State Review of Activities of the State Relief Administration of California, 1933–1935* (San Francisco, 1936), p. 46.

2. San Francisco Chamber of Commerce Research Department, *Annual Survey of Business Conditions in San Francisco* (San Francisco, 1934), p. 9; California, Emergency Relief Administration, "Economic Trends in California, 1929–1934," mimeographed (1935), p. 10; Norman Clark, *Washington: A Bicentennial History* (New York: W. W. Norton and American Association for State and Local History, 1976), p. 155; *Oregonian*, 5 March 1933 and 11 August 1933; *San Francisco Examiner*, 28 December 1933; Robert Burton, "The New Deal in Oregon," in John Braeman, Robert Bremner, and David Brody, eds., *The New Deal: The State and Local Levels*, vol. 2 (Columbus: Ohio State University Press, 1975), p. 356.

3. California, Emergency Relief Administration, "Economic Trends," p. 12; Los Angeles, Mayor, *Message to the City Council* (1936), p. 4; San Francisco Chamber of Commerce Research Department, *Annual Survey of Business Conditions in San Francisco*,

pp. 3, 7; West Coast Lumbermens' Association, *West Coast Lumber Facts*, pt. 1, (1941), p. 13; Seattle, Mayor, *Annual Message* (1935); Portland Chamber of Commerce, "Highlights of the Economy of Oregon with Particular Emphasis on the Portland Metropolitan Area," mimeographed (1950), p. 39; Washington Emergency Relief Administration, "Survey of Occupational Characteristics of Unemployed Persons," typewritten (1935).

4. Leonard Leader, "Los Angeles and the Great Depression" (Ph.D. diss., University of California at Los Angeles, 1972), p. 117.

5. "Self-help Movement: Self-help among the Unemployed in California," *Monthly Labor Review* 41 (December 1935): 1506.

6. Robert Glass Cleland, *From Wilderness to Empire: A History of California*, ed. Glenn Dumke (New York: Alfred Knopf, 1959), pp. 349–50.

7. Eugene P. Dvorin and Arthur J. Misner, eds., *California Politics and Policies* (Reading, Mass.: Addison–Wesley, 1966), p. 31.

8. Jackson K. Putnam, *Modern California Politics* (San Francisco: Boyd and Foster, 1980), p. 16.

9. Leader, "Los Angeles and the Great Depression," p. 251.

10. Burton, "New Deal in Oregon," p. 361.

11. Los Angeles City Council, "Comparative Tax Statistics: Twenty-five Cities of the United States over 300,000 Population," 1934, Council File 4027.

12. California, Emergency Relief Administration, "Survey of Financial Condition of California Counties," mimeographed (1935), p. 58.

13. Leader, "Los Angeles and the Great Depression," p. 86; *Los Angeles Times*, 7 March 1933; Los Angeles, Bureau of Budget and Efficiency, *Proposed Budget for the Fiscal Year Beginning July 1, 1934 Ending June 30, 1935* (Los Angeles, [1934?]), p. xi.

14. H. Brett Melendy and Benjamin F. Gilbert, *The Governors of California: Peter H. Burnett to Edmund G. Brown* (Georgetown, Calif.: Talisman Press, 1965), p. 77.

15. *Seattle Post-Intelligencer*, 10 April 1933.

16. Seattle City Council, Emergency Tax Commission, "Report and Supplemental Report," mimeographed, 1937.

17. King County Assessor, *Assessed Valuations, Tax Rates, and Taxes Levied*, 1933, p. 7, 1934, p. 7, and 1935, p. 4; Joseph P. Harris, *County Finances in the State of Washington* (Seattle: University of Washington Press, 1935), p. 313.

18. Multnomah County, Oregon, Tax Supervising and Conservation Commission, *Budget Facts and Financial Statistics* 1934, p. 46 and 1935, p. 9; Portland Chamber of Commerce, Research Department, "Relief Expenditures in Multnomah County, Oregon," mimeographed, n.d., p. 2.

19. *Oregonian*, 2 August 1933.

20. E. Kimbark MacColl, *The Growth of a City: Power and Politics in Portland, Oregon 1915 to 1950* (Portland: Georgian Press, 1979), p. 454; Terence O'Donnell and Thomas Vaughan, *Portland: A Historical Sketch and Guide* (Portland: Oregon Historical Society, 1976), p. 55.

21. *Oregonian*, 9 December 1933.

22. Washington, Governor, *Inaugural Message of Clarence Martin to the State Legislature*, 1933, passim.

23. California, State Relief Administration, *Review of Activities*, p. 77; Claude Arnold, *Review of Emergency Relief Activities of King County Welfare Board, February 1933 to April 1935* (Seattle: Washington State Department of Welfare [1935]), p. 30; Oregon, State Relief Committee, *Biennial Report of the State Relief Committee to the Governor and Legislative Assembly of Oregon* (1934), pp. 14, 53.

24. Frances Cahn and Valeska Barry, *Welfare Activities of Federal, State, and Local Governments in California: 1850–1934* (Berkeley and Los Angeles: University of California Press, 1936), p. 229; Arnold, *Review of Emergency Relief*, pp. 10–11.

25. Sanford A. Mosk, *Unemployment Relief in California under the State Emergency*

Relief Administrator, Essays in Social Economics, May 1935 (Berkeley and Los Angeles: University of California Press, 1935), pp. 253–54.

26. Bruce Blumell, *The Development of Public Assistance in the State of Washington during the Great Depression* (New York: Garland, 1984), p. 124.

27. Blumell, *Public Assistance in the State of Washington*, pp. 124, 127–28.

28. *Oregon Voter*, 74 (16 September 1933): 282–84.

29. California, State Relief Administration, "Summary Report," mimeographed [1934], p. 13.

30. Helen R. Jeter, "The Administration of Funds for Unemployment Relief by the Los Angeles Department of Charities prior to November 24, 1933," typewritten (Los Angeles: Los Angeles County Emergency Relief Committee, 1933), pp. iii, v.

31. Jeter, "Administration of Funds for Unemployment," pp. 5–6; *Los Angeles Times*, 3 May 1933 and 10 May 1933.

32. *Los Angeles Times*, 21 April 1934 and 21 November 1934.

33. *Los Angeles Times*, 10 October 1933.

34. *Oregonian*, 18 November 1933.

35. *Public Relief Projects, 1930–1942*. Series 8401–12, Portland Archives and Record Center.

36. Arnold, *Review of Emergency Relief*, pp. 18–19; *Oregonian*, 17 November 1933; *San Francisco Examiner*, 21 January 1934; *Los Angeles Times*, 14 December 1933.

37. Portland, Public Employment Bureau "Report," typewritten (1933).

38. *Los Angeles Times*, 1 January 1934.

39. Cahn and Barry, *Welfare Activities*, pp. 232–33; *San Francisco Examiner*, 9 February 1934; *Oregonian*, 1 April 1934.

40. *San Francisco Examiner*, 12, 14, 16 August 1934.

41. *Oregonian*, 22 September 1934.

42. Washington Legislature, Special Committee Investigating Washington Emergency Relief Administration, "Report," mimeographed, 1935, p. 2.

43. Federal Emergency Relief Administration, Works Division, "Activities, April 1, 1934 –June 30, 1935," typewritten [1935].

44. *Oregonian*, 8 June 1933 and 14 February 1935.

45. *Oregonian*, 21 May 1933; *Los Angeles Times*, 21 June 1933; *San Francisco Examiner*, 14 April 1934; *Seattle Post-Intelligencer*, 13 June 1933.

46. *Oregonian*, 4 January 1934.

47. *Oregonian*, 3 August 1933; U.S. National Emergency Council, "Report of the Proceedings of the Statewide Coordinating Meeting of Federal Agencies Working in Washington," mimeographed [1936?], p. 72.

Index

WILLIAM H. MULLINS teaches history at Oklahoma Baptist University.